WILD WICKLOW

WILD WICKLOW

Nature in the Garden of Ireland

Richard Nairn & Miriam Crowley

TOWN
HOUSE
DUBLIN

First published in 1998 by

Town House and Country House
Trinity House, Charleston Rd
Ranelagh, Dublin 6

ISBN: 1-86059-048-9

A CIP catalogue record for this book is available from the
British Library

Printed by L.E.G.O., Italy   Typeset by Typeform, Dublin

CONTENTS

Acknowledgements 6

Foreword 8

Preface 9

1: The Shape of the Land 11

2: Life in the Hills 41

3: Deep in the Woods 61

4: The Waters and the Wild 85

5: Down on the Farm .108

6: On the Seashore 122

7: Through the Ages 157

Gazetteer 188

Select Bibliography 225

Index 226

Complete List of Maps 236

Acknowledgements

Numerous people have helped us with this book, either by sharing their own information on the natural history of Wicklow, by accompanying us in the field or by reading and commenting on parts of the draft text. To them we express our sincere thanks: Wesley Atkinson, Dominic Berridge, Jim Bowman, Sean Casey, Dick Coombes, Mark Costello, Kevin and Aoife Crowley, Tom Curtis, Éamon de Buitléar, Terry Doherty, Katharine Duff, James Fairley, Padraig Farrelly, Una Farrington, Howard Fox, Jim Fox, Jim Haine, David Hickie, Howard Hudson, Mary Kelly-Quinn, Padhraig Kennan, Gabriel King, Mortimer Loftus, Brian Madden, Eleanor Mayes, Anthony McElheron, Andrew McMillan, Oscar Merne, the late Frank Mitchell, Frazer Mitchell, Paul Murphy, Anne Newton, Stephen Newton, Éanna ní Lamhna, Ciara O'Mahony, Marinus Otte, Karl Partridge, Adrian Phillips, Ann Porter, Lorcan Scott, Chris Smal, Geraldine Stout, Mary Tubridy, Suzanne Tynan, Jim Wilson, John Wilson.

For the use of their fine photographs, we thank Wesley Atkinson, Jaimie Blandford, Éamon de Buitléar, Frank Doyle, Con Hogan and Richard T. Mills. Tony Roche of Dúchas — The Heritage Service provided a set of archaeological maps. We are grateful to Matthew Stout for the preparation of the maps, and to Hugh McLindon for the line drawings. Much of the text was typed by Caroline Delahunt to whom we are grateful for transcribing our scribblings on paper and mumblings on tape.

We are very honoured to have a foreword written by Éamon de Buitléar, the best musical wildlife man in Wicklow.

We and the publishers are very grateful to Wicklow County Council for sponsorship of the book, and especially to Blaise Treacy, County Manager, and Tony O'Neill of the County Wicklow Development Team.

We could not have finished the long march to completion of this book without the support and tolerance of Wendy Nairn and Mel Howes, to whom we offer our thanks.

To the memory of the late Frank Mitchell,
scientist, teacher and mentor

Foreword

Out from the very doorstep of Ireland's capital city stretches a vast area which can only be described as a wonderland. A short bus-ride from the city can bring the visitor within easy reach of a splendid and ancient landscape.

Yet to many urban-dwellers the wilder parts of Wicklow are barely appreciated for their wonder and magic. Those who do not believe this to be a magic area should remember that it was in this very county that Oisín fell from his horse on his return from Tír na nÓg.

The varied habitats of mountain, bogland, forest, farmland, river, stream, lake, sea-cliff and beach make the county of Wicklow one of the best surviving wild areas in Europe. Some parts of Wicklow, such as the monastic site at Glendalough, are now major tourist attractions. Indeed the attraction of this area was felt from earliest times. On some of the mountain summits are the remains of the great tombs of stone, built to mark the territories of the earliest people of Dublin and Wicklow.

The wealth of information in this excellent and informative book, *Wild Wicklow*, will add greatly to the enjoyment of today's explorers.

Éamon de Buitléar

Wicklow County Council is delighted to be associated with and a major financier of *Wild Wicklow - Nature in the Garden of Ireland*. The County Council encourages all promotion of County Wicklow, The Garden of Ireland in an environmentally sensitive and sustainable way.

Preface

Wicklow, the 'Garden of Ireland', offers the visitor a unique combination of mountains, lakes, bogs, woodlands and coast. For many visitors, the scenery and fresh air are enough. For a growing number who come on walking holidays, the main attractions are the mountains and valleys and the freedom from crowds and noise. Added attractions such as ancient monuments, historic houses, heritage gardens and fine beaches make for a very special experience.

But for an increasing number of visitors, interested in the natural world, Wicklow offers more: habitats for an amazing range of wild plants and animals — from the herds of wild deer in the hills to the nesting terns on the beaches — all within an hour's drive of Dublin with its airport and ferries. This is the subject of our book — the wildlife and natural features of a county of great scenic beauty and steeped in history.

This book, like the great Avonmore river, began as a series of small tributaries, far apart yet similar in character. We have both known Wicklow since childhood. One of us spent a summer tramping the Wicklow hills for the Geological Survey of Ireland in the early 1970s, while much more recently, the other trained as a mountain leader in the area and studied the mountains for her master's thesis. We now live in Wicklow, one in Ashford and the other near Clara, ideal bases from which to explore both the mountains and the coast. We both work as environmental scientists in the county.

These are the personal histories that have contributed to our joint writing of this book. We have explored Wicklow's habitats from the highest summits to the seashore and this is the journey, down from the peaks through the woodlands, waters and farmlands to the shoreline, that we follow in the chapters of this book. We want to share with our readers what we have discovered about Wicklow's wild places and its natural secrets. We hope this book will be used by a new generation of naturalists who, like the intrepid pioneers of earlier decades, will record what they find and make their information available to a wider audience.

Richard Nairn, Ashford   Miriam Crowley, Clara

Editorial note

As a help to the reader, species that are discussed in the text or listed as typical of a particular place or habitat are printed in bold on their first or principal mention in any context. Passing references to species and subsequent mentions in context are in ordinary type.

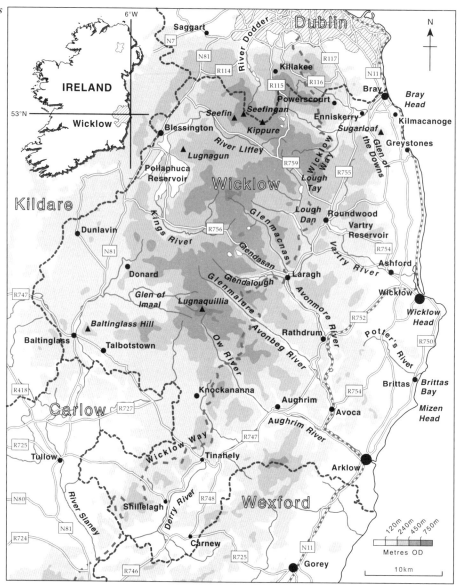

Map 1 Location and main features of County Wicklow

1. THE SHAPE OF THE LAND

A Wild Landscape

Ireland is shaped like a saucer. The low-lying central plain is surrounded by a rim of mountains, most noticeably on the north, west and south coasts. To the east the land is generally lower towards the Irish Sea, with one major exception: the county of Wicklow includes the largest continuous area of high ground in Ireland and it is isolated from most of the other mountain areas.

Through the millennia, from the Stone Age to the present, it has been colonised by successive waves of human settlers, each civilisation leaving its distinctive marks in the landscape. Yet Wicklow is still the wildest part of the east of Ireland. Even though it is highly modified from its original state, it still has the type of landscape that allows us to experience that feeling of wilderness so important for the human condition:

> *Still south I went and west and south again,*
> *Through Wicklow from the morning till the night,*
> *And far from cities and the sites of men,*
> *Lived with the sunshine and the moon's delight.*
>
> *I knew the stars, the flowers and the birds,*
> *The grey and wintry sides of many glens,*
> *And did but half remember human words,*
> *In converse with the mountain, moors and fens.*
>
> J. M. Synge

Wicklow is a county of great natural diversity. Its total area is about 781 square miles (2023 square kilometres). From the northern boundary at Bray to Clonegal at the southern limit is 41 miles (66km) and the greatest width from east to west is 27 miles (43km).

From sea-level on the east coast, the land rises to the majestic Wicklow mountain chain which occupies the whole centre of the county and stretches well outside its borders into Dublin, Carlow and Wexford. The highest peak, Lugnaquillia, at 3039 feet (925m) is among the four tallest mountains in Ireland and there are over twenty other summits in Wicklow above 2000 feet (610m). Twenty-six per cent of the surface of Wicklow lies above 1000 feet (305m).

The landscape of the flat coastal plain contrasts sharply with that of the windswept mountain peaks and dramatic glens, which yield to more gentle hills and valleys in the south of the county. In the extreme west of Wicklow, the land becomes less dramatic again as it eases towards the rolling fields of Kildare. Wicklow's landscape and scenery are the results of millennia of nature's actions and climatic changes imposed on the solid formation of the rocks beneath and overlain by centuries of human activities.

Time Out of Mind

The earth was congealed from the disparate matter of the universe about 4,600,000,000 years ago. In comparison, the oldest rocks in Wicklow are only 600 million years old. But our minds can hardly grasp or imagine such figures, so let's consider a different timescale. Imagine that those entire four thousand million years occurred in just one year — with the earth's birth on 1 January and today being midnight on the following New Year's Eve. On this imaginary calendar, Wicklow's oldest rocks would have been formed in early November, the dinosaurs lived for a few days in mid-December and humans only walked this earth a few seconds before midnight on 31 December.

The beginnings of Wicklow

During the Cambrian period — early November in our timescale — when ancient life forms were just beginning to expand and diversify, Ireland was under the troubled waters of an ocean. This great ocean, called Iapetus, was gradually closing, and the continents on either side were coming closer together. Enormous quantities of mud and sand were carried into the edges of the ocean and settled underwater in great thicknesses. Eventually these became compressed into the shale and sandstone rocks of Bray Head, which extend southwards as far as what is now Newcastle and inland to Roundwood.

Several million years later, during the Ordovician period — mid-November on our calendar — layers of muddy sand were still being deposited. But the earth's crust fractured under the pressure of the closing continents, gushing out layer upon layer of hot lava and ash through fissures onto the ocean floor. The resulting volcanic rocks, lavas and ash are interlayered with shale and sandstone, deposited concurrently in the ocean.

The formation of Wicklow granite

The closer the continents moved together, the more strained and fractured the earth's crust became. A few days later in November, in the Silurian period, the two continents finally collided and continued to push towards each other with tremendous force. The lower crust melted under the strain and large wedges of molten rock with the texture of porridge were forced up into the upper part of the crust.

This slowly cooled to become granite, a rock that commands the landscapes of Wicklow, as well as Connemara, Donegal and Down. The Leinster granite, solidified at great depth, was eventually exposed over time by erosion, revealing the greatest area of exposed granite in Ireland or Britain. It extends from the coast at Blackrock in County Dublin in a southwesterly direction and forms the backbone of the Wicklow mountains, stretches along County Carlow and the edge of the Blackstairs and continues almost as far as New Ross in County Wexford. Granite not only forms the rounded peaks of the Wicklow mountains, but also influences the vegetation that can grow there, which in turn affects the habitats for wildlife.

Granite is familiar as the beautiful cut stone of many fine buildings. The glimmering crystals are the product of the cooling and solidifying of the molten magma. If magma cools slowly, there is more time for each individual crystal to grow. The thick magmas in Wicklow never got near the surface and so were cocooned and insulated by a roof of earth's crust and took thousands of years to cool. As a consequence, the crystals of granite are large and visible; some even had the time to grow to the size of a thumb-print.

The baking of the envelope

At the edges of the fiery granite porridge, the adjacent rocks were being baked by the tremendous heat. This metamorphism occurred in Wicklow in a 1km (half-mile) zone all around the granite, converting the shales to smooth shiny mica-schists. The metamorphic aureole zone of warped layers of mica-schists can sometimes be picked out in the sharper peaks of some of the mountains such as Scarr and Djouce.

Scorching liquids, injected into this zone, crystallised into veins of minerals. Many of these contained metal ores in usable quantities, and iron, zinc, copper and tin were mined in the nineteenth century at Glendalough, Glendasan, Glenmalure and until recently at Avoca.

Meanwhile those same pressures that melted the lower crust were squeezing and heating the rocks of the upper crust. The mudstone was converted into slate and the sandstone was baked into quartzite. People sometimes think of the distinctive peak of the Sugarloaf mountain as looking like a volcano, but it is actually fashioned from hard, pale quartzite.

After the crash — drowning and scorching

After the final collision of the continents (in mid-November on our calender), Ireland became part of one large mountainous landmass. This is where the ancient rock record ceases in Wicklow, but we know from rocks elsewhere in Ireland that

13

this land was subsequently eroded by huge tropical rivers, which deposited the sandstones of Cork and Kerry. The land was then drowned in the Carboniferous period (early December on our calendar) under a tropical sea, which deposited vast areas of limestone over the entire country. (Wicklow has the distinction of being the only county in the whole of Ireland that has no Carboniferous limestone bedrock.)

After that, Ireland was being scorched under desert sun when suddenly, in the Jurassic period (mid-December), fissures developed in the landmass and the Atlantic Ocean was born. Dinosaurs evolved and became extinct, and another ocean started to open between Ireland and Scotland, but failed to materialise.

No record in the rocks

Many of these events were recorded in the rocks in various parts of Ireland, but Wicklow shows no evidence of them. This may be because Wicklow remained a mountain ridge throughout this time. Sediments are deposited in basins, so high ground collects no record of the rocks deposited. If any rocks were deposited after the Silurian period, they were probably eroded away again in the Cretaceous period (mid- to late December on our calender). Any vestiges of rocks that may have been overlying the granite were scraped away in the Ice Age.

Influence of the Rocky Skeleton

Different rocks have profound effects on the eventual landscape. Some rocks are much more vulnerable to weathering than others and each type of rock erodes in a different way, producing a characteristic landscape, such as the limestone of the Burren in County Clare which has weathered to a 'pavement'. Wicklow's rocks also show characteristic weathering patterns. The quartzite forms typical peaks with scree slopes, such as the Great and Little Sugarloaf. The granite mountain spine has been worn down to a softer, more rounded outline. It is flanked by more pointed mica-schist peaks such as Scarr, Djouce and Croghan Moira.

Crystals in the mountains

If you examine a granite outcrop in the Wicklow mountains you can pick out three distinct crystals. Quartz is translucent and very hard, feldspar is white or pink and mica is sheet-like, very shiny and colourless or brown. The granite forming the northern part of the range, such as that to the north of the Blessington lakes, has many large shiny mica crystals, which it is possible to peel into paper-thin transparent sheets, sometimes called 'books of mica'.

The granite of the Wicklow mountains is a reasonably hard rock, resistant to the ravages of the weather. However, even granite will eventually succumb as the feldspar crystals convert to clay and wash away, leaving the quartz crystals to fall

14

apart as a white gravel. This has given most of the mountains their rounded outlines. The rocks are now covered by a blanket of black peat, sometimes broken up and revealing the granite below. The black peat contrasts sharply with the white gravel.

Schist — hard and resistant

The thin zone of schist at the edges of the granite can often be picked out by the shape of a ridge or the peak of a mountain. Because it was baked, it became more resistant than either the granite on one side or the less baked rocks on the other. The schist thus forms peaks such as Djouce and the ridge of Scarr, and a tiny remnant even caps the highest peak, Lugnaquillia, which is otherwise forged in granite. A thin schist band also forms the cliffs west of the Wicklow Gap and the peak of Tonelagee.

The contact between the granite and the baked schist can be picked out in several areas in the landscape. A distinctive feature often reveals this contact, especially on the east side of the mountains. For example, waterfalls like those at Powerscourt and Glenmacnass mark the granite-schist junction in many valleys. The peak of Scarr and the cliffs at Luggala lie along the boundary, which can be seen on the slopes of Lough Dan. The resistant aureole also forms the low hill of Knockree, at the mouth of Glencree, which even the glaciers found it difficult to cut through.

In Glendalough, Glendasan and Glenmalure, the contact is close to the head of the deep glacial valleys. Its location is revealed by the mounds of white spoil heaps from past mining of the ore at the granite edges. In Glendalough the contrast between the layers of schist and the massive granite can be easily seen in the cliffs between the top of the Upper Lake and the miners' village, especially on the south side of the valley.

Ireland in the Ice Age

Almost two million years ago, the world climate began to cool significantly. The 'Ice Age' had started. This affected Ireland until 10,000 years ago and left a very important legacy on the topography of the entire country, and especially on mountainous areas.

Ireland was not blanketed in ice for the entire period. Instead the climate went through periods of cold — 'Ice Ages' or glaciations — when the ice sheets advanced to cover the land, and periods of relative warmth — interglacials — with weather similar to present conditions, when the ice retreated and the land became free of permanent ice. Humans had not reached Ireland at this time, but during the warmer periods woolly mammoths and bears roamed about.

The onset of a glacial period in Ireland was often very gradual. It might begin with a drop in average temperatures of only a few degrees, so that winter snow

1.1 Tony Farrington (1893-1973) was born in Cork and took a degree in engineering at UCC. He joined the staff of the Geological Survey of Ireland where he became involved in a survey of the Blessington area of County Wicklow. In 1927, he published an important paper on the granite-schist junction in the Leinster mountain chain which captures his excitement as he unravelled the jigsaw of the last glaciation. In 1928, he was appointed Resident Secretary to the Royal Irish Academy and from then until his death, Farrington devoted most of his spare time to glacial geology and geomorphology, contributing many significant works such as The Glaciation of the Wicklow Mountains *(1934),* The Glacial Drifts of the Wicklow Mountains *(1948) and* Glacial Lake Blessington *(1957). One of his major interests was in documenting the landscape history of the upper Liffey valley before it became permanently flooded by the present Pollaphuca reservoir in 1940. Anthony Farrington is buried in the old churchyard at Calary among his beloved glacial moraines and in view of the Great Sugarloaf mountain.*

falls did not fully melt in the summers. The snow would gradually accumulate and be compressed into ice, which slowly grew and covered the land. Much of the country was enveloped under large low-lying ice sheets, and areas of high ground like the Wicklow mountains also generated their own local ice caps. A number of times the climate improved for an interval, only for the process of glaciation to happen again.

Wicklow in the Ice Age

In the Ice Age, Wicklow was covered by three different expanses of ice. Two large ice sheets, one from the midlands and one from the Irish Sea, pushed slowly southwards on either side of the mountains. The midland ice sheet in particular abutted against the west side of the mountains, sometimes forcing its way up the valleys. Meanwhile, because of their altitude, the mountains themselves generated their own smaller ice caps, which pushed ice off the mountain ridge in both directions and down the hillsides.

On the west side, this mountain ice met the force of the midland ice, resulting in something of a stalemate. On the east side, however, the ice was able to flow and formed glaciers in the valleys, eroding and deepening them into the classic glaciated (U-shaped) glens, before continuing east and south to join the Irish Sea ice.

Legacy of the Ice Age
Valleys, corries, moraines, erratics

Glenmalure, Glendalough, Glendasan, Glenmacnass and the valleys of Lough Dan and Lough Tay are breath-taking examples of U-shaped valleys and, with the valleys of the Dargle and Glencree, are testimony to the mighty force of glacier ice. But rivalling the splendour of the deep glens are numerous precipitous corries high in the mountains where the snow and ice first started to accumulate, scooping out a hollow surrounded by steep crags.

The North and South Prisons of Lugnaquillia and Barravore Glen are dramatic corries. Many corries contain lakes, the waters dammed by glacial deposits: the two Loughs Bray, Lough Nahanagan, Lough Ouler, Cleevaun Lough below Mullaghcleevaun and Art's Lough and Kelly's Lough on the slopes of Lugnaquillia are examples.

The last glaciation had an enormous influence on the character of the Wicklow landscape, not only in what the ice scraped away but also in what it left behind. The most dramatic features are those that display the erosive power of the ice, but glacial deposits, while not so obvious, are every bit as important. Ice sheets and glaciers carry huge amounts of rock, which effectively makes the ice even more abrasive than it would otherwise be as it slowly moves across the bedrock. Thus even more rock is eroded to be carried away as debris by the ice. Scratches on the bedrock surface remain as clues to the direction of ice movement.

Whenever a valley glacier melted in Wicklow, it dumped what it had been carrying in great bouldery heaps of rock and debris called *moraines*. It is these heaps of boulder clay that block the escape of the corrie lakes and which can be seen as mounds in most of the glens. They are small moraines, however, and have only localised influence on the topography.

Another legacy, often much valued by sheltering walkers, are the huge scattered boulders dumped randomly by the melting ice. These boulders are usually of hard granite, and often they are perched on a hillside made of another rock type. This leads to their descriptive name of *erratics*, and when their source is known they can be an aid in the detective work revealing the direction of ice movement.

Boulder clay and limestone

The boulder clay left by the large ice sheets covers a very extensive area, moulding the landscape of the lowlands in both east and west Wicklow. There is no Carboniferous limestone bedrock in Wicklow, but, fortunately for Wicklow farmers, boulder clay from the midlands ice sheet consists of limestone debris. Dark grey limestone boulders can be picked up anywhere in north-west Wicklow from Baltinglass to Blessington, and in north-east Wicklow from Enniskerry to Kilcoole.

The Irish Sea ice sheet clothed east Wicklow with a clay containing many marine shelly fragments scoured from the seabed and occasional pebbles of a granite carried all the way from the tiny island rock of Ailsa Craig in Scotland. This clay also has a high calcium content and was often used as a soil improver, leaving many areas pock-marked with small holes where the clay was previously extracted. Much of the rolling topography between the flat coastal strip and the foothills of the mountains is the result of heaps of boulder clay deposited as moraines by the Irish Sea ice sheet.

Glacial lakes

During the short summer melting periods, an enormous amount of meltwater was produced. This drained away freely wherever possible, carrying the dropped load from the ice further along, either in front of or under the ice in ice-tunnels. However, the drainage of meltwater from the ice masses in Wicklow was often impeded by ice sheets on one side and by the mountains on the other. This resulted in ice-dammed glacial lakes in Blessington (bigger than the present, artificially dammed lake), Glencree and the Enniskerry/Fassaroe area. Eventually the ice blockage melted or moved and the lakes drained away but they may have existed at least a hundred years.

A small ice-dammed lake existed at one time in Glendalough, filling the whole

17

valley. Meltwater flowing from Glendasan entered the lake carrying large quantities of sediment. As the stream met the still lake water, it dropped its load as a delta, which gradually filled further out into the lake. Eventually the ice dam disappeared and the lake drained away, leaving the delta as a flat mound. It was on this glacial delta that the Glendalough monastic settlement was built, a raised plateau safe from the potential flooding of the rest of the valley floor.

V-shaped valleys

Wicklow has many examples of steep V-shaped valleys that are now dry or contain only tiny streams that are far too small to have eroded the valleys. These valleys were eroded by the huge volume of meltwater, which had tremendous erosive power. Many probably started life as streams surging in ice tunnels under the great weight of the ice and others as streams gushing along the ice margin. Dunran channel, which can be easily seen on the skyline from the Newtownmountkennedy bypass, and the Rocky Valley, beside the Great Sugarloaf, are examples of channels cut in this way.

The most striking meltwater channels, called 'glacial spillways', such as Hollywood Glen, the Scalp and the Glen of the Downs, were cut even deeper by water escaping from dammed-up glacial lakes.

Sand and gravel

The material deposited by meltwater is rather different from that dropped directly by the ice. Meltwater sorts the sediment into various sizes as it deposits its load. Most of the sorted sand and gravel mounds in Wicklow were deposited as deltas into the glacial lakes. These deposits are now valuable sources of concrete aggregate. The sediments at Kilpedder, Athdown, Fassaroe and Curtlestown in Glencree have all been quarried in the past and there is an active gravel quarry at Blessington.

There are many small disused pits in Wicklow, often providing habitats for wildlife, especially for burrowing animals and birds. Sand martins can be seen nesting in the pit behind the ruined barracks at Glenmalure. Areas overlying sand and gravel are very well drained and this leads to different soils and natural vegetation from that of the soggier boulder clay.

Return of Vegetation

During the warmer interglacials when the ice sheets retreated, the land could once again support soil development and plants began to establish themselves. This process of rebirth occurred several times between the Ice Ages, continuing until the temperatures plummeted once again into the grip of another glaciation.

When the ice sheets and glaciers of the last Ice Age were finally losing their hold on the land and starting to melt away, they unearthed a stark and barren landscape. The uplands had been scrubbed to bare bedrock and the lowlands had been coated with a lifeless clay. Yet slowly, hardy plants started to take hold, developing thin soils from the rock and clay, and gradually making way for other plants.

Eventually some trees were established and Ireland was colonised by animals such as the woolly mammoth, the giant Irish deer, wild horses, bears, hyenas, wolves, arctic foxes, reindeer, hares and lemmings. As soon as the ice sheets of the most recent glaciation withdrew from Ireland about 13,000 years ago, plants and animals again moved in, probably from warmer parts of Europe.

An enormous amount of seawater was still locked in the ice sheets, so the sea-level was then considerably lower than it is today. Consequently, Ireland was connected in several places by 'land bridges' to Britain. This connection undoubtedly speeded up the journey of plants and animals into Ireland, many of which probably first appeared on the east coast in what is now Wicklow, but this country probably became an island about 7500 years ago, cutting off the land to many species that had not yet reached here, and preventing Ireland from developing as diverse a flora and fauna as continental Europe and Britain.

A tundra landscape

At first, the emerging Ireland was a tundra-clothed place of snowy winters, perhaps similar to Iceland today. As the climate continued to warm, juniper and birch managed to take a hold in sheltered sites and herds of giant deer and reindeer wandered at the edges of the shrublands. Some animals that lived here then still survive today in Wicklow. The arctic charr is a cold-climate salmonid fish that became trapped in the isolated lakes of Glendalough and Lough Dan after the climate improved.

Before the familiar temperate climate returned, there was one last cold snap. The severity of the cold during this period was discovered in muds found under the water in Lough Nahanagan during the construction of Turlough Hill pump-storage station. This icy period, named after Lough Nahanagan, lasted between 11,000 and 10,000 years ago, and was cold enough for small glaciers to re-occupy the Wicklow corries.

Trees in the pollen record

After this last brief cold interval, the temperature gradually rose and Ireland was transformed from open grassland tundra to fully closed forest, surrounding great midland lakes. Over thousands of years, pollen-grain of plants has accumulated in peat and muds. It is possible to separate the pollen and identify different plant types. This pollen record provides us with a chronicle of vegetation changes since the end of the Ice Age.

19

The first trees to colonise were juniper, willow and birch, which became established around 10,000 years ago. Hazel and pine appeared around 9500 years ago, followed in succession by oak, elm, alder and ash about 9000 years ago. From then on, woodlands were originally dominated by pine and hazel until 8000 years ago, when oak and elm also became significant.

The peak of woodland growth occurred between 7000 and 5000 years ago, with hazel, oak, elm and alder shrouding the landscape. Elm thrived on calcareous soils, oak dominated areas with less lime, while pine held on mainly on the poorer soils of the Atlantic seaboard and mountainous areas like Wicklow. Many of these trees even grew on the tops of the mountains. Ancient tree stumps, preserved under the peat, show that the windswept Wicklow uplands were once cloaked in pine forests where few trees now grow. This tree-covered Wicklow hillscape is almost unimaginable today.

The first people

About 9000 years ago, people first appeared in Ireland. These were hunter–gatherer mesolithic people who had little effect on the wooded landscape. They hunted the forested country for wild pigs, fish and birds, and gathered hazelnuts and fruit.

Neolithic farmers appeared 6000 years ago, bringing cereal crops and domestic animals. They made the first small advances into Ireland's wooded countryside, initially along rivers and around the coastline, and eventually they cleared large areas of woodland for agriculture. Fen peat began to develop in the midland lakes 7000 years ago, slowly filling in the lakes.

The growth of the bogs

Around 4000 years ago, a combination of improved farming and another deterioration in the climate led to the growth of the bogs. Ireland's climate became cooler again. It was not cold enough for great ice sheets, but cool and damp enough for waterlogged and acid conditions to develop. This slowed down the decay of dead plant matter which eventually accumulated into peat. The midland lakes were gradually filled in to become domed raised bogs and uplands such as Wicklow became cloaked in the blanket bog we know today. This set the scene for the most recent changes in the Wicklow landscape — the impact of modern man. (This story continues in chapter 7.)

A Weather Eye

Along with the underlying rock, the climate is the most profound influence on a landscape, and not just during climatic extremes like the Ice Age. Although Wicklow is at about the same latitude as Moscow, its climate today, like that of most of Ireland, is dominated by the Atlantic Ocean. Mild, damp summers and cool, wet winters are the normal fare, but the weather patterns are ever-changing, never totally predictable.

Rain and shine, snow and wind

Annual rainfall reaches 2000mm on the highest summits, but can be less than half of that total on the coast. The more westerly peaks get the heaviest drenching, while there is a definite sheltering effect on the eastern slopes. Djouce mountain, for example, receives about 1630mm, while Duff Hill, a peak of similar height which is fully exposed to the westerly airflow, has 1950mm a year.

Winter months are generally the wettest and June and July the dryest, but extreme weather conditions can occur at almost any time of year and often have significant results for soil, vegetation and landscape. Hurricane Charlie, for example, resulted in a record of over 200mm of rain at Kilcoole on the night of 25/26 August 1986. The River Dargle burst its banks and caused major flooding in the Bray area and the Avonmore river became such a raging torrent that it swept away at least ten bridges, some of which were hundreds of years old.

Wicklow's position near the south-east corner of Ireland gives it a relatively high incidence of bright sunshine, averaging about four hours a day over the entire year. Together with the absence of extremes of temperature either in summer or winter, this allows certain plants and animals which are more at home on the European continent to maintain a foothold here.

Snow cover in winter increases with altitude and can reach an average of 30 days a year on some of the highest peaks. However, in the warmer lowlands, especially near the coast, snow rarely lies on the ground for more than a few days each winter. Even on the higher mountains wind often removes the snow cover quite quickly. There are extreme exceptions, however, such as the winter of 1947 when extensive parts of the Wicklow mountains were isolated by heavy snow cover for many months. Supplies of fresh food became short and some people in the higher mountain areas were forced to burn their furniture as fuel.

Wind is an important feature, especially on the higher hills where tree growth is often limited. Strong winds are an important factor in peat erosion on the summits and in the formation of sand dunes along the coast. Dominant wind directions are from the south and west, although there are times each year when an easterly airflow brings both snow and ice from the European continent together with waves of immigrant birds such as starlings, thrushes, lapwings and golden plovers. Easterly winds can also bring an ominous cargo of chemicals from the industries of Europe which has been implicated in the acidification of our waters.

1.2   Aerial view of Upper and Lower Lough Bray — two classic corrie lakes. (Cambridge University Collection of Air Photographs: copyright reserved)

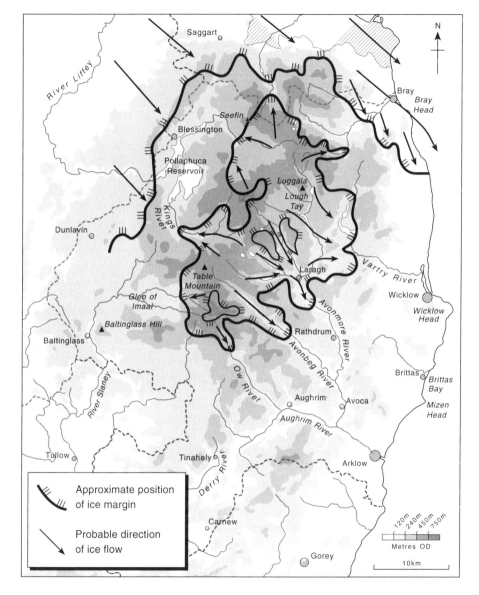

Map 2 Glaciers and ice movement during the later stages of the last Ice Age. At its greatest extent the ice sheets covered most of the Wicklow area but as the melt began, they separated into mountain glaciers and lowland ice sheets. The glaciers retreated into the upper valleys and some of the mountain summits poked out above the ice. (after Warren 1993)

1.3 Cloghoge Brook in spate. After a night of heavy rainfall a trickling stream can become a roaring torrent. Most of the invertebrates live under stones so they can remain in place under such high energy conditions. (Richard Nairn)

Map 3 Simplified geological map of County Wicklow and surrounding area. The Leinster Granite forms the mountain spine while the Bray Group contains some of the oldest rocks in Ireland. (after Warren 1993)

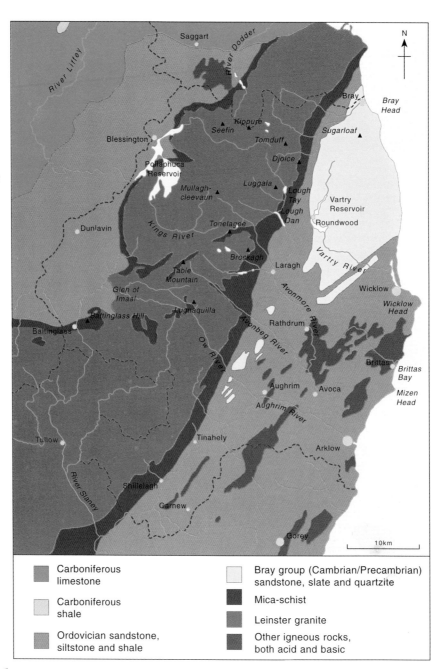

N

River Liffey
Saggart
River Dodder
Bray
Bray Head
Kippure
Seefin
Tomduff
Sugarloaf
Blessington
Djoice
Luggala
Pollaphuca Reservoir
Lough Tay
Lough Dan
Vartry Reservoir
Mullagh-cleevaun
Roundwood
Kings River
Tonelagee
Dunlavin
Vartry River
Brockagh
Laragh
Avonmore River
Table Mountain
Wicklow
Glen of Imaal
Wicklow Head
Lugnaquilla
Rathdrum
Balinglass Hill
Avonbeg River
Baltinglass
Brittas
Ow River
Brittas Bay
Aughrim
Avoca
Mizen Head
Aughrim River
Tullow
Tinahely
Arklow
Shillelagh
River Slaney
Carnew
Gorey

10km

Carboniferous limestone	Bray group (Cambrian/Precambrian) sandstone, slate and quartzite
Carboniferous shale	Mica-schist
Ordovician sandstone, siltstone and shale	Leinster granite
	Other igneous rocks, both acid and basic

26

1.4

1.4　Brent geese in flight with the Great Sugarloaf mountain in the background. This conical summit is unusual in Wicklow where most of the mountains have a rounded shape. It is formed of very hard quartzite, whose white colour has contributed to the sugar-like appearance. (Frank Doyle)

1.5　Feral goats among granite boulders at the old mining village in Glendalough. The boulders here are typical of the large blocks into which granite fractures when subjected to extremes of weather. The goats, which live here thoughout the year, may be descended from domestic animals once kept by the miners. (Richard Nairn)

1.5

27

1.8

1.9

1.6   On the slopes in the upper part of Glendalough, the white waste material from the old mines marks the contact between granite to the left and mica schist to the right. This is where the mineralisation took place as molten granite came into contact with the surrounding rocks. (Richard Nairn)

1.7   The Glenealo River meanders across the flat valley floor to join the Upper Lake at Glendalough. During the last Ice Age the valley would have been filled with a glacier, and the ice carved the steep sides as it moved slowly down the slope. In the nineteenth century the river was harnessed to provide power for crushing the ore from the mines in the valley. (Richard Nairn)

1.8   A winter view over the Cloghoge valley highlights some features formed during the last Ice Age. A glacier moving down the valley plucked rocks from the side of Knocknacloghoge, leaving rugged slopes to the left. The mountain tops are all rounded by the ice sheets and a corrie, or depression, scraped out by the ice on the north-east side of Tonelagee mountain, is visible in the background. (Richard Nairn)

1.9   The Glen of the Downs is the largest example in Ireland of a meltwater channel. It was formed by melting water draining from beneath the edge of the Irish Sea ice sheet about 15,000 years ago. Later the ice thawed to form large glacial lakes around Enniskerry and the glen formed an outlet channel to the south. Native woodland now covers the valley slopes. (Richard Nairn)

1.10 This tundra landscape in east Greenland today gives an impression of how Wicklow may have looked after the glaciers of the last Ice Age retreated. The mountain summits are still snow-covered in summer, there are snow patches on the low ground and meltwater carves channels across the valley floor. Vegetation is sparse and trees are completely absent. (Richard Nairn)

1.11 The Cloghoge River winds its way down from Lough Tay. The farm in the foreground is built on a series of glacial moraines, gravel and boulders left behind by a glacier. In the background, the cliffs of Luggala mark the contact between granite to the left and mica schist to the right. (Richard Nairn)

1.10

1.11

30

1.12 Professor Frank Mitchell examining the glacial deposits in a quarry at Athdown in the Upper Liffey valley. This moraine and its associated gravels were dumped here by a local mountain glacier towards the end of the last Ice Age. A line of recent sand martin burrows may be seen near the top of the profile. (Richard Nairn)

1.13 The rolling landscape of west Wicklow has deep boulder clay deposits laid down by ice sheets. The more fertile soils in the river valley are intensively farmed with a dense network of hedges. Forestry plantations occupy the thinner soils on the slopes. (Con ORourke)

1.14 High winds whip up the surface of Lough Tay. Dominant wind directions are from the south and west, although there are times when an easterly airflow brings snow and ice from the European continent. (Éamon de Buitléar)

2.4

2.5

2.1 *Glendasan with heather and gorse in flower in September. Both plants thrive in the drier acid soils which are typical of the valley slopes. (Richard Nairn)*

2.2 *Bare peat on the slopes of Mullaghcleevaun. Erosion such as this can be caused by a number of factors including burning, overgrazing, water and wind. Intensive use of some peat soils for hill walking or mountain biking can also cause serious damage to mountain paths. In the background a television mast marks the summit of Kippure. (Richard Nairn)*

2.3 *A badger sett on the slopes of Lybagh mountain at over 2000 feet above sea level. Wicklow's highest mountain, Lugnaquillia, is enveloped by cloud in the background. Although surrounded by granite mountains, the summit is formed of mica schist. (Richard Nairn)*

2.4 *Two well-grown raven chicks sit in a cliff nest lined with discarded sheep's wool. The birds nest early in the year to take advantage of the supply of dead animals in the mountains in late winter. In some years there is competition for nesting sites between the raven and peregrine falcon. (Frank Doyle)*

2.5 *A female hen harrier defends its territory. During the 1960s the population of these raptors expanded with the widespread afforestation of the hills. However, the maturing of the conifers and the extensive improvement of mountain land has left very little suitable breeding habitat. (Richard T. Mills)*

35

2.6

2.7

2.8

2.6   A wet flush in the mountain grassland at Brockagh. The vegetation here is dominated by sedges and bog mosses with heather on the dryer hummocks. In the background, the distinctive shape of the Turlough Hill pump storage station marks the skyline. (Richard Nairn)

2.7   Ling heather is one of the commonest plants of the mountains. It gives the hills a purple tint in late summer and autumn. The woody stems of the heather are very susceptible to burning but, if the fire is not too intense, the plants will produce new shoots from the base. (Richard Nairn)

2.8   Scree slopes above the ruined miners' village in Glendalough. Scree is a jumble of collapsed boulders and stones which have fallen from the cliffs above. Some rare plants gain a foothold among the boulders and the tiny wren finds enough food and shelter in the crevices to survive the winter here. (Richard Nairn)

2.9   Snipe are found during the breeding season in some of the wetter mountain bogs. They use their long bills for probing in the soft peaty soil. One of the best ways to confirm the presence of snipe is to hear the distinctive drumming sound made by the male birds in spring. (Richard T. Mills)

2.10 The fluffy white heads of bog cotton are typical of the wetter bogs, including the pools left by former peat cutting. It is a useful indicator of ground which is unsafe for walking. In the background, heather is being burnt to encourage the growth of new grass for sheep. (Frank Doyle)

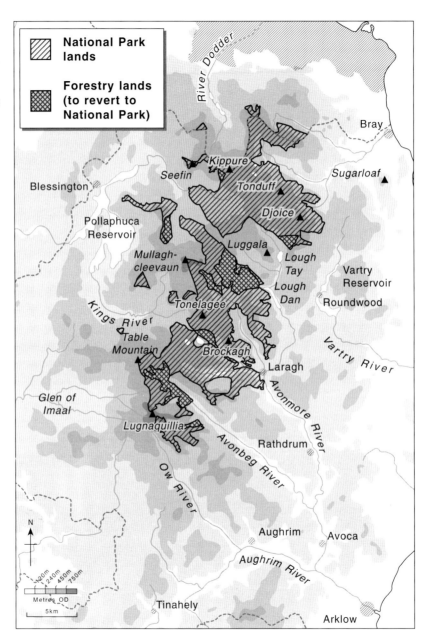

Map 4 National Park covering almost 20,000 hectares. Most of the central mountain spine and some of the highest summits are state-owned. Afforested lands within the park boundary will revert to semi-natural vegetation when the conifers have been harvested.

National Park lands

Forestry lands (to revert to National Park)

River Dodder

Bray

Kippure

Seefin

Sugarloaf

Blessington

Tonduff

Djoice

Pollaphuca Reservoir

Luggala

Lough Tay

Vartry Reservoir

Mullagh-cleevaun

Lough Dan

Roundwood

Tonelagee

Kings River

Table Mountain

Brockagh

Laragh

Avonmore River

Vartry River

Glen of Imaal

Lugnaquillia

Rathdrum

Avonbeg River

Ow River

Aughrim

Avoca

Aughrim River

N

120m 240m 450m 750m

Metres OD

5km

Tinahely

Arklow

38

2.11

2.11 This group of hybrid deer in Glenealo valley show some characteristics of both red and sika deer. The sika were introduced to Powerscourt Demense in north Wicklow in the nineteenth century. They later escaped and interbred with the native red deer. Some deer can be found on the hills while other prefer the cover of forests. (Wesley Atkinson)

2.12

2.12 An adult frog among the bog mosses in Liffey Head bog. The tadpoles live in the bog pools where they feed on tiny aquatic insects. The presence of multi-coloured Sphagnum moss is a sign of an actively growing blanket bog. (Richard Nairn)

2.13

2.13 Red grouse in its preferred habitat among the heather. The birds nest in dense heather and the chicks are fed on heathland insects and spiders. Once common enough to support regular hunting in winter the grouse has declined because of overgrazing and burning of the heather. (Frank Doyle)

2.14 The merlin feeds its young mainly on small birds such as meadow pipits. Although these small falcons are widespread on the hills, most now breed in conifer plantations, using the abandoned nests of crows. (Richard T. Mills)

2.15 The peregrine falcon nests on steep cliffs and crags all over Wicklow. It has largely recovered from the population decline which occurred in the 1960s due to the effects of pesticide poisoning. Pigeons are the favourite prey but female falcons are large enough to kill an adult red grouse. (Frank Doyle)

2. LIFE IN THE HILLS

The Wicklow mountains are not the highest in Ireland, but they do constitute the largest unbroken area of high ground in the country. Indeed they are hardly mountains at all when compared with the Alps, for example, but the dark rounded shapes of these hills, their tops often lost in the clouds, are a forbidding enough place for animals and plants to forge an existence.

A hillwalker in Wicklow can expect to spend at least part of the day without seeing another person. But the mountains are far from empty. Behind the next rock there may be a mountain hare ready to explode across the heathery hill. Overhead there will usually be a raven playing in the updrafts and announcing its presence with a deep-throated croak. The plant and animal life in these rolling uplands is company indeed for an observant walker.

BILBERRY

Up the Airy Mountain

The exposed summits of Wicklow's mountains are typical high-altitude habitats, and some are just high enough to harbour a few alpine and tundra plants. On the domed summits above 500m, such as Mullaghcleevaun, Tonelagee and Table Mountain, where severe erosion has left little peat detritus behind, heathers are stunted, often giving way almost entirely to dwarfed grasses, especially **bent grass** and **sheep's fescue**, and sedges, while **bilberry** is common.

Lugnaquillia

The summit of Lugnaquillia, Wicklow's highest mountain, is really a wide plateau of short grass, bounded on three sides by steep corries, the North and South Prison and the Barravore cirque. Although surrounded by granite mountains, the summit of Lugnaquillia itself is of mica-schist, thought to be the remnants of the 'roof' rocks above the granite. The baked schist is more resistant to erosion than the granite, which probably accounts for the loftiness of this summit.

The plateau harbours unusual plantlife. After walking through ankle- or even knee-high heathers and grasses, it is a surprise to find oneself walking over a stiff mat of short grass. This mat is especially well developed where the peat has been almost entirely eroded away, as on the Cloghernagh ridge. Rosettes of club moss, like miniature lime-green fir trees, stick up from the short grass carpet. What on first glance appears to be heather, may turn out to be **crowberry**, another of the heath family, with tiny, stiff, waxy leaves, rolled backwards, revealing a white stripe on the underside. It has tiny pink flowers in summer and black berries in autumn.

41

COWBERRY

Overgrazing and the cowberry

Overgrazing — along with the weather and impact of human feet — is one of the main pressures on Wicklow mountain habitats, and one species that is susceptible to grazing pressure is the **cowberry**. This is a tiny heather-like plant that grows on the summits and steeper slopes. Looking not unlike its larger relative the bilberry, it has pale pink flowers in spring and by autumn the berries are scarlet and often hidden among the foliage.

In some places, such as Mullaghcleevaun, on Tonelagee and at various places around Lugnaquillia it was abundant in the early years of this century. J P Brunker recorded it on the mountain heaths and rocks ranging from 1500 to 2900 feet above sea-level, but as early as 1934, he recorded that it was becoming scarcer on the west face of Kippure, owing to the weathering of the peat. The 1977 edition of Webb's *An Irish Flora* listed the cowberry as rather rare in the north and east of the country, and by the 1990s it had become difficult to find. The disappearance of cowberry may be a direct result of increasing grazing by both deer and sheep.

Rocky Cliffs

Diverse plants in varied habitats

Surrounding Lugnaquillia's plateau summit, the rocky cliffs of the corries harbour a diverse community of plants, owing to the variety of tiny habitats among the rocks. Alpine species such as **starry saxifrage, mossy saxifrage**, **dwarf willow** and **alpine lady's mantle**, grow on the isolated cliffs, and the unusual saxifrage, **St Patrick's cabbage**, has also been found in this imposing hanging valley.

Mineral-rich rainwater flushing down the steep slopes adds to the diversity. Ferns, mosses and liverworts thrive on the wet crags, and often the wetter north-facing slopes are more diverse than the drier cliffs with a southerly aspect.

The cliffs above Lough Ouler have **golden saxifrage** as well as **starry saxifrage** occurring in rivulets. Cliffs at Glendalough have the annual **fairy flax** and the woodland species **sanicle** occurring alongside heathers, grasses and ferns. The constantly moist cliffs around Powerscourt waterfall shelter a community of ferns including **Wilson's filmy fern**, **hart's tongue fern**, as well as **clubmoss**, **woodrush** and **sorrels**.

Birdlife on the cliffs

Wicklow's steep cliffs provide nesting sites for the best-known of Wicklow's birds of prey, the **peregrine falcons**, which are enjoying a recovery after years of persecution and the effects of pesticide poisoning.

The call of the peregrine must surely be the wildest 'cry of the mountain' but its high-pitched calling is often echoed by the deep croak of the **raven,** with which it may compete for nesting space on the crags. The raven is a constant presence in the mountains, where it is at home, summer and winter. This largest member of the crow family is well known as a scavenger and feeder on carrion, and to survive they must be wide-ranging in their diet. We have several times come upon a dead deer in the hills, our attention drawn to it by ravens.

The raven tends to nest early in the year, even when snow is lying on the ground. Late winter is the time when weaker prey are most likely to succumb to malnutrition or exposure, so carrion tends to be plentiful at this time. Traditionally, lambs were also born in the hills in early spring, so a supply of afterbirth was available. Nowadays, Wicklow ewes are removed from the hills during the winter months and most lambing takes place in sheds in the lowlands and valleys, yet ravens appear to be as common as — if not more plentiful than — they were several decades ago.

One reason for this is probably a reduction in shooting pressure — in the past, ravens were persecuted by gamekeepers and sheep farmers —as ravens no longer pose a serious threat to farmers' income at lambing time. Secondly, there has been a continued growth in deer populations in the hills and some of the weaker animals generally die in the hungry months of late winter and early spring — a deer carcass could sustain a family of ravens for several weeks. Then there is a variety of other food sources such as mountain hares and rabbits. Ravens are opportunistic feeders. They will take almost anything edible that presents itself and have even been known to feed on rubbish tips alongside hooded crows and jackdaws.

The traditional nesting sites for ravens in Wicklow have been on the rocky crags in the mountains and along the coast but increasingly nests are recorded in trees. The nest is a large and unwieldy structure which may survive from one year to the next. It is possible that ravens now occupy the ecological niche formerly held by large birds of prey, such as eagles, in Ireland.

Scree Slopes

Below most of Wicklow's cliffs is a talus of scree, collapsed boulders and stones which were once part of the cliff above. There are extensive scree slopes in Glenmalure, Glendalough and around Lough Dan and Lough Tay.

Loose scree slopes are hostile places for plants to gain a foothold. However, the most stable parts of the scree slowly build up a community of lichens and mosses and eventually grasses and shrubs establish, their roots in turn stabilising the scree. Once established, **bilberry**, originally a woodland plant, can flourish among large block screes, where there is a certain amount of shade and shelter. Some rare plants also find a niche among the boulders, sheltered from grazing animals, and a look into the cracks may reveal species such as **hard fern** or even, at higher altitudes, **St Patrick's cabbage**.

2.16 James P Brunker (1885-1960) is best known for his botanical work which was published in 1950 as Flora of the County Wicklow. He devoted most of his spare time to exploring the plants of Co Wicklow, which he subdivided into eight regions. He records that his interest in the flora of the county began in 1918 when, on holiday in the town of Wicklow, he 'happened to blunder on the remarkable variety of clovers to be found there… So began a long series of excursions at weekends and during holidays, sometimes alone, but often with willing and enthusiastic helpers; and continuing over a quarter of a century.' His book records over 800 species and still forms the best account of the higher plants of the county. Many of the rare plants which he found have not been seen (or searched for) since.

43

A stable scree slope provides many nesting sites for small animals and birds. Perhaps the most persistent bird of upland scree slopes is the tiny **wren** which survives here throughout the year, even finding food and shelter among the crevices when deep snow blankets the ground. Often the only sign of its presence is a thrilling delivery of high-speed clicking song from deep in the boulders.

In spring it is joined by the **wheatear**, a smart grey and black bird, which arrives back in the mountains in late March from its African wintering grounds just in time to exploit the abundance of insect food among the heather and the rocks. It seems to prefer areas of bare rock or short vegetation where it can easily catch insects on the ground.

A much rarer breeder on these scree slopes is the **ring ousel**, the mountain relative of the blackbird. It looks rather similar to its lowland cousin, except for the distinctive white band across its lower throat, and the silvery feathers on the wing margins. The ring ousel was once widespread in Wicklow, probably nesting on coastal cliffs as well as mountain crags. Nowadays it is found sparingly in some of the corries and big valleys; it is almost certainly under-recorded.

The Boggy Blanket

Peat, which turns the mountain streams a russet brown, is an integral part of the Wicklow landscape. The blanket bog of the uplands is windswept and very often drenched in thick mist or rain. The wet and acid surroundings mean that only the hardiest of plants can survive. Conditions in the mountains are usually too harsh to allow an annual plant to complete all its growing and flowering in one season, so nearly all the mountain plants are perennials, surviving from year to year, using the stored nutrients from the previous year to flower each spring.

Most mountain plants have particular physical adaptations to allow them to survive the wind and cold. A hummock or a rosette shape gives some wind shelter, while narrow or thick waxy leaves reduce drying out by the wind. Some plants like the bilberry and the tussocky grasses have buds at ground level to protect them from frost over the winter.

Much of the peat has been cut in the past, leaving high faces of cut turf. Some regeneration of the peat surface has since taken place, but the vegetation of previously cut areas is mixed, reflecting the varying thicknesses of the remaining peat. Thus, in some areas, plants characteristic of two different habitats occur side by side.

We are fortunate to have some places among the Wicklow moorland where active peat building is still taking place. The Liffey Head bog is one and there are other smaller patches throughout the mountains with a wonderful array of hummocks and pools filled with *Sphagnum* mosses. These 'bog' mosses are the most important builders of the peat structure. When they die, their stems and leaves build up and eventually form the bulk of the peat framework.

BOGBEAN

Mosses and other plants

The Liffey Head bog has several species of **bog moss** or *Sphagnum* in a variety of colours, each specially adapted to life in such nutrient-starved surroundings. Bog moss obtains its nutrients from the water, but because bog water is extremely low in minerals, it has to filter vast quantities of water to obtain the nourishment it needs. Bog moss is just like a sponge, bulging full of water, with specialised internal cells to extract minerals from the water. Some bog moss species, especially the yellowish *Sphagnum papillosum*, first colonise the open water of the bog pools, making it like a thick soup. As these plants die, the dead matter that will eventually become peat builds up and the soup becomes more solid until finally hummocks of moss bulge out of the water. Different moss species such as the red *Sphagnum rubellum* will take over the drier hummocks.

A fascinating collection of other plants and animals can then begin to inhabit the spongy bog mosses, and manage to live in this inhospitable environment. Poking through the dense moss carpet are scattered grasses and sedges, with shoots of heather, occasional **tormentil** flowers and the fragrant **bog myrtle**.

Those carnivorous plants, sundew and butterwort, which trap midges, flies and froghoppers to supplement their diet with nutrients and minerals, may be found here. The **sundews** are beautiful miniature plants with a fleshy disc at their leaf tips, surrounded by tiny red shiny hairs. These hairs have a droplet of sweet sticky liquid, irresistible to insects. As the insect struggles to get free, it becomes more and more ensnared, inducing the sundew to release enzymes to digest its catch.

The **butterworts** look less alien, but they are just as deadly to insects as the sundew. They have long, lime-green leaves, radiating out flat against the peat, sometimes with a single violet-like flower on a long stem reaching out from the centre. Like the sundew, they trap insects on their sticky leaves, and absorb the nutrients.

Other bog plants, such as the **bog asphodel** and **cotton grasses**, which cannot take advantage of insects, have other adaptations: they carefully recycle their nutrients by storing them in their roots.

Insect life in the boggy uplands

Insects such as mayflies, stoneflies, midges, **dragonflies** and **damselflies** need the bog waters for reproduction and the first stages of their life cycle. The larvae of dragonflies and their smaller relatives, damselflies, are voracious carnivores in the water. In spring, the larvae climb out of the water and may be seen in May or June clinging to a stalk to emerge into adults. The spectacular irridescent adult dragonflies circle the bog pools hunting for small insects on the wing, often returning to a favourite perch to eat their prey and keep watch.

Long-legged **pond skaters** skim the surface of the water, while tiny **whirligig**

beetles can be seen gyrating among them. **Water boatmen** use their specialised pair of legs as oars, and have hairs on their bellies to trap an air bubble, allowing them to swim down into the bog pool in search of food.

One common inhabitant of the bogs and other water sources is the **midge**. These tiny speckled biting flies of the Ceratopogonidae and Simuliidae families manage to irritate the human skin out of all proportion to their size. It is only the females that bite, to nourish their eggs. A cloud of midges tends to comprise only one sex, which may account for some midge clouds seeming more voracious than others.

Midges' eggs are laid in a sticky mass onto floating aquatic plants and sometimes the female submerges herself beneath the water to lay. The microscopic larvae attach themselves to plants and rocks, feeding by filtering the water through mouth brushes. The young adults emerge from a bubble of air at the water surface and take to the wing.

Frogs in bogs

The healthy insect population in turn provides abundant food for frogs and birds who feed on them. With its ability to live in or out of the water, the **common frog** is ideally suited to the bog habitat. Frog spawn can regularly be seen in bog pools in spring, but remember that it is illegal to collect it. The active tadpoles are a joy to observe, dredging the pool bottom for food.

Bog birds

Although the wet *Sphagnum* and **bog cottons** are unattractive to most nesting birds, **snipe** breed frequently around the wet bogs, feeding on the edges of the boggy pools, locating food by touch. There are few areas where snipe have been surveyed accurately but at Carrigower bog, in the upper Vartry catchment near Newtownmountkennedy, over 120 were counted one winter.

The haunting cry of another wader, the **curlew**, can occasionally be heard around the wet bogs in summer, although the number of nesting pairs in Wicklow has declined to a very low level. The nest, if present, is camouflaged in the moorland plants and curlews will often fly in to the wet bogs to feed.

Golden plover, which nested in Wicklow 'on the desolate moors that cap the highest mountains' in the early years of the twentieth century has now disappeared. This is probably due to disturbance, as there is still suitable habitat available.

High and Dry on the Moors

Growth of peat bogs relies on frequently waterlogged conditions for the bog mosses to survive, so bogs are very vulnerable to damage by drainage. Bogs may be deliberately drained for farming or forestry purposes, but drainage is also caused incidentally by overburning, overgrazing by sheep, tracks made by mountain users

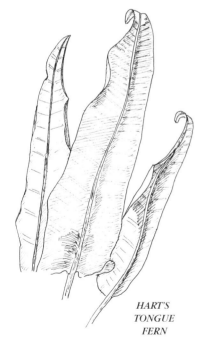

HART'S TONGUE FERN

and natural dissection of the bog. Because most of Wicklow's peat has dried out too much for mosses to thrive, moorland or heath vegetation has taken over and strictly speaking, most of the blanket bog in Wicklow should properly be called moorland or heathland.

Heathland vegetation

The moorland plant that most people will recognise is the heather, one of the most crucial plants in the habitat. Much of the heather in Wicklow is **ling** or **common heather** with tiny rounded flowers. Dotted among this is **bell heather** with its elongated, cowbell-shaped flowers. Occasionally **cross-leaved heath** can be found in the wetter parts of the moor. Large areas of heather moor in the Wicklow mountains show a wonderful range of dark browns, dark greens and purples, constantly changing with the seasons. Heather grows best on reasonably well-drained ground, so it can often show a drier path across a soggy mire.

CROSS-LEAVED HEATH

The other common shrub in the hills, **bilberry** (commonly known as **fraughan**, from the Irish *fraochán*), is recognised by its bright green stems, bare in winter, and with small green or reddish leaves hiding the blue-black berries (fraughans) in autumn. Bilberry likes shade and is more accustomed to flourishing under deciduous woodland or mature conifer plantations. However, on the exposed uplands bilberry can survive where the soil is relatively dry, or where there is a certain amount of shade and shelter. Bilberry is very sensitive to moor burning and to grazing and often reaches its most profuse in crags and crevices where sheep and deer cannot reach.

The rest of the upland vegetation is a mosaic of grasses, sedges, rushes, bog cottons and a few other shrubs. The mixture of species varies depending on the slope, drainage or depth of peat.

The commonest plants in the Wicklow uplands are those that can persist after burning. The bog cottons, **deer grass** and **purple moor grass** survive by virtue of their dense tufts which prevent the burning of the leaf bases. **Mat grass** and **heath rush** on the wetter grasslands can regrow readily from their underground parts.

At a distance, with colours of faded red brick, large swathes of deep peat covered with **cotton grasses** and **deer grasses** seem like prairies, patterned with the white fluffy seed heads of the cotton grass and dotted with raised patches of darker heather. Although the two 'bog cottons' occur together, they prefer slightly different conditions. The deep peat where deer grasses are common has a smooth, hard, wet surface with many bare peat patches, while those areas with cotton grasses dominant are spongy and yielding underfoot and have complete plant cover. **Bog rosemary**, a member of the heath family with delicate pink bell-like flowers, occurs in the damp deer grass areas, accompanied by the orange-yellow **bog asphodel**.

47

Animal Life in the Hills

Although the Wicklow uplands may seem devoid of life, there is a hardy community of animals camouflaged and scattered among the moorland vegetation. The biggest of these are the elusive deer.

Once, the large **red deer** were native in Wicklow, but they were hunted to extinction here probably before 1850. Viscount Powerscourt had a special interest in breeding deer on his estate near Enniskerry, and a herd of red deer from Germany was introduced into the Powerscourt estate in the eighteenth century. Japanese sika deer with white rumps were also imported and these have since interbred with the red deer to produce a **red–sika** hybrid which is now the most common deer in the mountains.

Deer predominantly live in separate female and male herds, except during the rutting season in late autumn. Male deer grow and lose their antlers every year and the older the stag, the larger and more branched the antlers will grow each year. The antlers are soft and velvety in spring but become hard and pointed to enable them to vie for dominance of the herd in the autumn rut.

Originally woodland animals, deer in Wicklow had to adapt to open land as the forests became scarcer. They are now more characteristic of open moorland than forests, which is the usual red deer habitat in mainland Europe. The Wicklow deer live and graze on the open moorland, but some herds will shelter in deciduous or coniferous forests if available.

Although they are often well camouflaged, deer can be found throughout the mountains, often grazing on the moorland grasses and heathers around the Military Road at dawn and dusk. They will also browse in forests, eating young shoots and leaves, and they can damage young trees by stripping off the bark to obtain minerals. Deer have also been known to lick or eat old bones and antlers on moors to get phosphate and calcium which the peatland vegetation lacks.

The absence of large predators such as wolves in Wicklow means that the deer must be culled to prevent excessive tree damage and overgrazing of moorlands as the population grows. This culling is carried out by experienced marksmen and the resulting post-mortem examination of the carcases provides much useful information on the herds.

Another characteristic mammal of the mountains, russet mountain **hares** are well camouflaged and wary, quickly disappearing when disturbed. Hares do not burrow but instead make a hollow in the vegetation, which enables them to live in the wet, boggy mountain areas. They rely on their speed over the open ground to escape from danger. They feed on all types of vegetation, building up a healthy diet from a variety of plants, none of which is particularly nutritious in itself. This means they have to travel over large areas, so hares are rarely seen. The true density of hares becomes evident when snow lies on the mountains and their tracks can be found everywhere, criss-crossing the slopes.

An animal that is even less visible, except unfortunately dead on the roads, is the **badger**. It is usually thought of as a woodland animal, but setts can be found on open ground up to 600m, such as on the slopes of Djouce mountain, Tonelagee and in the Glenealo valley, where the soil is easy to dig and there is little disturbance. We have also seen a single badger sett on the slopes of Lybagh, the southern ridge of Lugnaquillia at about 600m. Although they won't find their favourite earthworms up in the acid peat, badgers will take small mammals such as mice and shrews, and will eat beetles and slugs and, if available, blackberries, acorns and beechnuts.

The **fox** also occurs in a variety of habitats throughout Wicklow. It breeds in earths, but outside the breeding season, it spends most of its time above ground, resting in vegetation cover. It ranges over a large territory and fox droppings can be found in the uplands, where they have carefully marked the edges of their territory.

Feral **goats** with long shaggy coats and curved horns are regularly seen on the remote mountains and cliffs. Originating from escaped domestic goats, they live in small groups of up to ten females with one or more males during the rutting season. They can often be seen in upper Glendalough, Glendasan and on other steep cliffs in the mountains. They will eat almost any plant, including the bark and shoots of trees. The goats thrive on the old mountain pastures close to the mining village at the Upper Lake in Glendalough. Here they live among the ruins of the houses where their ancestors were probably kept for milk and meat by the mining community.

Smaller animals

Because of low calcium availability, there are no snails in the peatlands but the large **black slug** has found a niche instead and probably forms an important part of the diet for the upland carnivores. **Bumble bees** and **wasps** burrow into dry banks or nest in trees and visit the heather moors to feed.

The commonest butterfly is a dull brown species, the **small heath**, whose caterpillars feed on various grasses. The caterpillars of the **emperor** and **fox moths** live and feed on the foliage of bog plants. Occasionally large counterparts of the black beetles of suburban gardens can be found, with shining greenish-brown wing-cases. This is a species of **ground beetle**, which, apart from looking rather colourful, has the distinction of being able to release an unpleasant smell when picked up.

The vast bulk of blanket bog fauna is made up of soil organisms. Because of the high acidity, earthworms cannot survive in the peat. Instead **mites** and **spring-tails** are abundant in the Wicklow peat, living in the surface layers of plant debris. They penetrate to greater depths when the bog dries out a little in summer, and retreat back towards the bog surface via pockets of trapped air when the lower levels again become flooded. The carnivorous **centipede** can also be found here and the bog is very important for the larval stages of **two-winged flies, click beetles** and many types of **spiders**. The **viviparous lizard**, Ireland's only lizard, is surprisingly frequent on upland bogs and moorlands, feeding on the insects.

Birds of the moors

Insects are an important food source for birds on the mountains and moorlands. In the drier parts of the uplands where the heather grows thickly, the air is often filled with the songs of **meadow pipi**t and **skylark**. The meadow pipit is common in the mountains, where the purple moor grass grows in dense tangled tussocks providing good nesting sites. It runs after insects on the ground, snapping them up with extraordinary speed. In spring, the male performs a display flight. This is a quivering descent to the ground like a tiny parachute, with wings and tail fanned out, accompanied by a stream of musical notes.

The distinctive tapping of **stonechats** and the call of the **cuckoo** is frequently heard in summer. Cuckoos often use the nests of pipits. **Whitethroats** may be seen in the wetter and scrub areas. The male's plumage is particularly obvious in summer, with a grey cap, white throat and reddish wings. They feed on insects and their larvae, spiders and fruit. On bare rocky uplands, where grazing keeps vegetation low, the **wheatear** can be found. The handsome **hooded crows** scavenge for carrion throughout the county.

The **red grouse** glides low across the hill to an accompaniment of clucking alarm calls. Its distribution is influenced by a complex of factors including geology, topography, land use, vegetation and food supply. The chicks are fed on a variety of insects including flies, beetles and spiders, but as the birds get older, their diet consists almost entirely of young heather shoots, bilberry leaves and fraughans.

Burning of the moors encourages regrowth of young heather shoots and purple moor grass, which improves the food supply for red grouse. However, it also needs taller, unburnt heather for cover and nesting. In September 1991, a census of grouse in the Liffey Head bog estimated about 44 birds on approximately 500 hectares (over 1200 acres), which gives a density of just under one grouse per 10 hectares (250 acres) of the bog. Red grouse in the uplands occur in highest numbers where there are more minerals in the soil.

Until the middle of the last century, the **white-tailed eagle** was breeding in Wicklow, but it became extinct in Ireland because of persecution, including shooting, egg-collecting, trapping and poisoning. It would be possible to reintroduce this bird to Wicklow, but this is unlikely to be well received by the local sheep farmers. While most farmers recognise the importance of nature conservation, they are not prepared to lose lambs to wild predators, and the laying of poison, mainly targeted at foxes and crows, is still widespread in Wicklow.

One of the most interesting birds of prey in the Wicklow mountains is the **hen harrier**. Like all the other raptors, this species has undergone a series of expansions and contractions in Wicklow over the centuries. There was a remarkable expansion of hen harriers during the 1960s with the widespread afforestation of upland areas in Wicklow. As the young spruce trees grew up, they were accompanied by an impenetrable cover of brambles, bracken and other scrub which provided the harriers with just the security they needed and a high population of small song birds, which are their major prey. In 1961, David Scott found as many as seven breeding pairs of hen harriers in a single ten-kilometre square in east Wicklow

By 1982, however, it was estimated that there were no more than two or three pairs remaining in all of Wicklow. One theory for this decline is that the majority of the forestry plantations, which had encouraged the hen harriers, had grown to maturity, with a closed canopy producing a different habitat for birds. The typical species now were **goldcrest** and **coal tit**, which are not common prey for hen harriers because they prefer the denser cover of the trees. In Antrim, however, harriers nest mainly in conifers, so a question remains as to why the Wicklow birds have been unable to adapt to the changed situation.

The maturing of the forest plantations coincided with Ireland's accession to the EU, and the resulting rise in farm incomes brought a sudden increase in the amount of clearance and 'improvement' of mountain land. Large areas of scrub and heather-covered marginal land, which were suitable hunting ground for hen harriers, were bulldozed and reseeded with grass for sheep. These changes undoubtedly had a significant impact on the harrier population of Wicklow but other factors such as illegal shooting, nest destruction and predation by foxes may well have contributed to the widespread decline.

Today, it is still just possible in March or early April to find a pair of hen harriers circling on the rising air on a Wicklow moorland, far above the effects of intensive farming. Alternatively they can be seen hunting low across the heather moor, with deep wing beats, searching for the small birds that are their staple diet. With the widespread clearance and replanting of forest areas in the foothills of the mountains, we may yet see another return of the hen harrier in coming years.

Kestrels are perhaps the commonest bird of prey throughout Wicklow. They occur not only in the remote mountain areas but also in the lowlands and along the coast, even hunting along newly planted roadsides where the long grass provides suitable habitat for their main prey, the wood mouse. The kestrel, known in some parts of Wicklow as the windhover, can regularly be seen hanging in a stationary position with its wings fluttering like a butterfly and its broad tail fanned out like a rudder holding it in position. From this height, it can detect the slightest movement in the vegetation below and if it sees a mouse it will drop like a stone to take the prey.

A much less common falcon, the **merlin**, also occurs in Wicklow but is largely confined to the upland area in spring and summer. In an extensive in the early 1990s, Anthony McElheron mapped up to twenty-three merlin territories in Wicklow, mainly in the northern half of the mountains, although only about sixteen of these are occupied, in any one year, by pairs which attempt breeding.

The merlin population declined in the 1960s and 1970s, probably because of extensive burning of the heather moorland, and most merlins in Wicklow are now breeding in conifer plantations, using the abandoned nests of crows and other forest birds, even though their hunting grounds remain the open landscape of the hills. Perhaps, as for so many other mountain species, it is the mosaic of different habitats that makes the mountains a suitable breeding area.

Merlins are less easy to find because they hunt low across the hillsides barely skimming the tops of the heather. They feed mainly on small birds such as meadow pipits and large insects such as the emperor moth, which is a common species on the moorland. Even long hours of searching the hills may be rewarded with only a few fleeting glimpses of these enigmatic birds of prey as they flit across their territory.

There is no sound that is more characteristic of the Wicklow mountains in spring than the high pitched 'kee-kee-kee' of the **peregrine**, the lord of the hills. These beautiful falcons soar and dive among the crags on their long sickle-shaped wings. They are the most spectacular flyers of the bird world, achieving speeds of over 100 miles per hour in the downward swoop on an unfortunate victim.

Peregrines are large enough to kill an adult red grouse with a single blow of their powerful talons. However, grouse are relatively scarce on the hills and the peregrine has turned to an easier source of prey — the **pigeon**, which uses the valleys as a handy fly-way. It is a stunning site to see a peregrine drop from the sky on a slow-moving wood pigeon and, with a scattering of feathers, carry off its victim for plucking on a favourite crag.

In winter, peregrines leave their traditional nesting areas and wander widely across the countryside and along the coast in search of prey. As well as their favourite targets, the pigeons, peregrines also hunt flocks of waders and wildfowl in such places as Broadlough and Kilcoole Marshes.

Down the Rushy Glen

Wicklow's valleys are quite different from the broad open expanses of the uplands. Most of the seven valleys on the east of the mountains are narrow, deep glacial troughs, while the three on the west side are wider, more open river valleys.

Valley soils and vegetation

In the eastern glens, moorland species or conifer forests cling to the steep slopes among the scree, while the valley floors have pastures enclosed by dry stone walls or hedgerows. Soils are a complex mixture of peaty podzols, iron humus podzols or skeletal soils, while the gentler improved slopes have brown podzolics, brown earths and reclaimed podzols, often freely drained owing to the morainic and alluvial foundation.

The upper valley slopes have a dwarf-shrub vegetation in which **ling** and **bell heather** dominate, but here it is interspersed with **dwarf gorse**. On the more friable schists and shales the vegetation is often dominated by the thin wiry **mat grass** while heather is more common over the granite. On the lower slopes, just above farmed land, the taller **European gorse** becomes more apparent, with **sheep's fescue**, **bent grasses** and **heath bedstraw** in the ground layer.

The upper edge of good agricultural land coincides roughly with the edge of the limestone drift of the most recent Ice Age, over which well-drained brown podzolics and brown earth soils developed. Grassland and even tillage may extend above this, but only if the farmer continually fights against the inroads of gorse and bracken. Areas which were previously farmed or forested and have now been clear-felled are commonly taken over by bracken, especially in more sheltered areas.

Bracken is a tall, robust fern which has no nutritional value to grazing animals, so it is usually avoided and can completely engulf the smaller plants. It seems to thrive on abandoned farmland — old potato ridges in some of the valleys are now entirely covered with bracken — and is a more aggressive invader than gorse. As the shoots come up in the spring, it turns whole hillsides a beautiful pale green, which becomes a lovely shade of russet in the autumn, as the plants die back for the winter.

Valley animals

The animal community in the valleys is a mixture of mountain and lowland animals. The diversity of habitats allows grassland, woodland and riverbank species to live almost side by side. Hedgerows, fields and woodland provide many niches for common birds such as **tits**, **chaffinches**, **wrens** and **blackbirds**.

A host of mammals lives in the varied habitats of the valleys, including **badgers**, **foxes**, **hares**, **otters**, **rabbits**, **stoats**, **hedgehogs**, **squirrels**, **shrews**, **fieldmice** and **rats**. The **deer** in the area stray occasionally down into the valleys, especially in winter, but they prefer to remain away from human interference and near their upland grazing area. An exception is the Cloghoge valley between Lough Tay and Lough Dan where deer are so plentiful even in summer that they far outnumber the sheep, and the air of the Luggala estate is punctuated everywhere by the shrill warning cries of **sika deer**. Here the herds graze mainly undisturbed across the parkland of the valley floor.

Managing the Mountains

Although the windswept upland area seems like a wilderness, in fact the landscape is very much the result of human intervention. Heather can grow to the height of a deer, but it is usually below knee height in the Wicklow mountains, because of management practices.

Tall heather provides shelter, especially for red grouse, and its young vigorous shoots are essential grazing for these birds in the winter. Traditional management of heather moors involves burning patches of heather every ten years to kill the old shoots, allowing fresh regrowth and ensuring a mosaic of young and mature plants. The moor is also drained to encourage heather growth. However, the main land use in the Wicklow mountains is sheep grazing, and landowners often burn more frequently to encourage the growth of grasses instead of heather. Moor burning generally decreases the diversity of plants on the hills, as it kills off some plants entirely and leaves fewer niches for other species to colonise.

Sheep grazing and moor burning ensure that the vegetation is kept in check and never allowed to revert to natural scrub and woodland. Grazing also determines the distribution of plant species. One example of this is the pale buff clumps of mat grass, which are avoided by grazing animals, who prefer the sweeter grasses. This gives the unpalatable mat grass more space and light, and if the land is overgrazed or too heavily burnt, it will tend to encroach further on areas once covered by heather.

Especially severe fires in the dry summer of 1995 devastated many areas, burning not only the plants, but also the dry peat, reducing large parts of the Sugarloaf mountains to bare rock. Many plants will recover after a controlled fire, but if the peat itself is destroyed or exposed, it can be eroded away, leaving some areas forever stripped of their blanket of peat.

Grazing in the Hills

Grazing in the Wicklow muntains has had a major effect on the distribution of native woodland, blanket bog and heather moorland. The less extreme climate in Wicklow means that soil erosion is not such a problem as in the western uplands, but grazing pressure is a major factor in vegetation change. It is also linked to the practice of burning on the mountains, which takes place frequently after dry periods in the spring and summer. The combined effects are to remove the woody vegetation of heather and to allow invasion by a variety of grasses which are favoured by the sheep. As a result some large sections of the Wicklow mountains are largely devoid of heather and are instead dominated by grassland. This is very evident in a walk from the Sally Gap along the ridge to Mullaghcleevaun, which goes from deep heather moorland to a grassy sward overlooking the reservoir at Blessington. In certain areas, around Laragh for example, there is serious erosion of the blanket bogs which can be partly attributed to grazing pressures. The combined pressures of overgrazing and intensive rereational use in some parts of the mountains are among the major challenges facing the new National Park (see page 58).

The Power of the Elements

Erosion involves the breakup and removal of rocks, peats and soils by the physical forces of water, ice, wind and gravity, helped by human activities.

Erosion by water

Rain falling on the mountains either is taken up by surface vegetation, percolates through the ground, or flows downslope over the ground surface. This continual downward passage of water from the hills gradually erodes the soil, peat and rock in its path.

A number of V-shaped valleys in Wicklow provide evidence of rivers exerting a downward eroding force, but most of them, such as the Scalp near Enniskerry, are the result of glacial meltwater. Water can freeze in cracks in the rocks and act to break them up. Scree slopes occur commonly at the base of rock faces in Wicklow, the result of gravity removing frost-shattered material downslope.

Where the vegetation cover is intact it protects the soil, but if it is damaged or removed the fragile peat is exposed to the processes of erosion. As rain falls on bare peat each drop displaces a tiny amount of the peat, which can then be removed as the rain forms a sheet of water flowing over the surface. This surface flow occurs especially where the peat has been compacted, and the water cannot percolate into it. Water flowing over the surface tends to concentrate, and erodes small closely spaced channels or 'rills', low structures with peat exposed on one side only.

When the water becomes distinctly channelled, it starts to erode larger gullies, which can be seen dissecting many of the Wicklow hills, such as parts of Kippure, Tonduff and Barnacullian. Water in the gully scours even deeper, often to bedrock, and wind erodes it laterally, undercutting the vegetation, so the gully gets wider and deeper.

Freezing of the peat also loosens it and aids other erosion processes. In extreme cases, the only remains of the former peat surface are isolated hummocks or 'haggs', exposed on all sides, but capped by a mat of vegetation, as on Table Mountain, at the head of Glenmalure.

A much less obvious form of erosion occurs *within* the bog. Rootlets of plants expose tiny channels when they die, leaving a network of tubes through which water can flow. These become more eroded until they are large channels or pipes,

55

2.17   Percy's Table, Lugnaquillia
(Cambridge University Collection of Air
Photographs: copyright reserved)

which eventually flow into the surface channel network. The roofs of these pipes finally collapse, leaving surface gullies which continue to act as drainage channels and are thus subject to further surface erosion. Peat pipes can be seen throughout the Wicklow mountains, especially in areas of thick peat accumulation such as around Liffey Head and the Sally Gap.

A more catastrophic erosion of peat by water is known as a bog-burst. This happens occasionally when the peat becomes over-saturated with rainwater and, under the weight of the bog itself and the force of gravity, the water gushes out at the lowest point, dragging the more solid layers with it. If the bog is large and deep, a great flood of semi-liquid peat may be ejected. If the slope below the point of ejection is steep, a devastating torrent may result. Small bog-bursts occur occasionally in the Wicklow mountains, leaving a hollow scar above the mound of displaced peat.

Erosion by wind
Strong winds are common in the mountains and their eroding power is considerable, especially where the surface material is dry or unconsolidated. The drier, upper surfaces of bare peat faces can be undercut by the wind, causing the sides to collapse, thus acting to widen gullies and rills, and aiding in the formation of haggs.

Generally the Wicklow mounains are too wet for wind erosion to have any great effect, but in the hot summer of 1995 the peat surface dried, and much bare peat became loosened and was then susceptible to further erosion. Unconsolidated peat caused by freeze-thaw can also be removed by strong winds. Artificial drainage of the peat for turf cutting or afforestation also dries the upper parts of the bog and allows wind erosion to occur.

The Hand (and Feet) of Man
Erosion
Human activity is an important factor in erosion. The afforestation of land involves the cutting of access roads, which encourages erosion by water, and the growth of the trees may help to drain the adjacent peat, thus subjecting it to erosion. Sheep grazing in the mountains creates muddy tracks where vegetation is damaged, and where erosion can be initiated. Overgrazing by sheep destroys the protective vegetation cover.

The extraction of rocks, minerals and fuels is the most immediately obvious erosion process occurring in the mountains today. Quarrying removes hundreds of tonnes of rock every year. Exposed rock faces in quarries are susceptible to further erosion, especially by freeze-thaw. Mining in Glendalough and Glendasan ceased at the end of the last century, but the scars remain.

Cutting of peat for fuel can have devastating effects. Not only is part of the bog removed, but the bog is also drained and bare peat is exposed to natural processes. Peat cutting has been carried out throughout the mountains, but especially in areas of deep bog, such as around the Military Road near the Sally Gap.

Hill-walking is a popular pastime, and the increasing numbers of walkers over the past few years have resulted in increased erosion of paths in the Wicklow mountains. Severe gullying can be seen along much-used routes, such as parts of the Wicklow Way, the track known as 'the Spink' along the clifftop south of Glendalough Upper Lake and the track to the top of Djouce mountain.

When the ground is frozen, trampling loosens the soil even more and then rain or wind can remove this downslope. Some of the Wicklow Way has been re-routed to avoid extremely fragile wet bog and wooden walkways have been erected along vulnerable sections. Added to the effects of walkers are the problems caused by mountain bikes and motorbike scramblers. These plough up the already incised track, further damaging the fibre base of the bog.

Most of the visitors to the Wicklow mountains have traditionally been concentrated in a few popular places, such as Glendalough and Glencree, and the Military Road has become a popular tourist route through the mountains. By the 1980s there was already considerable evidence of recreational pressure on the hills especially associated with the Wicklow Way. Parts of the path, on Djouce mountain and White Hill are already severely damaged and wooden walkways have had to be placed along some vulnerable sections.

Wicklow Mountains National Park

During the 1980s there was considerable debate about the management of the Wicklow mountains, and the idea of a National Park was mooted by several environmental, conservationist and hillwalking groups. These proposals met with opposition from local farmers, who didn't want to be told how to manage their own environment by lobby groups based mainly in Dublin. The reaction of many local people, when the Taoiseach of the day made the dramatic announcement in 1988 that a National Park was to be created, was to see this as a victory for the Dublin-based recreation and conservation movement. This split in attitudes was the beginning of significant division in the local community on the issue of the national park.

In April 1990, the National Park was formally established, and it was announced that the park would eventually cover an area of more than 30,000 hectares (74,000 acres). Sheep owners and other local residents expressed considerable concern about this development. The main concern focused on the threats to the future of hill-farming and fears that park designation would lead to a massive increase in visitors.

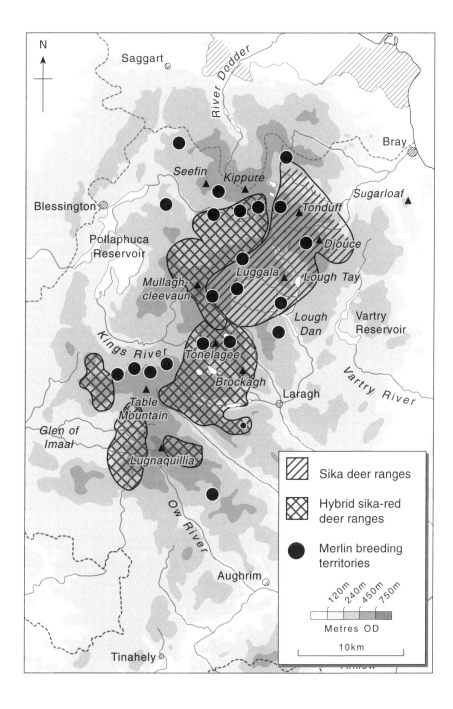

N

Saggart

River Dodder

Seefin

Kippure

Bray

Sugarloaf

Tonduff

Blessington

Pollaphuca Reservoir

Djouce

Mullagh-cleevaun

Luggala

Lough Tay

Lough Dan

Vartry Reservoir

Kings River

Tonelagee

Vartry River

Brockagh

Table Mountain

Laragh

Glen of Imaal

Lugnaquillia

Ow River

Aughrim

Sika deer ranges

Hybrid sika-red deer ranges

Merlin breeding territories

120m 240m 450m 750m

Metres OD

10km

Tinahely

The Wicklow Uplands: A Management Strategy, a study commissioned by Wicklow County Council and published in 1992, was quite critical of the National Park proposal as it existed at that time and suggested instead that an uplands partnership committee should be established under the aegis of Wicklow County Council.

The Luggala Centre

Meanwhile, in 1990, the government approved the provision of a visitor-cum-administrative centre for the National Park. When it was discovered that the visitor centre was to be sited in a forestry plantation on the south side of White Hill, overlooking the spectacular Luggala valley, there was widespread and negative reaction from local residents and environmentalists. Various alternative proposals were made, for example that an existing building, such as Glendalough House near Annamoe, should be used for the centre, or that the existing Glendalough visitor centre could be expanded, but these were rejected.

Several studies and submissions were made, and some of the major objections were that the proposed development would attract large numbers of people onto some of the most sensitive landscapes in Wicklow and the likelihood of damage to the forestry plantation by wind-throw and fires. Eventually, after much bitter controversy, plans for the centre were shelved, when planning permission was refused by An Bord Pleanála.

Uplands Partnership/Council

In 1995 the Department of Arts, Culture and the Gaeltacht commissioned a new management study of the Wicklow uplands, with special reference to the National Park and other designated areas. This study, prepared after wide consultation with interested parties and published in 1996, proposed a new structure for management of the uplands, based on the idea of a Wicklow Uplands Partnership. Most interested groups, including farmers, conservationists, landowners and hillwalkers were strongly in favour of the proposed partnership.

Around the same time, a Wicklow Uplands Council was formed, representing a broad range of community, farming, recreation and environmental organisations. This group believed that, 'It is vital that those who live and work in the uplands and those who use the area should be fundamentally involved in the formulation of strategies for the area and in the execution of those strategies.' This initiative is one of the more hopeful signs for the future of the Wicklow mountains.

3. DEEP IN THE WOODS

Imagine walking in the cool spring air inside an oak woodland on a Wicklow hillside. The ground underfoot is carpeted in deep mosses and last year's leaves, while in the clearings there is a sea of bluebells. A red squirrel clatters up the trunk of a tall tree, spiralling, leaping and occasionally pausing to watch the intruder below. High above there is the sweet song of a wood warbler newly arrived in its breeding territory. All of Wicklow was once clothed in forest like this, teeming with wildlife.

History of Woods in Wicklow
Neolithic farming
When the first neolithic farmers arrived in Wicklow, around 6000 years ago, they found dense forests with mixed species, varying with the topography. Pine, birch and oak forests covered the hills, and oak, elm, ash and hazel woods grew on the better soils of the valleys. It must have been an enchanting place, with vast areas cloaked by lush green trees, and even the waterlogged hollows smothered with willow and alder woods.

These early farmers probably cut a ring around the bark of the trees to kill them. They then grew their crops and grazed their animals underneath the standing dead trees. It is possible that neolithic farming encouraged depletion of the soil and waterlogging, eventually initiating the development of blanket bog. Peat developed on the uplands, enveloping the pine and birch, while the lowlands and valleys remained heavily forested. The stumps of pine trees can still be found in the peat; some found at Turlough Hill are estimated to be 4200 years old.

Bronze Age to Viking times
In the Bronze Age (about 2200-500 BC) more widespread forest clearance occurred, to provide fuel for mining. Some authorities think that Wicklow had become a grassland with scattered trees by the early Iron Age (which lasted from about 500 BC to AD 500) but numerous townland names in Wicklow suggest that the county was still heavily forested by the early Christian period (from about AD 500 onwards). However, the *lo* element in the Viking names Wicklow and Arklow means meadow, which suggests few trees around these coastal settlements by Viking times (about AD 800 to 1150). In any case, the area of woodland in Wicklow had undoubtedly been severely reduced and the composition had been changed by the Middle Ages. It seems that native Scots pine and elm were extinct by the twelfth century, and hazel scrub had expanded into the abandoned farmland of former forest areas.

61

Placenames of Wicklow derived from trees and woodland

Irish word	English translation	Placename examples
Carthann	Mountain ash	Carrick Carthyn
Coill, coillidh	Wood	Kilmore, Quill, Killybeg, Lugnaquillia
Coilleach	Woodland, forest	Killough
Coillseach	Wooded place	Kelsha, Kelshamore
Coll	Hazel	Fiddancoyle, Barnacoyle
Coll-coill	Hazelwood	Callowhill
Crann	Tree	Cransillagh, Ballynagran
Crannagh	Wooded place	Cranagh, Mullanacranna
Craobhach	Wooded land	Crewagh, Annacrivey
Creamh-choill	Garlic wood	Craffield
Daragh	Abounding in oaks	Lackandarragh, Glendarragh
Doire	Oakwood	Ballinderry, Knockaderry
Doirin	Little oakwood	Derreen
Eochoill	Yew wood	Oghil
Fearnach	Place of alder trees	Farnees
Rosachan	Wooded place	Rosahane
Saileach	Willow	Corrasillagh
Saileog	Willow	Ballinsilloge, Parknasilloge
Sailearnan	Willow grove	Barneballaghsilurnan

Source: Liam Price (1967) The Place-Names of Co. Wicklow

Norman times

After the Anglo–Norman invasion of 1170, Wicklow's woods began to be exploited for the English market. The concept of private ownership of land and English 'forest law' was introduced, and the wild woodland of Glencree became the 'Royal Forest', a playground for hunting. Timber works were established at Glencree for the export of timber to build the castle at Haverford. The Royal Forest was eventually abandoned in the early fourteenth century, and pollen analysis at Glencree suggests the complete disappearance of oak from Glencree around this time.

The forests were an important shelter for Gaelic clans. Several deliberate forest clearances were undertaken but were unsuccessful in eliminating the clans, and towards the end of this period, disturbances and clashes probably resulted in forest rejuvenation on abandoned farmland. (Another target of these largely unsuccessful clearances were the wolves that the woods harboured.)

'Plantation' of Wicklow

The final assault on Wicklow's woods started in the 'plantation' period in the sixteenth and seventeenth centuries, when the land was planted not with trees but with Protestant English settlers. Probably because of the rugged terrain, the county seems still to have had more than average forest cover, although many areas called 'woods' were probably unfenced wooded pastures. The forests were now exploited to the full for timber for ships, houses and barrel staves, and also to fuel the wood-hungry iron works which had been established in several sites in south Wicklow in the seventeenth century. The smelting of iron, imported from Wales, required 2¼ tonnes of charcoal for production of each tonne of bar iron.

The forest of Shillelagh became celebrated for its oak timber in the mid-1600s. Timber was exported from it in vast quantities, and was used in buildings in England, France and Holland. Vast amounts of timber went to build merchant and navy ships, which had a lifespan of only 30 years. Oak, elm and beech were favoured for the hull, while pine or spruce were selected for the masts. Queen Elizabeth I again introduced a deliberate policy of destruction of wild woodlands, with the double intention of flushing out rebels and wolves while also supplying timber to England. However, the woods were nearly exhausted and by the end of the century, Ireland had become a net importer of timber.

More recent times

By the early 1700s, timber had become so scarce that landowners were advised to encourage new planting on their estates. New tree species appeared on the estates at this time, including **sycamore, Spanish chestnut, lime, walnut, hornbeam, plane, English** and **Dutch elm** and the once-native **Scots pine.** There was a tradition of woodland management in Wicklow, with coppicing carried out on the Meath, Malton, Mount Kennedy and Fitzwilliam estates. The copses included pure oak stands and mixtures of birch, ash and holly, which were cut at 25–30-year intervals.

In the eighteenth and nineteenth centuries, new woods were planted within the demesnes, introducing more new species to the county, such as **horse chestnut, turkey oak, holm oak** and various ornamental conifers.

There seems to have been sufficient timber in Wicklow to support a variety of industries, including the mining operations in Glendalough, Glendasan and Glenmalure. However, a Bartlett drawing of 1818 depicts Glendalough entirely bare of trees, as the valley was stripped of timber for fuel and charcoal for smelting. This led the mining company to plant a quarter of a million trees around Glendalough in 1857 to provide future pit props and fuel. Fortunately, mining ceased before the timber was mature, and many **Scots pine** and **larch** survive today in the valley. The adjacent Derrybawn woods also survived and were managed throughout this period and the oaks still show evidence of former coppicing.

Another major pressure on the woods was the increasing demand for farmland in a phase of unprecedented population growth and hunger. The struggle for fuel intensified on the remaining woods, scrub and bushes, reaching a peak as famine gripped the country in the mid-nineteenth century. Much of Wicklow was stripped bare of trees, but the first edition ordnance maps (1830s) show good woodland surviving in many eastern parts, including the Arklow area and the Avonmore valley. West Wicklow seems to have had little woodland cover, and tenants were 'glad of hedge trimmings for firewood'. It was here in Glenbride that pure conifer stands were first established later in the nineteenth century, to redress the balance.

Conifers such as larch, spruce, firs and pine were increasingly planted, especially as nurse crops for hardwoods, but subsequently on their own. The Coronation Plantation of Scots pine in the Liffey valley was named for the crowning of William IV in 1831. Larch, spruce and Scots pine were planted in Rathdrum in 1850 and Ballyreagh in 1870. Beech was the most popular broadleaf species planted in Wicklow in the nineteenth century; very little oak was planted at that time.

Twentieth century

By the beginning of the twentieth century, a fraction of broadleaved woods remained, mainly in old demesnes, ornamental plantations or former coppice areas. With the collapse of the landlord system, the state took charge of timber production. A forestry school was established at Avondale, and trial plots of many tree species were planted, including **eucalyptus.** Many of the first modern plantations were established in Wicklow, encouraged by the presence of this school.

The 1920s saw the afforestation of Wicklow's valleys, with new plantations in Crone and Ballyreagh in Glencree, Lugduff in Glendalough, Ballyboy and Cloghernagh in Glenmalure and the Aughrim to Aghavannagh valley. The war and post-war period exerted great pressure on forests, but the 1950s saw the acceleration of conifer afforestation, especially the planting of stands in upland moorland areas previously considered unplantable. Many of the last remaining deciduous woodlands in state ownership were shamelessly underplanted with conifers.

The transformation of Wicklow's landscape from extensive broadleaved woodland cover to open land represents an enormous habitat change, which has had huge implications for woodland wildlife. Several species that were once widespread in Wicklow are no longer found today, in particular wolves, which were deliberately hunted and persecuted, mainly because they were a threat to farm animals.

3.1

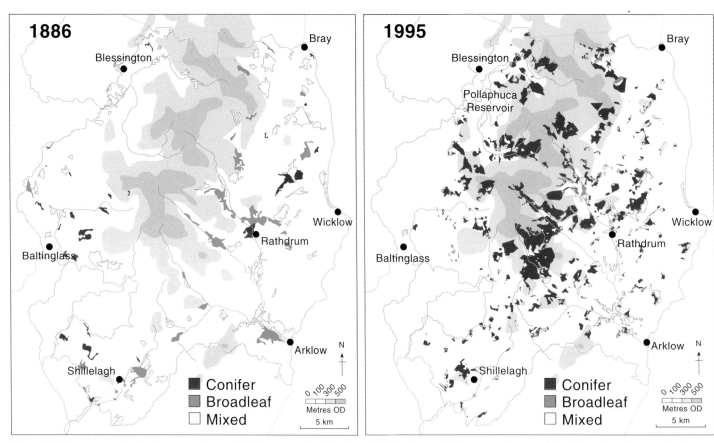

Maps 6a.b *The changes in forest cover in County Wicklow as mapped by Mary Kelly-Quinn. By 1886 most of the remaining broadleaved and mixed woodlands were on the east of the mountains. A few conifer plantations had been established but most of the state afforestation took place in the mid-1900s. By 1995 only a few tiny fragments of native woodland remained in nature reserves. (after Tomlinson in: Aalen, Whelan & Stout, Atlas of the Rural Irish Landscape, 1997)*

3.1 *The Coronation plantation in the Upper Liffey valley. One of the earliest plantations in Wicklow, it was named in honour of King William IV in 1831. With a mixture of oak and Scots pine, it has matured to resemble native woodland and provides a rich habitat for wildlife. (Frank Doyle)*

3.2 *The wood mouse is probably Ireland's commonest mammal. It lives in a network of runs beneath the ground or under vegetation. It is a common prey species for owls, kestrels and foxes. (Frank Doyle)*

3.3 *Fly agarics are among the most poisonous fungi in woodland. However, they are eaten by slugs and snails without causing them any apparent harm. (Richard T. Mills)*

3.4 *Primroses are typical of open sunny glades in woodland and long-established hedgerows. (Frank Doyle)*

3.5 *The long-eared owl is the commonest species of owl in Ireland. Old crows' nests in conifer woods are often used for breeding. The adults are normally silent but in summer the young birds make a wheezing sound when calling for food. Wood mice are the most frequent prey, followed by brown rats. (Richard T. Mills)*

3.8

3.9

3.6   Oak sapling in a protective tube at Tomnafinnoge Wood. Selective felling of mature oaks over the centuries has reduced the Shillelagh woods to a remnant of their former glory. However, public ownership and some enlightened management may save the remainder from extinction. (Richard Nairn)

3.7   A badger sett in woodland. The main setts are distinguished by a large number of entrances with piles of earth and discarded bedding outside each hole. The woodland floor near an active sett is criss-crossed with well worn tracks. Some undisturbed setts may be hundreds of years old with extensive networks of underground tunnels. (Richard T. Mills)

3.8   Siskin among lichens. This small finch breeds mainly in coniferous forests but it feeds in the autumn on the fruits of the alder tree which grow abundantly on river banks. The bark of old alder trees can be festooned with lichens which act as indicators of good air quality. (Richard T. Mills)

3.9   Goldcrest. Ireland's smallest resident bird is a common breeding species in both broadleaved and coniferous woodland. It spends most of the time in the woodland canopy searching for insects among the tree tops. (Richard T. Mills)

3.10   Red squirrel. This native species is still quite common in mature woodlands in Wicklow despite competition from the introduced grey squirrel. They spend most of the time foraging for seeds, fruits and fungi. Breeding takes place in special nests or dreys built high in the fork of a mature tree. (Richard T. Mills)

3.11   Feral goats regularly eat the bark of trees causing significant damage to woodlands. They also graze the understorey and, in doing so, remove young seedling trees, thus preventing natural regeneration. (Wesley Atkinson)

3.12   Foxgloves in a forestry plantation. These large colourful flowers favour the acidic soils which are common in Wicklow. They can tolerate the dense shade of coniferous woods and often grow along old stone walls within the plantations. (Richard T. Mills)

3.13   Beech woodland in autumn. The density of the foliage allows little light to penetrate to the woodland floor and the ground flora is naturally sparse. The fallen leaves are slow to decompose and build up a deep litter layer. (Richard T. Mills)

3.14 A carpet of bluebells in the broad-leaved woodland at Luggala. Woodland flowers appear early in the year to take advantage of increased light before the canopy casts a deep shade. (Éamon de Buitléar)

3.15 Silver-washed fritillary. This large butterfly is associated with old broad-leaved woodland. The eggs are usually laid on the bark of a mature tree in an area where the larval food plant, common dog violet, is available. The adults fly in sunny glades in late summer. (Richard Nairn)

3.16 Native woodland along the shores of the Upper Lake at Glendalough. In the early nineteenth century this area had been stripped bare of timber as the rising population scoured the area for fuel and charcoal for smelting. The secondary woodland is now dominated by oak and birch but contains a variety of non-native species such as Scots pine, beech and sycamore. (Richard Nairn)

3.15

72

Oakwoods

Oakwoods, with their wide-spreading branches cloaked in soft green mosses, are some of the most beautiful and diverse habitats in Wicklow. The **sessile oak** — also known as the **Irish oak,** although it occurs in acidic mountain areas throughout Europe — is Ireland's national tree and is the primary species of Wicklow's oak woods. The sessile oak is distinguished from the lowland pedunculate oak by its acorns being clutched tight against the branches and its stalked leaves.

Oaks are not the only trees in oak woods — other common species are **ash,** hazel and holly — but they are the most important to the forest ecology, as oaks directly feed several hundred insect species, and so indirectly support a vast number of animals further along the food chain.

The mature large trees in an oakwood (mainly oak and ash) form the tall *canopy layer*, towering above the *understorey* trees of holly and **hazel**, which in turn overlook the *shrub* and *ground* layers of brambles, shrubs, ferns and flowers. It is this 'layering' in a deciduous forest that makes it such a diverse habitat, with plenty of niches for a great variety of life to colonise.

Holly, which forms the understorey, is intimately connected to Irish oakwoods and it is well adapted to the habitat, its shiny evergreen leaves able to take advantage of the spring light before the oaks are ready to start growing. The prickly leaves are the holly's protection against grazing animals. Though holly is usually a bush, there are actual holly trees, some as tall as a house, in Glendalough. The leaves near the top of these trees are perfectly smooth, with not a prickle in sight — the holly has cleverly not wasted its resources on producing prickles where no goat or deer could reach to graze. Unlike most trees, holly has separate male and female trees, the female ones bearing the familiar red berries only after pollination from the male tree by insects.

Flowers of the forest

In summer when the trees are in full leaf, it is shady in the woods, but a verdant, dappled light does filter through so that at least some light reaches the plants of the lower layers. When a large tree eventually falls, it leaves a gaping hole in the canopy, letting even more light through, which allows light-hungry plants such as grasses to thrive for a few years, before the canopy closes in again.

Spring is the traditional time for a walk in woods, to marvel at the flowers of the woodland floor. The **bluebells, wild garlic, wood anemones** and **celandines** that live under the trees are specially adapted to the reduced amount of light. These plants grow and flower in early spring as soon as it becomes warm enough but before the leaves have appeared on the trees, so they get maximum light. For the rest of the season, all they need to do is disperse their seed, which will lie dormant until the warmth and light of the following spring.

Enchanted woodlands

Non-flowering woodland plants create their own enchantment in the dappled light. In a moist shady wood, soft **moss** coats every available surface — forest floor, boulders, dead branches or living trees — large trees drip with **lichens, woodrush** and **bilberry** display their greens and reds, and **ferns** growing from damp ground or mossy tree trunks uncurl their new leaves from a pale furry spiral.

Lichens, unique combinations of algae and fungi — which can take many forms, from smooth black coatings to bright yellow rings — take hold on tree trunks and rocks. The most eye-catching are shaggy olive-green tufts that cling to trunks and branches. Lichens are a good indicator of air quality. The stemmed and bushy lichens are especially vulnerable to pollutants in the air. That is why they never grow close to cities or anywhere the air quality is poor. Grey-green branched lichens draping the trees mean the air is clean and fresh.

Where moss has gathered, plants like **wood sorrel** can grasp a hold on a tree trunk and the tangle of green gives the forest a jungly feel. The trailing stems of the climbing **honeysuckle** drape the trees with fragrant flowers and fuzzy seed heads. **Ivy** too climbs thickly along the ground and up the trunks, clinging on with myriads of false roots, flouting forest-layer rules in search of light. Although popularly supposed to choke trees, it only really damages young or very old, unhealthy trees and it has a very important place in the woodland community. The thick foliage provides vital shelter for woodland animals, and cover and food sources for nesting birds, both from its black berries and from the healthy insect population sheltering under its tendrils.

In autumn, as the leaves fall, the forest floor again comes alive. Different species of fungi produce their spore-bearing bodies (mushrooms and toadstools) in various seasons, but a majority sprout up in the autumn, creating a display of brash, vibrant reds and yellows blended with softer tones of rust and grey. The tall shaggy **ink-cap** is easy to recognise, as is the yellow spongy **boletus.** The **puffballs** are unmistakable, thin-skinned spherical mushrooms containing spores, sometimes on a short stalk. When they mature, a raindrop or a gentle tap will release a puff of spores into the air through a tiny hole.

Fungi are important to the woodland ecosystem, living throughout the year under the soil or on dead wood (the **bracket fungus** for example), and helping to decompose the forest leaves. **Basidiomycetes** particularly are responsible for the breakdown of wood, both in living trees and in dead wood.

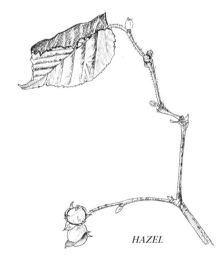

HAZEL

Threats to the woods

Many of Wicklow's oakwoods, in particular those adjacent to the mountains such as the Glendalough oakwoods, are habitually visited by deer, sheep and goats from the neighbouring hills, which efficiently nip off the sweet young tree shoots, and will eat the entire stem of a young sapling. This is a serious threat to a forest. When large trees eventually die, younger trees should take their place so that the forest is continuously regenerated. If the young trees are eaten, there will not be a next generation to take over, and the forest will gradually come to an end. This problem can only be overcome by the erection of high deer fencing, and constant monitoring.

Fortunately, few of Wicklow's oakwoods — apart from the private woods near Greenan — suffer from the choking effects of rhododendron. **Laurel**, however, is threatening some of Wicklow's oakwoods. Its long waxy leaves look similar to the rhododendron, but are arranged flat along the stem, not radiating. Laurel invasion can be halted by laboriously cutting the plants and painting the cut stalks to prevent regrowth.

Other Broadleaved Woods

Apart from the oakwoods, there are scattered patches of broadleaved forests throughout the county. Birch woods comprise **silver birch** and **downy birch,** both native Irish trees. In winter delicate patches of birch woods show their beautiful reddish hue on the lower slopes of Faninerin mountain, in Glenmalure. Birch is a light-hungry coloniser, one of the first trees to take over a neglected hillside, and, together with Scots pine, formed the major upland woodland of Wicklow after the Ice Age. Today, given time, birch usually gives way to other trees, and the forest would eventually culminate in oak or ash woodland.

Ash–hazel woodland occurs in parts of the Glen of the Downs woods, on base-rich soils on shallow slopes. **Holly** and **hawthorn** occur in the understorey. Hazel is common as an understorey tree also in Wicklow's oakwoods and the familiar hazelnuts are an important source of food for many of the mammals. They can be found split by a squirrel or punctured by mice.

Beech woods or stands of beech in other woods are a common relict of nineteenth-century planting in large estates. They are enchanting places, with only dim light seeping through the dense foliage. However, they are poor in ground flora as very few plants can grow in such dense shade. Nevertheless, they yield a good supply of prickly beech mast, containing the triangular nuts, a favoured food source for **squirrels** and other woodland mammals. The summer migrant **chiffchaff** is commonly found associated with beech stands in the Glen of the Downs woods.

The beech can be a threat to oakwoods, however. Its arrangement of branches and leaves casts a very dense shade, and only its own seedlings can tolerate

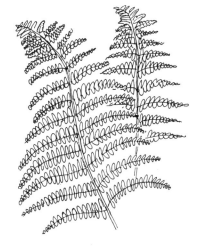

BRACKEN

75

growing underneath. Thus the young beech trees tend to be more successful than the other trees, and gradually the wood becomes more and more dominated by beech trees instead of oak. Management of Wicklow's oakwoods thus has to include the removal of beech from important but vulnerable oakwoods.

Scrub vegetation is a very important habitat, as it consists of a mixture of bushes and tree seedlings at various stages of growth. The wide variety of plant species often contributes to a rich wildlife. The bird population includes woodland species as well as birds more characteristic of open ground. The scrub near Broadlough includes thick gorse patches, on which **linnets** sing. **Willows** and **alders** are found in the damper places, in marshy ground, along rivers, beside lakes.

Life in the Wildwoods

Of all Wicklow's habitats, woodlands have the greatest diversity of wildlife. The variety of animals, interconnected in a complex of food webs, ranges from the hordes of tiny caterpillars to more limited numbers of voracious predators, both mammals and birds.

Mammals

With woodland loss, many mammals have become adapted to a variety of other habitats, even though woodland is their original and preferred home. Woodlands are important habitats for **field mice, stoats, badgers, deer, rabbits** and **foxes,** which are all found also in a variety of other habitats in Wicklow.

Wicklow harbours six out of the seven species of bat found in Ireland. **Pipistrelle, long-eared, Leisler's, Daubenton's, whiskered** and **natterer bats** have all been recorded in Glendalough by staff of the National Park. Bats need the shelter of trees or caves, often feeding close to water, which is a good source of flying insects. They feed from dusk, navigating in the dark by means of the echoes from their shrill cries. They hibernate from October to March in caves, mines, cellars and buildings, and give birth in the spring to a single young, which is constantly carried by the mother for three weeks until it can fly.

A quiet summer's evening walk through Wicklow's open woods is quite likely to be rewarded with the sight of a **red squirrel.** Although once indigenous, the red squirrel is thought to have become extinct in Ireland by the early eighteenth century, a casualty of the extensive woodland loss. It was re-introduced from England in the nineteenth century. With the extensive reafforestation it has spread again throughout much of the country.

The red squirrel is one of our most attractive woodland animals, often heard before it is seen, noisily searching for nuts high in the branches. It is originally a conifer woodland animal, and favours woods with some Scots pine or larch. It feeds on cones, nuts, beech mast, berries, mushrooms and occasionally insects,

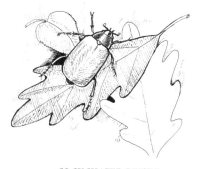

COCKCHAFER BEETLE

young birds and eggs. In times of plenty, squirrels often bury stores of nuts and acorns. These may germinate — an unintentional aid to forest regeneration.

Squirrels feed by day and sleep at night in covered dreys in the fork of a tree. Nature detectives can find evidence of red squirrels in tiny toothmarks at the edge of a split hazelnut, or in the eaten remains of a pine cone, like an apple core.

An American native, the **grey squirrel** was introduced into Longford in 1913. Now common in woods and parks of the north and east of Ireland, it is also present in a number of Wicklow woods. The grey squirrel seems to have a competitive edge over the red, especially in broadleaved woodland, so it is to be hoped that the widespread replacement of the red with the grey squirrel that has happened in Britain will not be repeated here.

WOOD SORREL

There have been occasional reports of sightings of the rare **pine marten** in Wicklow, the most recent in 1961. The pine marten is a long, low, shy animal with a beautiful chocolate-brown coat and pale bib and ears, which lives in woodlands and scrub. It nests in holes under tree roots or boulders and it feeds on a range of prey, mainly mice and rats, sometimes squirrels. Seasonally it may turn to small birds, beetles, berries or fish.

The pine marten was once widespread in Wicklow and was holding its own in the county at the end of the nineteenth century. Woodland loss, together with trapping for fur and in the mistaken belief that it was a pest, severely reduced the population. It is now confirmed only in the west and south of Ireland, but it seems to be on the increase. With increased tree planting, it may spread back to Wicklow in the future.

Woodland insects

The continuous droning one can hear on a summer's day in the Wicklow woods comes from thousands of flying insects of various sizes and shapes, each individually making only a tiny sound. **Bees, wasps, flies, ants** and **beetles** all contribute to the woodland community.

The caterpillars of several butterflies — **peacock, silver-washed fritillaries, painted ladies, tortoiseshells, speckled woods, wood whites** — and **moths** feed on the trees and plants. Both the caterpillars and the butterflies themselves are eaten by birds and spiders.

Woodland birds

Broadleaved woods have a high diversity of songbirds. In spring the woodlands are alive with the songs and chatterings of many birds. The most common species are **wren, robin, blue tit, chaffinch** and **great tit. Goldcrest, chaffinch** and the summer migrant, **chiffchaff,** flit through the canopy, searching for insects in the tree tops. **Wrens** fly low through the woods, and can often be mistaken for a small mammal as they skulk in the undergrowth in search of food.

Small woodlands and copses support tits of all species, and these essentially woodland birds show a certain loyalty to particular woodland habitats. The **great tit** is by far the commonest in beechwoods, while the **blue tit** is dominant in oakwoods, and the **coal tit** is fairly constant in both, but holds its own in conifer woods, where it is adapted to finding food among needles. The **long-tailed tit** makes use of a variety of habitats, such as hedgerows, scrub and open canopy, and they travel in twittering flocks from tree to tree. The long-tailed tit has the most spectacular hole nest, carefully constructed of moss, cobwebs, hair and lichen, and lined with feathers.

If one sits long enough in a Wicklow oakwood, there is a good chance of spotting a **treecreeper.** The exploits of this bird are fascinating to watch. It flies to the base of a tree trunk and then scurries up the trunk, often in a spiral pattern, in search of insects and larvae in the cracks of the bark. It then flies down to the base of the next tree and repeats the process. When it stays still against the tree bark, its speckled brown back is perfectly camouflaged. It finds insects mostly in trees with rough bark like oak and pine and it nests behind the loose bark of mature trees or ivy.

3.17 Aerial view of native broadleaved woodlands at Luggala near Sally Gap. The waters of Lough Tay can be seen in the foreground. (Cambridge University Collection of Air Photographs: copyright reserved)

Some of the deciduous woods have great diversity on the ground among the shrubs and trees. The elusive **jays,** colourful arboreal members of the crow family, feed on bulbs and fruit, and are famous for burying stores of acorns like squirrels. They can be found throughout the Wicklow woods, but usually only as a distinctive excited rasping chirr and flash of blue and bronze as they fly away. We have found their tiny, electric-blue-and-black-striped wing feathers in Knocksink wood.

The abundance of small birds and small mammals in the Wicklow woodlands provide enough food to support **sparrowhawks,** which hunt low through the trees and skim the shrubs to surprise their prey.

Owls are scarce in Ireland. Wicklow has two breeding species. The **long-eared owl,** which breeds in woodlands, often nests in old crows' nests in pine woods. Beautiful ghostly **barn owls** have been spotted at night around various parts of Wicklow, often near buildings and towns.

Some of the larger woodlands support occasional nesting of the rare **redstart** and **wood warbler**, which are associated with mature woodland. Redstarts sometimes breed at Luggala and Glendalough, while the wood warbler visits remnants of high forest at Powerscourt and is an annual visitor to Glendalough, its ecstatic melody echoing through the valley on summer evenings.

The **blackcap** is a graceful woodland summer visitor to Wicklow, now quite widespread, occurring in mature oak woodland with good shrub layer such as at Powerscourt, and Lough Dan woods.

The **pied flycatcher** is a very occasional summer visitor, and has bred at least once in Wicklow. The much commoner **spotted flycatcher** catches insects on the wing at the edges of thin woods and farm copses.

Woodcock are perfectly camouflaged against the ground, living where there is an open canopy, dry nesting ground and wet feeding areas.

Saving the Woods

The oakwood known as **Tomnafinnoge Wood** (part of the Coolatin woodlands), in south Wicklow, is widely regarded as the last surviving remnant of the ancient Shillelagh woods which once stretched for many thousand of acres across the south of the mountains. Like all the former woods in this area it was managed in the past by a method involving coppicing. All the estate records for the Shillelagh area show that cutting cycles in these oakwoods varied from 16 to 33 years with an average cycle of 25 years. The woodland managers of previous centuries found it more economical and efficient to use a system of rotational harvesting of existing woodland rather than felling and replanting. These early estate managers were expert conservationists but, unfortunately, the value of the timber was so high and pressures to exploit and remove all of the woodland were so great that large areas were cleared during the seventeenth and eighteenth centuries.

79

A proposal in 1991 to grant a felling licence for Tomnafinnoge Wood was strongly resisted by both local and national conservation bodies, but the County Council was unable to enforce a tree preservation order here because of the likely enormous costs of compensation which would be required by the owners. A voluntary group, called Friends of Coolatin Wood, was established and set about fundraising for purchase of the site. The end result has been purchase of the site by Wicklow County Council, with joint funding from the voluntary movement and from the Office of Public Works. However, although the immediate danger has passed, there is still no management plan for its future nor any detailed proposals for public access to the site.

Another remnant of the woodland heritage that has come under pressure is the **Glen of the Downs,** near Delgany. A deep gorge which was carved by meltwater escaping from the front of a glacier during the last Ice Age, this valley is now clothed in deciduous woodland with a mixture of oak, ash, hazel and some planted beech and Scots pine. As state-owned land, it was one of the first statutory nature reserves to be declared under the Wildlife Act, 1976.

The floor of the valley also contains the N11 road, one of the busiest traffic routes in the country, which is now designated a 'Euroroute', linking Dublin with the ferry port at Rosslare and the rest of Europe. Section by section, the N11 had been upgraded to cope with increasing volumes of heavy traffic and the resultant congestion, but the narrow section through the tree-lined Glen of the Downs remained as a bottleneck, especially at weekends. It was proposed to widen the existing road to provide a dual carriageway from Kilmacanogue to the Glen of the Downs to relieve the pressure.

The original route proposed for the new road would have had a direct impact on approximately 2% of the nature reserve, with serious effects on the ash–hazel woodland on the valley floor and the stream which runs through it. The County Council accordingly revised its proposals, reducing the width of the road and finding a new alignment further west, which avoided serious damage to the wetter parts of the glen and reused some older sections of road that had lain idle as lay-bys since completion of a previous road improvement.

Local opposition to the new road was largely satisfied with this compromise, and the County Council commissioned a special study to design a retaining structure for the western side of the new road. The study recommended an innovative technique using 'geotextile' materials to achieve a high visual and ecological compatibility with the rest of the glen. It also recommended that the importation of non-local topsoil should be discouraged, to prevent accidental introduction of exotic species to the nature reserve. Large numbers of acorns were collected from the oak trees in the glen and grown in a nursery for planting out after road construction, in order to protect the genetic stock in the nature reserve.

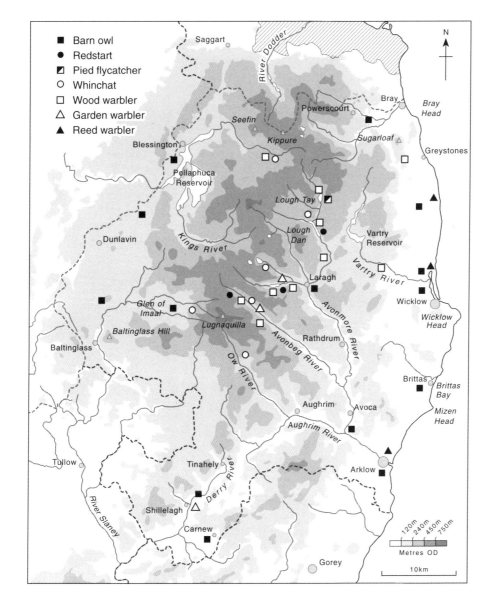

Legend:
- ■ Barn owl
- ● Redstart
- ◪ Pied flycatcher
- ○ Whinchat
- □ Wood warbler
- △ Garden warbler
- ▲ Reed warbler

Map 7 Some scarce breeding birds in County Wicklow in the 1990s. Several of these species – wood warbler, redstart and pied flycatcher – are woodland specialists preferring the remaining areas of oak woodland in the valleys. The barn owl is confined to the lowlands and especially favours river valleys. Records of this elusive owl have been collected by Brian Madden and Dominic Berridge.

With work on the new road due to begin in a few months, events took a dramatic turn in late 1997. Environmental campaigners, including some seasoned 'eco-warriors' from different parts of the world, set up camp in the glen. Amid a blaze of publicity, they built large tree houses high in the branches of some old beeches between the road and the stream. A growing encampment on the ground was marked by a pall of smoke from the wood fires, as the campaigners placed themselves in the line of fire. They argued that the new road was not necessary and that the trees were threatened as part of an arrangement with 'the developers' to sell off the timber for profit. This type of radical direct action was a new feature in the Irish conservation scene but the entire argument quickly became embroiled in court actions.

Coniferous Plantations

Some conifer plantations in Wicklow date from the last century: the Coronation Plantation started in 1831 for the crowning of William IV, and Glendalough's mature Scots pine was planted by the miners in the 1850s. The character of much of Wicklow's open land has been radically altered by the planting of dark green tracts of conifer trees over the last century. Large-scale planting of conifers by the state started in the Wicklow glens in the 1920s, with Crone and Ballyreagh woods. With increased planting in the last thirty years, forests have been established at higher elevations on the bog, but a combination of inadequate soils, competition from the native vegetation and exposure resulted in a poor crop.

The dominant tree planted in Wicklow is **sitka spruce**, with **lodgepole pine** on poorer ground as well as **Norway spruce**, **larch**, **Scots pine** and **Douglas fir**. None of these species is native to Ireland, although the introduced Scots pine is considered semi-native because it is similar to the ancient Irish pine we once had.

Because they are not native to Ireland, there is a far smaller number of insects that can live on these trees, and so there is an even smaller number of birds and mammals feeding on them. This means much lower species diversity in these conifer plantations. Since these forests are planted for commercial reasons, they are very densely spaced, allowing no light to penetrate to the forest floor, which is dark and lifeless.

Conservationists generally denounce coniferous forestry plantations, because of their effect on the landscape and habitats and their tendency to acidify their surroundings. However, even though they are 'alien' in the landscape, conifer forests can provide limited habitats for wildlife, and sheltered spots for wildlife watching, especially where the conifers have been sympathetically mixed or edged with broadleaved trees.

Recently some thought has been given to creating plantations that are more wildlife-friendly and aesthetically acceptable. More deciduous trees are being planted at forest edges and in isolated groups within the plantation, and some consideration is being given to the shape of the whole forest, a factor that is vital to the appearance of a planted hillside. The shape of the whole plantation is also important in making the wood look 'natural'. This is essential for planting on slopes, where the entire form of the plantation is clearly visible.

There is also much more scope for planting small groups of broadleaves within large conifer plantations. Small deciduous stands support more species than the same area planted in one single large block within a conifer plantation. Recent oak plantings in Glencree are much welcomed and with current environmental awareness, deciduous planting should play a much larger part in forestry plantation in the future. These will provide many more wildlife habitats and may partially restore the character of the wildwoods that Wicklow once supported.

Birds and beasts

For some bird species, conifer forests are the major habitat in Wicklow. The **siskin** is characteristic of coniferous plantations, and the Wicklow mountains are considered a stronghold of the species. Another occasional resident of old coniferous plantations such as the Coronation Plantation is the **crossbill**, a relatively rare bird in Ireland. Numbers vary from year to year, depending on eruptions from the continent, but the species appears to be well established now in Wicklow. In the past, very young plantations have provided perfect cover to nesting **hen harriers**, prompting the hope that, with so much re-afforestation, hen harriers may once again return to Wicklow.

The more mixed plantations, especially when mature, harbour a mammal and bird community that is comparable to that of broadleaved woodlands. **Red squirrels** feed on cones and deer, which can do considerable damage to young trees, shelter in the conifer plantations. Most animals which make their homes in the conifer plantations usually stay at the forest edges, where light allows a mixed covering of plants to grow, rather than venturing into the dark interior rows where the only carpet is of dead needles.

Forestry in the landscape

While the area of deciduous woods in Wicklow has been steadily eroded, coniferous forests have continued to expand. The effects of blanket forestry are obvious in places such as the Ow valley, where the entire landscape is filled with forestry right to the summits of the hills, closing off extensive areas of formerly open land.

Of the 36,000 hectares (89,000 acres) of existing plantation in Wicklow, 80% is under the control of Coillte, the state-owned forestry company. The peak planting period of Coillte plantations was between 1950 and 1960, when an average of 132 hectares (326 acres) was planted each year. Much of this land was purchased by the State Forest Service from local farmers. Unfortunately, broadleaved trees have never made up more than 10% of the total area planted since 1920, and between 1960 and 1985 no broadleaves at all were planted by the state. A total of 17 different conifer species have been planted in Wicklow's forest, but of these, sitka spruce makes up some 58%, and Douglas fir and Norway spruce between them a further 14%.

The development of the National Park in the Wicklow mountains has effectively put an end to state planting in the uplands. A number of existing Coillte plantations within the National Park target area will not be replanted following clear-felling and will be assimilated into the park. Coillte forestry is now largely confined to lower ground and to replanting of existing land holdings once the commercial timber has been harvested.

Approximately 1500 hectares (3700 acres) of proposed Natural Heritage Areas are located on Coillte property throughout Wicklow. Much of this is composed of oak and oak regrowth in mixture with conifers. These will be managed in future by agreement with the National Parks and Wildlife Service and we can assume that much of it will be allowed to regenerate as oak once the conifers are removed.

Coillte has adopted a policy of landscape planning in its approach to both planting and felling to ensure the minimum impact on the natural landscape. An example of some landscape projects now under way in the area of clear-fell include the Avoca and Hollywood valleys. However, many plantations still remain which are unsympathetic to the landscape and these need attention as they fall due for clear-felling. In practice, Coillte is now reafforesting almost six times as much as it is planting from scratch and it has set targets to achieve a mix of species within all its plantations. A minimum of 15% larch and 10% broadleaves has been set for the annual planting from 1996 on.

The proportion of the county that is privately planted is relatively low, at 7000 hectares (17,297 acres). Unfortunately, the premium rates of grant aid for planting broadleaved trees have not been sufficiently attractive to offset the long period required for a return on investment.

Tomorrow's Woodlands

Some way must be found to overcome the resistance among farmers to planting broadleaved trees, as this would be more valuable than conifers in the long term and would fit in very well with the existing network of hedgerow trees which dominate the lowland landscape of Wicklow. Woodlands were the main feature of the landscape that greeted the earliest humans in this part of Ireland. The plants and animals of these habitats have clung on in a few places as the woods were cleared but they could expand again to occupy the new woods of the future.

4. THE WATERS AND THE WILD

Stand for a moment by the side of a rushing mountain stream and feel the cool damp water splashing over granite boulders. Look carefully and see a dipper bobbing about among the stones. Or stare into the deep mysterious waters of Glendalough and marvel at the sparkling sunlight on the surface. These life-giving waters have been here since the glaciers of the last Ice Age carved out this valley.

The Wicklow mountains are the source for six major river systems. The headwaters of the Liffey flow west before the river curves around the north of the mountains to reach Dublin, while the Dodder follows a more direct route from Kippure towards the city and suburbs. The Derry river and other tributaries of the Slaney drain to the south-west before flowing towards Wexford. On the east side, the mountains are drained by the Dargle, the Vartry and the numerous streams and rivers which eventually form the Avonmore and then the Avoca rivers.

These rivers and their valleys have inspired poets and songwriters, such as Thomas Moore, who wrote in 'The Meeting of the Waters':

> *There is not in this wide world a valley so sweet,*
> *As that vale in whose bosom the bright waters meet.*

The River Dargle plunges over Ireland's highest waterfall into the Powerscourt estate. The Liffey and the Vartry rivers have been dammed to make Wicklow's biggest lakes, the Pollaphuca reservoir near Blessington and the Vartry reservoir at Roundwood, which, between them, supply much of the water needed by Dublin and the eastern counties. The mountain area also contains many small but exquisite natural lakes. Most are corrie lakes, their dark deep waters bounded by steep and imposing cliffs.

Life in the Rivers

The Wicklow mountains are criss-crossed by numerous small streams — peat-stained and oxygen-filled — which can swell from a trickle to a torrent after heavy rain.

Most of Wicklow's rivers are flashy, filling rapidly after heavy rain and rushing headlong to the sea. The thin peats of the blanket boglands cannot capture such great quantities of water, so the excess flows quickly into the streams. A mountain river in spate is an awesome sight as boulders, which normally provide stepping stones, are moved along by the power of the water.

Acidification

Wicklow's waters are soft (lacking in calcium) and naturally acid, because of the acid nature of the underlying rocks, especially the granite. There is evidence, however, that the rivers are becoming more acid, because of atmospheric pollutants containing compounds of sulphur and nitrogen. Although the air in Wicklow is relatively free of pollution most of the time, recent studies have shown that some freshwater systems in Wicklow receive moderate levels of acidification under easterly wind conditions.

Coniferous plantation forestry may further accelerate the acidification process. In the 1990s a major research project in Wicklow on the effects of forestry on freshwaters was co-ordinated by Dr Mary Kelly-Quinn. The headwater tributaries of the King's, Liffey and Avonmore rivers and the feeder streams of the Vartry reservoir were sampled, and over a two-year period 63 sites on 33 rivers were investigated. The results show that the freshwater animals in these streams are already living near the limit of their tolerance of natural acidity. Increased acidity causes physiological stress, resulting in an impoverished fauna. This may interact with the reduced nutrient levels in the water, causing a decrease in animal life.

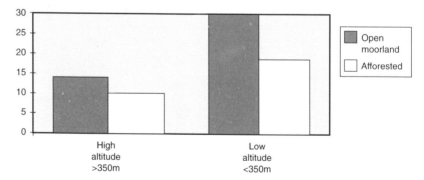

Average number of invertebrate species in mountain streams in County Wicklow (after Kelly-Quinn, Tierney & Bracken 1996)

Streams running through afforested areas often experience sudden changes in acidity, with waters remaining acidified for longer periods than in open moorland streams. At high altitudes this doesn't seem to affect animal life, but in the lower reaches of the streams, forest sites have a much poorer fauna than comparable moorland sites. Heavily shaded streams with forestry running right to the bank show the lowest number of invertebrate animals.

Fish in the rivers

Fish populations were also sampled by Dr Kelly–Quinn and her research team. Common species including minnow, **stoneloach** and sticklebacks were present in the Vartry catchment. Otherwise the only fish found were small brown trout. Population densities were low, and some of the streams in both open moorland and afforested sites contained no fish at all. This may be because fast-flowing waters are less likely to contain fish. However, a small number of afforested streams carried fish populations below the densities expected of such waters. The study concluded that plantation forestry should be discontinued in these mountain catchments.

STICKLEBACK

Stickleback and **minnow,** both commonly called pinkeen, occur in all Wicklow's rivers, some making it as far as the higher reaches. The stickleback is a native fish, able to live in both salt and fresh water, and very territorial on its own patch. The male builds a barrel-shaped nest and encourages females to lay their eggs in it. The male then single-handedly protects the nest and the young. Minnows, on the other hand, live in large shoals and are not such conscientious parents, letting their eggs fall on the gravel and abandoning them. In winter individual fish retreat to deep water and shelter under stones to escape floods which may otherwise be fatal.

There are several designated **salmon** rivers in Wicklow including the Dargle, the Vartry and the Slaney. This designation gives effect to the EU Freshwater Fish Directive of 1978, which requires regular monitoring of water quality and compliance with strict quality standards. It is generally considered that waters which can support salmon are clean enough for most other uses.

Young salmon live for two years in the upper reaches of those rivers in Wicklow that are not blocked by deep weirs or dams. They then migrate to the sea, where most spend a few years before returning to spawn in the same river in which they grew. Strangely, although they can be tempted to take bait, the adults never actually feed in the rivers, despite spending months working their way upstream during floods to seek out the spawning ground. In November the females lay eggs in hollows, often in the very gravel where they themselves hatched, and the males immediately cover the eggs with sperm. Most salmon die after spawning. Only some Atlantic salmon will survive to return to the sea. The eggs develop slowly under the gravel during the winter, emerging as young salmon late in the following spring.

The clean water bubbling over gravel in the young rivers of the mountain glens is also a perfect spawning ground for **brown trout**, which, unlike the salmon, live all their lives in fresh water. They scoop out hollows in which to lay their eggs, which hatch in spring into the 'fry' stage and become fiercely territorial. The survivors of this stage continue downstream as they grow bigger, often moving to live in the lakes. Trout lead very active lives, always swimming gently against the current, on the lookout for any passing food and darting around to chase away other fish. To keep up this endless activity the trout requires a plentiful supply of oxygen in the water. The water in the upper reaches of the rivers is full of oxygen, dissolved from the mountain air as the stream splashes over the bouldery riverbeds and waterfalls, producing the ideal habitat for brown trout.

An experiment was undertaken recently, by Dr John Bracken and Dr Jim Bowman, involving two groups of fifteen brown trout fry, which were put in nets in two separate rivers flowing into the Upper Lake at Glendalough. One of these rivers, the Lugduff, drains a catchment which is over 90% afforested; by contrast the Glenealo river flows from an unforested high mountain valley. All the fish in the Glenealo river nets behaved normally throughout the experiment, but twelve of the fifteen brown trout monitored in the Lugduff river died over the seven-day period. All of the Lugduff fish had extensive coating of aluminium and mucus on their gills. It is well known that highly acid waters cause aluminium to leach from surrounding soils and it becomes mobile in the water. The mucus on the gills may be protective, binding the aluminium and so delaying its absorption into the blood of the fish.

Sea or **white trout** live most of their lives in the sea and only come into the rivers to breed and spawn. In the lowland reaches of the rivers, the trout have to compete with introduced fish such as **pike, perch, rudd** and **roach.** The pike is the top fish carnivore of the river.

The **eel** is a remarkable fish species found in the lower reaches of Wicklow rivers. Eels don't breed in Ireland — they spawn in the Sargasso Sea, off the West Indies, and the tiny larvae are carried by currents across the Atlantic. The elvers swim up the mouths of European rivers in spring. They remain in our rivers for ten to fifteen years, after which they are ready for their once-in-a-lifetime breeding. Then, when the rivers are flooded, the eels start downstream for the ocean. They manage to navigate across over a thousand miles of ocean to find the Sargasso Sea. After breeding they die and the whole cycle begins again.

Birdlife by the streams

The **dipper** is a small plump bird that looks rather like a large blackbird with a prominent white bib from the throat down to the belly. Walking along the banks of almost any stream or river in Wicklow one can expect to see a dipper perched on a stone in the centre of the white water. It has a distinctive bobbing action, a movement which gives the dipper its name.

Dippers can be found on virtually any waterway from the highest summits right to the coast but they prefer the fast-flowing waters in the foothills of the mountains because these have a rich invertebrate fauna on the stream bed. These birds have an extraordinary method of feeding. They dive under the water and, using their wings for propulsion, walk along the bed of the stream turning over stones and picking off the caddis flies and other insect larvae to eat.

Dippers are one of the few birds which remain on in the upland streams over winter. They are very territorial and while they will fly along the river to the boundaries of their territory they will not stray into the next stretch which is occupied by a neighbour. In early spring, often while snow is still on the ground, dippers begin to build their dome-shaped nests, usually beneath an over-hanging bank or hidden under an old stone bridge. Occasionally, dippers will build in the rock crevices behind a waterfall and adult birds fly backwards and forwards through the curtain of falling water to feed the chicks in the nest.

The decline in insect life in many of the upland streams as a direct result of afforestation in the catchments has almost certainly caused a parallel decline in the number of dippers on these waters.

The other typical bird of upland streams is the **grey wagtail.** Despite its name this bird's most distinctive colour is yellow, which is splashed on the plumage of the body and tail. The wagtail flies with a bounding flight, calling as it goes and constantly flicking its long tail up and down. The grey wagtail also feeds on insects but has a wide-ranging diet and prefers to feed on surface-dwelling adults rather than the submerged larvae favoured by the dipper. The wagtail concentrates on those stretches of river which have the richest insect fauna and seems to prefer stretches with gravel banks on which it can perch.

In Britain, one of the characteristic breeding birds of fast rocky streams in the hills is the **goosander,** a large and rather beautiful fish-eating duck. In Ireland, these birds had, until recently, been recorded as breeding only in Donegal, but as the range of the species expanded in Britain they began to colonise the east coast of Ireland. There has been a series of reports of goosanders seen on Wicklow lakes and rivers, especially on the Avonmore system, since 1993. Given the abundance of suitable habitat in Wicklow and the recent expansion of breeding in Britain, we can expect to find them on many other river systems in the county in the future.

The males and females are easily distinguishable by the colour of the head. The drake has a dark green head and upper neck with a long red bill while the female has a lovely chestnut red head and crest. Males are known to desert the breeding area early in the incubation period so it is not surprising that most of the records refer to females (or 'redheads').

Waterfall spectacles
Perhaps the most spectacular features of Wicklow's rivers are the waterfalls at such places as Powerscourt on the Dargle, at Pollaphuca on the Liffey and at the head of Glenmacnass. The steep cliff over which the River Dargle plunges is nearly 100m

(600ft) high. It is formed at the contact between the two rock types, granite and mica schist, where it was carved by the action of a glacier.

Within the spray zone of the waterfall there are many interesting **mosses** and **liverworts** with **hart's tongue** and **filmy fern** growing luxuriantly in the damp atmosphere. The cliff ledges near the waterfall hold breeding **kestrel** and **peregrine,** the latter preying on **wood pigeons** and occasionally on the **stock doves** which also nest in the trees below.

In west Wicklow the waterfall at Pollaphuca was a favourite tourist destination for centuries before the creation, in 1940, of the present hydro-electric dam which reduced the water flow over the falls. In the 1820s the engineer Alexander Nimmo designed and built a spectacular bridge over the gorge allowing travellers to look straight down on the top of the waterfall.

Mountain Lakes

Most of the highest lakes in the Wicklow mountains were formed during the last Ice Age as cirques or corries. They generally formed on the north and east side of the summits in areas that were most protected from sunshine and wind. Up to twice as much snow can accumulate in the lee of a mountain compared with the windward side. As the ice accumulated a great thickness it began to slip from the mountain side with a rotational movement, thus scooping out a deep basin with steep cliffs at the back and sides and a rock lip at the front.

Such deep hollows filled with rainwater after the ice retreated, forming the beautiful mountain lakes which we know today at Cleevaun Lough, Lough Ouler, Lough Nahanagan, Lough Firrib, Art's Lough and Kelly's Lough. In some cases, such as at Upper and Lower Lough Bray, there are sizeable heaps of boulders and clay (moraines) which were dumped by the moving glacier as it slid out of the corrie. Most of Wicklow's corrie lakes have small streams draining from their lower sides.

As the ice built up in the high mountain areas all the glaciers probably joined together to form an extended ice cap which spread well beyond the coast to the east and into the lowlands to the west. The glaciers, which may have been greater than 400m in thickness, began to move down from the mountain heights and in so doing carved the beautiful U-shaped valleys of Glenmalure, Glendalough, Glendasan, Glenmacnass and the Cloghoge valley. The glacial debris dumped along the valley floors formed natural dams causing later formation of long ribbon lakes at Glendalough, Lough Dan and Lough Tay. These are generally larger than the high corrie lakes, but are also deep and cold.

Acidity levels

Research by Dr Jim Bowman has shown that the levels of acidity are generally normal in the Upper Lake at Glendalough and in the streams that flow into it, with the exception of the Lugduff river, which drains an afforested catchment at the south side of the lake. The waters of Lough Dan, and Upper and Lower Lough Bray are also characterised by high acidity, low calcium and high aluminium and a peaty colour to the water. By contrast, Lough Nahanagan and the Vartry reservoir are less acidic and have slightly higher calcium and magnesium concentrations. They are surrounded by shallower and less extensive peat.

Although the waters of these mountain lakes may appear to be devoid of life, they contain a large number of microscopic organisms. Most important of these are the tiny plant forms known as **phytoplankton.** In the Upper Lake at Glendalough the density of phytoplankton is low. Even so, over a hundred different types of phytoplankton have been recorded from this lake. However, there is very little (sometimes no) acid-sensitive zooplankton. There is also a prominence of certain organisms with a tolerance for acidity, that is the **Cladocerans**, which suggests that the increased acidity and aluminium measured in the lake are having a selective influence on animal life in the lake.

This is also reflected in the larger invertebrate animals from the lake. Some species of mayflies, molluscs and crustaceans are very sensitive to acidification and will not survive where the pH is less than 6.0. However, certain insect larvae, such as **stoneflies**, can survive in acid conditions. In the Upper Lake at Glendalough the shoreline fauna is dominated by **midge** larvae, stoneflies and **mayflies**. However, the mayflies encountered were exclusively acid-tolerant species and acid-sensitive forms were absent.

Research by Dr Marinus Otte has also shown that the marsh at the Upper Lake in Glendalough has 40 times the level of iron as Lough Dan, 6000 times the levels of zinc, 1200 times for arsenic and 2800 times for lead. This contamination of the soils has clearly influenced the water quality in the Upper Lake at Glendalough.

BLACK DARTER DRAGONFLY

Fish in the lakes

The fish populations of the Upper Lake at Glendalough were sampled in 1989 by the Central Fisheries Board using gill nets. **Minnow** and **brown trout** were both recorded in the lake. However, difficulties with the sampling technique caused by the steep contours of the lake bottom resulted in only a single brown trout, about three years old, being captured. This fish was shown to have a slower overall growth rate than any trout captured in upland lakes throughout Ireland, which reflects the low productivity of this lake. It is likely that trout stocks in Glendalough are under immediate threat due to acidification.

Lough Ouler, an isolated corrie lake on Tonelagee, has a population of very small brown trout, typical of acid mountain lakes. The naturally low levels of nutrients in the lake would never allow trout to attain their usual breeding size here. But the Lough Ouler trout manage to breed at a much smaller size than most trout. The lake waters of Lough Dan also contain brown trout and minnow, while the edges have some fen habitats, providing homes for a variety of wading birds and cormorants, which feed on the minnow and trout.

The Arctic **charr**, a relative of salmon and trout, is at the southern end of its global range in Ireland. It is found in some lakes in the west of Ireland and in Lough Dan, and may have been isolated here since the end of the last Ice Age. Although the populations of charr in Ireland are isolated from one another they are considered to be descended from a common ancestor. The Arctic charr is threatened by deterioration in water quality and it is very unlikely that it still occurs in Glendalough, given the evidence of increased acidification there. The charr is also subject to predation by and competition with native brown trout and introduced coarse fish species, so its future does not seem assured in Wicklow.

Animal life around the lakes
The upland lakes often seem desolate and barren, but **little grebes** and **moorhens** breed around them, and they occasionally support the **common sandpiper**. The lakes are occasionally visited by **whooper swans, cormorants** and **herons**, especially Lough Dan and the Glendalough lakes. **Mallard** are common on all wetland habitats except for the highest hills. **Reed bunting** frequent the marshes, lakes and streams of Wicklow, and **lapwings**, though more common at the coast, occasionally visit and breed at the upland lakes.

The amphibians of the area consist of the **common frog** and the **common newt**. These occur throughout the county, especially in damp areas, in bogs and streams, feeding on a wide variety of insects. The **common newt** grows up to 10cm long and lives under stones and vegetation on lake and pool shores. Frogs are especially suited to survival in blanket bog conditions. They can shelter under the low-growing vegetation and are perfectly adapted to fluctuations in water levels. Their slow metabolic rate enables them to survive for long periods without food. They don't waste much energy chasing their food either, they just sit and wait for the food to come to them.

Some mammals such as otter and mink rely mainly on aquatic habitats, as both feed primarily on fish. The **otter** is a native species for which Ireland and Scotland are the main strongholds in Europe. Otters require stretches of unpolluted rivers, lakes or coast, as they have long territorial ranges (up to 40km or 25 miles for a male), and so they occur at naturally low densities. They live along waterways with a good supply of fish, although they will also eat frogs, small mammals and birds. Otters breed in 'holts' below the ground at river banks. Despite their widespread occurrence they are shy and nocturnal and are rarely seen, even by inhabitants of the countryside. The best way of detecting their presence is by their droppings or 'spraints' with which they mark their territories along the waterways. Spraints can be found in 'worn' raised patches along the banks of rivers.

In the mountain area otters are frequently seen at Lough Dan, Lough Tay, Glenasmole Lodge, and Glencullen river, and are likely to occur at many other sites in the foothills. The Vartry river system in the east of the county is also well used by otters. We have seen spraints on various parts of the river bank from the reservoir at Roundwood to the estuary at Broadlough. This includes semi-natural areas like the Devil's Glen, artificial sites like Mount Usher Gardens in Ashford and even in the garden of Hunter's Hotel at Newrath Bridge. The occurrence of the otter on the Wicklow coast is little known but it certainly occurs at the mouths of rivers.

The **mink** is a North American species which became naturalised in Ireland after escaping from mink farms in the 1960s. It spends most of its time around rivers and other waterways although it will readily travel across farmland, using the cover of hedges and undergrowth for safety. The mink is an efficient carnivore which will eat whatever is freely available including large insects, frogs, rabbits, fish and birds. It can be quite destructive to poultry and waterfowl if the opportunity arises. Nevertheless, we have seen a mink crossing a road near the Vartry within 30m of a flock of domestic ducks without any apparent attempt to attack.

Mink are now widespread in Wicklow in all but the high mountain areas where, presumably, there is a shortage of potential prey. In some upland areas densities may be as low as one mink per 4km (2.5 miles) of river, while in the richer lowlands there may be up to one mink per kilometre.

Reservoirs

Wicklow is largely lacking in natural lowland lakes, but two of the major rivers which flow from the Wicklow mountains, the Liffey and the Vartry, have been dammed to produce artificial lakes or reservoirs supplying essential drinking water for the ever-increasing demand from Dublin and its hinterland.

The earliest reservoir in the Wicklow mountains was that developed on the upper catchment of the **Vartry** river, about 200m (600ft) above sea-level. This short river rises on the southern slopes of the Great Sugarloaf and the eastern side of Djouce mountain and its passage to the sea was blocked in the 1860s by the construction of a major dam close to the village of Roundwood. This was followed by a second dam, creating the upper reservoir in 1924. The combined Vartry reservoir now covers an area of 280 hectares (691 acres) and supplies approximately 80 million litres of water daily to Dublin city, south County Dublin and parts of north County Wicklow.

As living standards in Dublin increased in the early part of the twentieth century, a growing demand for water led to the proposal for a dam on the River

Liffey on the west side of the Wicklow mountains. In 1938, construction work began on the **Pollaphuca** hydro-electric scheme, which was designed both to harness the power of the Liffey and to provide a major reservoir for supply of water. The upper valley of the Liffey at this time was an attractive mixture of small farms, fields, hedgerows and bogs. A previous resident of the valley, Billy Crowley described the area before the flooding:

> *There was a lovely valley where the lake is now. All along there we had rolling fields and cattle grazing. Our house was very close to the river in an old wood and it was called the Mill Bank. That was the road leading to Lacken then. It went down by the house I lived in. Now you can't walk down there — it's flooded, the trees are gone. There were great beech trees, elm and all sorts of trees and a lot of wildlife — rabbits, hares, badgers and otters.*

Up to 300 landowners were affected by the flooding, with seventy-six farmhouses and cottages covered by water. Over the preceding few years these families had been resettled nearby and compensated for the loss of their land. The project even involved the removal of bodies from a graveyard at Burgage and their re-burial near Blessington.

In March 1940, the sluice gates were closed at Pollaphuca and the reservoir began to flood. This was, in effect, history repeating itself. Some 10,000–15,000 years ago, a large meltwater lake arising from the front of an Ice Age glacier filled this same valley. Now the Pollaphuca (or Blessington) reservoir covers an area of 22 square kilometres (8.5 square miles) supplying Dublin and the eastern region with large amounts of water.

Wicklow also supplies Dublin with electricity. The Pollaphuca dam has two turbines which are about 400m from the reservoir. The total output of this station is about 30 million kilowatt hours per year. The water released from Pollaphuca is trapped again 1.5km (one mile) downstream at the Golden Falls dam. The water here is released much more slowly through a turbine which produces 4 megawatts of power.

The growth of Irish industry in the 1960s also put extra pressure on the national grid. This was especially the case in times of peak demand during the day, although there was a net surplus of generating capacity during the night-time hours. To cope with this imbalance the Electricity Supply Board developed the pump storage station at Turlough Hill in the centre of the Wicklow mountains. A large storage reservoir was built at about 650 metres (2100 feet) above sea-level near the Wicklow Gap. Water from the lower natural corrie lake of Lough Nahanagan is pumped up to the reservoir at night and released during the day to fall by gravity through turbines back to the lower lake again. The regular outline of the Turlough Hill reservoir is visible from many directions in the Wicklow mountains and, while it seems now to have been accepted as part of the landscape, it would be unlikely that such a massive engineering development would be permitted here if it were proposed today.

Reservoir flora

Water levels in both the Vartry and Blessington reservoirs fluctuate considerably throughout the year in relation to rainfall amounts. Lowest levels are generally reached in September/October and the levels recover over the winter to reach capacity between February and May. Annual fluctuations can range up to 5m (15ft) from highest to lowest levels, which is much greater than the range in a natural lake. This produces a series of characteristic habitats.

In the area between high water and low water levels, there is an unusual type of vegetation, mainly dominated by annual species. These include **marsh cudweed** and some **redshank** growing on the silty lake bed. On gently sloping shores of gravel the vegetation is dominated by **shoreweed**, which is a grass-like plantain species. This plant is one of the few which can tolerate such large and sudden variations in water level and will persist over many months of drought until water returns again in the winter. Other common plants in this zone are the **common spike-rush, reed canary grass, bulbous rush** and **broadleaved pondweed.**

At Vartry, the main areas of species-rich shore vegetation occur at the northern end of both reservoirs. Further south near the dams the shoreline is steeper and stony and largely bare of vegetation.

At the northern end of the Vartry reservoir there is also an extensive area of marsh grassland where grasses, sedges and rushes predominate with other plants including **meadowsweet, wild angelica, devil's bit scabious** and **common valerian.** On the extensive embankments which support both the upper and lower dams there are large areas of species-rich grassland. These can be classified as acid grassland because of the acidity of the soil but, due to the absence of fertiliser and the late seasonal mowing, a wide variety of species occurs here. The main grasses are **fescues, cock's-foot, false oat-grass** and **Yorkshire fog**. Other plant species include **knapweed, yarrow, sneezewort, smooth hawk's beard, field scabious** and **milkwort.**

The area immediately below the upper embankment at the Vartry reservoir has all the appearance of semi-natural woodland established on the edge of a lake. This is dominated by **birch** and young **sessile oak** with a ground flora of grasses and occasional **gorse**. More open areas have a ground flora of **bramble**, grasses,

95

heather, **billberry** and occasional **rowan**. In the wetter areas, which are regularly flooded, there are small areas of willow scrub, dominated by **grey willow**. This area has a diverse ground flora including **bog myrtle, bogbean, sharp-flowered rush, marsh cinquefoil, carnation sedge** and **bottle sedge.**

Shoreline and woodland are the main habitats around the Blessington lakes. The sandy shoreline is colonised by **spike-rush, shoreweed, lesser spearwort** and **reed canary grass.** Annual fluctuations in water level are too great for common reed but there are some marshy areas of shoreline which support a variety of wetland plants such as **water mint, sneezewort** and **yellow flag. Willow** and **hawthorn** scrub is common on the shoreline, which is generally backed by a fringe of coniferous plantation. There are a number of species here such as **yellow rattle**, which are indicators of long-established grassland managed as hay meadow.

Reservoir birds and mammals

In the absence of natural lowland lakes, the birds of the Vartry reservoir provide an interesting spectacle for bird watchers. The main interest is in winter months when waterfowl such as geese, ducks and swans arrive from their arctic breeding grounds to feed on the reservoir.

Counts carried out here by Padraig Farrelly show that the overall numbers are relatively small but fairly consistent from year to year. However, **greylag geese** have declined from an average of 240 in the 1980s to relatively small numbers in recent years. This is the same flock of geese which uses the coastal strip of the Murrough and it may be that farmland in this area is more attractive than the grazing around the Vartry reservoir at present. This is confirmed by a similar decline of about two-thirds in the flock of whooper swans, which are also grazers. These birds may be increasingly attracted to improved grassland in the Kilcoole area.

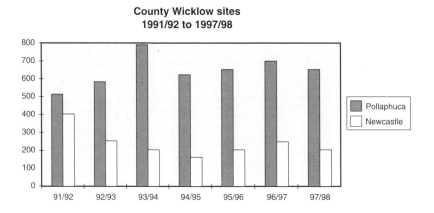

County Wicklow sites
1991/92 to 1997/98

4.4

4.5

4.1   Lough Dan is a ribbon lake, surrounded by mountains and woodlands. Its waters are dark and deep with high levels of acidity. The arctic charr, a rare fish species has survived here since the last Ice Age. (Jaimie Blandford, Slidefile)

4.2   Mountain stream in the Glen of Imaal. Wicklow's streams are oxygen-filled and naturally acidic due to the underlying granite rocks. However, those catchments with a high proportion of forestry are more acidified. This causes a decrease in animal life in the water. (Richard Nairn)

4.3   Sea trout smolt. This species has evolved for life in both freshwater and the sea. The silvery colour indicates that it is on its way down river to the sea in spring. When mature this fish will return to spawn in its natal river. Despite significant declines in the west of Ireland, sea trout are still caught each year in Wicklow rivers. (Éamon de Buitléar)

4.4   Dipper on a mountain stream. These birds depend for food on the insect life in the water. They have favourite stone perches from which they plunge-dive to catch their prey. The nest is often built in the stonework of old bridges, from which they can drop vertically into the water. (Richard T. Mills)

4.5   Grey wagtail. This bird swoops across the river picking insects off the water surface. Gravel banks and stretches of fast moving water seem to provide the best feeding opportunities. (Richard T. Mills)

99

4.6 *Avonmore River, Trooperstown. Entering its lowland stage, the river carries a load of sediment and there is silting on the slower stretches. Aquatic plants become more abundant with an increase in nutrients in the water. (Richard Nairn)*

4.7 *Powerscourt waterfall, at nearly 100 metres (300 feet), is the highest waterfall in Ireland. Several species of mosses, liverworts and ferns grow in the spray zone, which is kept constantly damp. (Richard Nairn)*

4.8 *Mute swans. These are common inhabitants of lowland lakes and rivers. Due to shortage of suitable inland territories they occasionally attempt to nest on coastal marshes. In winter, flocks of swans gather in locations such as Bray harbour and the rivers in Wicklow and Arklow towns where they are fed by local residents. (Richard T. Mills)*

4.9 *Glendalough Upper Lake. Despite the tranquil waters, increased levels of acidity in the lake have affected the invertebrate life, favouring species such as midges, stoneflies and acid-tolerant mayflies. Few fish occur in the lake due to the naturally low productivity of its waters. (Richard Nairn)*

4.10 *Reflections in the Vartry reservoir. Built over a century ago, the reservoir now harbours a variety of natural habitats from marsh to broadleaved woodland There are significant numbers of wintering waterfowl and breeding birds, while the fish populations attract both otter and mink. (Éamon de Buitléar)*

4.9

4.10

4.11

4.11 Stone loach. An inhabitant of running water, this small fish is a frequent food of trout, eels, water birds and mammals. It usually spends the daylight hours hiding under stones and emerges at night to feed on bottom-living invertebrates. The long barbels around the mouth act as antennae in the darkness. (Éamon de Buitléar)

4.12 Common darter damselflies mating. Lakes, slow-flowing rivers and even small ponds can hold a variety of dragonflies and damselflies. The larvae are entirely aquatic. When ready to emerge as adults, they crawl up the stem of a rush and spread their wings to dry in the sun. (Richard T. Mills)

4.13 Common or smooth newt. An amphibian of ponds and lakes, the adult lives both on land and in the water. The female lays individual eggs attached to the leaves of water plants. She will spend the winter hibernating underground or beneath rocks. (Richard T. Mills)

4.12

4.13

4.14 Cowslips on the embankment of the Vartry reservoir. These grasslands, while artificial in origin, are managed as hay meadows, and now hold a rich variety of native plants and insects. (Éamon de Buitléar)

4.15 Greylag goose displaying. Flocks of these geese spend the winter around Blessington and on coastal farmland near Newcastle. They feed by day on grass fields and roost on the reservoirs at night for safety from predators. They return to Iceland in summer to breed. (Richard T. Mills)

In the spring most of these birds depart for breeding grounds elsewhere, but teal have been recorded breeding in two summers in the early 1990s. Great crested grebes have also started to breed in the 1990s with an average of two pairs each summer. These birds have a spectacular courtship dance on the water, in which they offer water weed as a 'love token' to each other.

The absence of natural islands limits the number of breeding birds at Blessington, but there are some great crested grebe, **mute swan, mallard, moorhen, coot** and **snipe**, especially in the less disturbed areas. **Sand martins** nest in colonies in the steep sand cliffs on the west side near Russborough House. Solitary herons feed in the shallower bays and on streams entering the lake. The forestry plantations hold **sparrowhawk** and a variety of common songbirds such as **coal tit, blue tit, wren, robin** and **chaffinch**.

Wintering water birds at Blessington include greylag goose; whooper swan, mallard, wigeon, teal, **shoveler**, pochard, tufted duck, **lapwing** and **curlew. Mallard, wigeon** and **teal** are the commonest ducks with an average of over 1,500 present during the 1980s although numbers seem to have decreased in the 1990s. These are surface-feeding ducks which like to graze on the vegetation or eat seeds. By contrast, the **pochard, tufted duck** and **coot** dive for food on the lake bed. **Greylag geese** and **whooper swans** prefer to graze on surrounding fields but use the lake as a safe roosting area. The reservoir also has a very large night-time roost of **lesser black-backed gulls** (up to 1000 birds) in the autumn. The best places to see the birds are from Crosscoolharbour (at the north end of lake) and from the various bridges.

Mammals which regularly use the Blessington lake shore include **deer, badger, fox, mink** and **otter**. Although these are mostly nocturnal, their tracks and sometimes food remains (such as fish scales in the case of otters) are often visible on the exposed mud and sand around the lake.

Managing the reservoirs

Although the Vartry reservoir originated as an artificial lake, it has developed over time a range of vegetation types, some of which are naturally going through a succession, for example, from marsh to valley mire to wet heath. The Vartry reservoir has more diverse habitats than Blessington lake. This is largely due to the greater variation in soil type, allowing the development of wetland vegetation such as willow scrub and greater species diversity.

The range of habitats present and the waterfowl populations make Vartry reservoir a site of national importance for nature conservation. It is managed by Dublin Corporation primarily for water supply, but there is great potential for management of the habitats around the reservoir in the interests of nature. The paths around the reservoir provide a wonderful amenity for local people and tourists alike while the water body itself is a valuable angling amenity.

The entire lake at Blessington and a strip around the shoreline are owned by the Electricity Supply Board (ESB). Safe car-parking, picnic areas and access to the shoreline have been provided at nine points around the lake. Swimming in the reservoir is prohibited and fishing and boating are allowed only under permit from the ESB. While there are many interesting locations around the lakes, the best variety of habitat is found at the northern end (car-park at Crosscoolharbour) which includes an extensive marsh area at the mouth of the Liffey.

In 1995 the Minister for the Environment commissioned a major strategic study of the water needs of Dublin and its surrounding area. The report of the study, which was published in 1996, sets out a broad range of recommendations for the development and management of Dublin's water supply over the next 20 years. The effective capacity of the combined water treatment works serving Dublin in 1996 was 442 megalitres per day, but even so, the water supply situation in Dublin was considered to be 'finely balanced'. Some 44% of water produced in the Dublin region is lost as a result of leakage from the system, and over the next 20 years a major investment programme has been recommended to upgrade the supply network, which should help significantly with water conservation. However, it is proposed that in the early years of the twenty-first century, additional water supplies should come from Ballymore Eustace on the River Liffey, which will draw further on the storage capacity of the Blessington reservoir.

The ever-greater demands for water from the main reservoir at Pollaphuca and the Golden Falls have produced generally lower water levels in the rest of the River Liffey. This has affected its function as a fisheries resource and its capacity for dilution of waste water from the growing conurbations of north Kildare. Similar problems have arisen with the Vartry reservoir where demand regularly exceeds supply and the amount of water released to the lower stretches of the Vartry river in recent summers has been little more than a trickle. This has caused problems of inadequate dilution of sewage effluent from the growing town of Ashford.

River Valley Management

An integrated approach to landscape management and development is clearly needed in large river valleys such as that of the Avonmore river, which reaches the sea at Arklow. The catchment of the Avoca–Avonmore rivers covers some 650 square kilometres (250 square miles) and is the largest in Wicklow. Stretching as far north as Lough Tay and Lough Dan, it includes most of the spectacular east Wicklow glens as well as the rolling lowland country around Rathdrum, Avoca and Aughrim.

The Avoca copper mines are now disused, although the crumbling remains of the chimneys and mine machinery stand as a legacy to the workers of a bygone age. The extensive mine tailings (or settling ponds) continue to leach heavy metals into the waterways making the Avoca one of the most toxic in the country. In the lower valley, among the remains of former broadleaved woods, a giant fertiliser factory dominates the landscape, releasing a pall of smoke over the town of Arklow.

Between 1994 and 1997 Wicklow County Council prepared the Avoca–Avonmore Catchment Conversion Plan to try to address some of the environmental problems in this extensive river valley. The plan set out to develop a strategy to remedy past environmental damage and apply the concept of an area-based environmental management system. Two pilot projects on mine rehabilitation were introduced, one to treat the leacheate from the mine tailings and another to revegetate the spoil heaps. An ammonia reduction unit was introduced at the fertiliser plant to reduce losses and increase nitrogen efficiency of the factory.

Environmental managment systems have been introduced by several companies in the catchment. This project has been funded by the European Union to help balance economic development with environmental quality, but converting attitudes to exploitation of the landscape and its natural resources may take somewhat longer.

Water of life

Water is an essential feature of the Wicklow landscape, whether it is trickling from a mountain bog or thundering over a waterfall into one of the valleys. Some of the most outstanding views in Wicklow — Glendalough, Blessington, Lough Tay, and Lough Dan — are over large expanses of water. The light of the sun sparkling on the surface of a mountain lake, the reflections of trees and cliffs in the dark waters and the sight of a dipper on a bubbling stream are all images that lodge in the memory. But the future of Wicklow's waters may rest with the insatiable demand for this valuable resource from the growing city of Dublin.

5. DOWN ON THE FARM

Looking down from the sides of the Wicklow mountains the walker can see a patchwork of fields and hedges, which is characteristic of the Irish landscape in every county. Almost everywhere there is an abundance of mature trees, the white blossom of hawthorn and the yellow flower of the gorse in the spring.

These lowland parts of Wicklow, shown in yellow or green on the Ordnance Survey maps, are largely confined to the fringes of the county, with the greatest area in the eastern and southern foothills and on the coastal plain. To the west, the mountains drop steeply to the central plain of Ireland, a small part of which is in Wicklow. The great majority of the lowlands of Wicklow are under farmland and the rich soils with their extensive hedgerow network give the impression of a wooded landscape. The soils are deep and generally well-drained, and lowland bogs are almost completely absent in Wicklow.

Down to Earth

On the east side of the county the soils are dominated by acid **brown earths**, which extend in a strip from Delgany to Rathnew and then in a south-westerly direction towards Shillelagh. The soils are generally well drained and contain large quantities of small stones. These are the soils most frequently used for arable crops in Wicklow.

On the slightly higher ground of the Roundwood plateau the soils are mainly **brown podzolics.** These soils are generally shallower than the brown earth and their use is mainly limited to grazing.

On the extreme coastal area of the county the soils are principally **gleys** which are derived from calcareous marine muds originating on the bed of the Irish Sea. These are generally poorly draining and unsuitable for tillage — they tend to be dominated by rushes and may be badly poached by cattle if not well managed.

To the west of the mountains the soils of the lowlands are again dominated by podzolics. **Brown podzolics** are mainly derived from the granite of the mountains and occur in a narrow strip between Kilbride in the north and Shillelagh to the south. Further west, around Dunlavin and Stratford, the soils are grey–brown podzolics, which are mainly derived from the limestone and shale of the midlands.

This diversity of soil types leads to a range of suitability for cultivation, with the most productive soils being on the eastern coastal plain between Greystones and Wicklow town. Virtually the entire lowland area is suitable for grassland, with the best soils in the coastal plain and the area south-west of Blessington.

Farming the Land

Land use in Wicklow has changed considerably over the last century or two. An extreme situation was reached in the 1840s when the population of the county was over 126,000 people. At that time some 56% of Wicklow's land was arable with most farmland in the lowland part of the county under crops and comparatively little meadow or pasture. Most of the farm holdings were tiny, some even less than one acre (0.4ha). Even so, Wicklow was one of the better-off counties in Ireland at this time, and the landed gentry enjoyed a comfortable life moving between their country mansions and their town houses in Dublin.

After the Great Famine in the late 1840s things changed dramatically in the lowland landscape. Much of the arable land was returned to pasture and livestock numbers increased accordingly. In a period of some 60 years, the area under crops was reduced by two-thirds. The later nineteenth century was also a period of extensive planting of large estates and many of the mature deciduous trees we see today in the lowland landscape date from this period. By the mid-twentieth century the scene had changed again with grazing assuming even greater importance. This decline in arable land has continued to the present day, leaving an intimate mixture of lowland fields, hedgerows and small woodlands and providing a number of habitat types for particular animals and plants.

Hedgerows

The southern and western fringes of the county have the densest network of hedgerows, giving the appearance of a wooded landscape. In the eighteenth century, however, much of Ireland was farmed on the open field or *rundale* system. Each small *clachán* or group of houses was surrounded by strips of open field with no fences or hedges between them. The widespread enclosure of fields began in the early eighteenth century, when the quality of pasture land was being improved by draining, digging ditches and planting hawthorns to stabilise the earth banks.

To encourage this work, the Royal Dublin Society offered grants to landlords for the planting of hedgerow trees. The improved pasture land was stocked with larger numbers of cattle and the newly planted hedges helped to stop the cattle wandering. Hedging improvements on the large estates were followed in the rest of the county over the next hundred years. By about 1850, the patchwork of small fields we know today was already in existence. Hedges are not found everywhere in Wicklow, though. They are absent from the large areas of unenclosed blanket bog and moorland in the mountains over about 400m (1300 feet) in height.

Growing in the hedgerows

Hedges vary greatly in the shrubs and trees they contain, depending on the soils and underlying rocks. In the eastern plateau between Roundwood and Shillelagh and on the western lowlands between Manor Kilbride and Baltinglass there are extensive networks of luxuriant hedges containing **hawthorn** and **blackthorn.** Hedgerow trees usually consist of **ash, elm, oak, sycamore** and **Scots pine.** In some areas, especially on the foothills of the mountains, **gorse** becomes especially common in hedgerows and is most obvious in the spring when its yellow flowers light up the countryside.

At Ballynabarney, just south of Rathnew, the hedges contain lines of **Scots pine.** This was a favourite hedgerow tree for planting in the late nineteenth century. Natural vegetation on these soils would probably be **oak–holly** woodland, and in fact holly is locally quite common in these areas. In a few places holly and ash have been planted together and the evergreen holly gives the hedges a dark green colour throughout the year. Common herbs in these hedges often include the tall purple flowers of the **foxglove** with the white **stitchwort** shining out from below.

Moving higher up the flanks of the mountains, especially in the south and east of the county where the soils are acid and stony, hedges are low-growing structures dominated by **gorse** with a mixture of holly, **birch, rowan,** ash, **broom** and **bracken.** The trees may be few and there are gaps in these poorly developed hedges. The banks or ditches on which the hedges are planted are often made up of stones which have been cleared from the fields. Natural vegetation here would probably be **oak–birch** woodland.

In some small areas where wet gley soils predominate, hedges are dominated by **willow** with occasionally some **gorse, alder, hawthorn, elder** and birch. Typical flowers below these hedges include **wild angelica** and **meadowsweet.** A possible natural vegetation in these areas might be **alder–willow** woodland.

A walk along a leafy back-road in south Wicklow in spring or early summer is a delightful experience. Damp shady conditions favour woodland flowers like **bluebell, wood anemone** and **wood sorrel. Lords and ladies,** with its pointed hood, has a cluster of poisonous bright red berries in the autumn. In April and May, before the trees are fully in leaf, hedgebanks are bright with **primroses** and the occasional bunch of early **purple orchids.** Long **briars** stretch out in all directions, the tip of each shoot taking root where it touches the ground. The hedgebank in spring may be smothered in a mass of tall white-flowered **cow parsley.** The similar looking **hogweed** takes over in mid-summer. In May the **stitchwort** spreads a carpet of white flowers among the gorse and hawthorn. On stony banks there may be the tall purple flowers of **foxglove.** Other delicate flowers of the hedgebank include the purple **herb robert,** the yellow **lady's bedstraw** and the common **dog violet.** In damper soils the tall hollow-stemmed **angelica** flowers in late summer, and there may be the creamy white flowers of **meadowsweet** and delicate pale pink **spotted orchids.** In marshy areas and wet drains the pink or white **lady's smock** stands alongside the large exotic flowers of **yellow flag.**

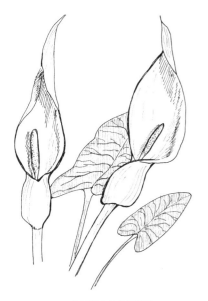

LORDS & LADIES

Animals under cover

The most important advantage offered by hedges to the larger animals — the birds and mammals — is cover. In addition they provide abundant food supply and, in the case of birds, nesting places and singing perches.

Among the brambles and other low plants on the hedgebank is the place to find the nest of the **willow warbler.** This delicate yellow-brown bird spends the winter months in the warmer climate of Africa returning to us each spring. A cock **pheasant** may take off with a loud crow and fly along the hedges. There is always a danger that the unguarded nest with its large clutch of green eggs may be robbed by a scavenging **magpie** or **hooded crow.**

Yellowhammers are heard calling out their melodious song from many of the lowland hedgerows in Wicklow. The **wheatear** prefers to nest in stone walls with sparse hedgerow.

Bushy hawthorn hedges throughout Wicklow provide nest sites for a wide variety of species including **hedge sparrow** (or dunnock), **linnet, greenfinch** and **chaffinch,** as well as for the more familiar garden birds such as **robin, song thrush** and **blackbird.** Holes in the trunks of old trees are used by **blue tit, great tit, starling** and **jackdaw** while the **wren** will build its spherical nest among the ivy on trees. **Treecreepers** sometimes move up the trunk of a hedgerow tree, feeding on the insects in the bark. The upper branches of trees are used by **wood pigeon, magpie** and **mistle thrush.**

A newcomer to the hedgerow scene in Wicklow is the delicate **collared dove.** It was first recorded breeding in Greystones and Killincarrig in the north-east of County Wicklow in 1964, and the following year it bred in Wicklow town. Since then the birds have spread throughout the lowlands of Wicklow and indeed the rest of Ireland.

Lines of mature hedgerow trees, especially Scots pine and beech, are favourite nesting places for colonies of **rooks.** Around the beginning of March they begin the noisy business of setting up home as they fly backwards and forwards carrying sticks to rebuild the substantial nests which have been broken up during the winter storms. Most rookeries contain fewer than twenty nests but there are some much more numerous colonies. In a survey of one 10km (16-mile) square in east Wicklow in the 1970s we found a total of over a thousand rook nests. The majority were in several very large colonies located in tall trees in old estates. Most of the nests are well out of reach and often out of sight in the foliage of the tall trees. However, in some of the mountain areas where there are few tall trees rooks will nest in more accessible places. In 1915, the naturalist, Robert Lloyd Praeger, reported rooks' nests only fifteen feet (5m) above the ground at Aghavannagh. Rooks are specialist grassland feeders and move across the fields probing the ground with their strong, pointed beaks for earthworms and leatherjackets.

111

Wildlife corridors

The importance of hedgerows and lines of trees in the lowland landscape cannot be over-emphasised. They contribute enormously to the wooded appearance of the valleys and foothills and provide a substitute for the former natural woodland habitat. Hedges function as corridors for wildlife, moving between areas of woodland cover, and an isolated hedge is of much lower value than one that is connected to other field boundaries.

Of special importance in the Wicklow landscape are the so-called spine hedges which are usually old parish or townland boundaries to which many younger hedges and other areas of woodland are connected. Hedges are important for all wild animals in farmland especially the large animals such as foxes which use them for territorial markings and for refuge from disturbance.

Many insects use the shelter provided in the lee of the hedges to lay their eggs. For example, **bumblebees** like to burrow into sunny southfacing hedge banks to lay their eggs. Generally, the older the hedge the greater the variety of woody species it will contain but there are few hedges in Wicklow more than two or three centuries old. Before that most of the country was farmed on the open field system without any hedges or fences at all, with the exception of the large walled estates.

House and Garden

Among the best-known old estates in Wicklow are Powerscourt in the north, Coolatin in the south and Russborough in the west. To wander inside their high stone walls is like entering a world frozen in the nineteenth century, with avenues of mature **lime** and **beech** trees, crumbling stone walls covered in **ivy** and old mixed plantations.

A species which was once common in lowland estates was the **buzzard,** a large bird of prey. This was probably a rare breeding bird in Wicklow in the early nineteenth century but by the end of the century the buzzard had been eliminated completely from Ireland as a breeding species. By the early 1960s it had re-colonised Northern Ireland. Since then the population has slowly spread throughout the northern half of Ireland and there have been increasing reports of breeding attempts in Wicklow.

Buzzards seem to prefer a combination of small fields and open countryside for hunting, with trees and small woodlands for shelter and nesting. Today, you could hear the plaintive mewing call of a buzzard through the woodland canopy in any part of lowland Wicklow. You could be lucky enough to see a pair of buzzards soaring above the trees, wheeling and diving on slightly upturned wings which are

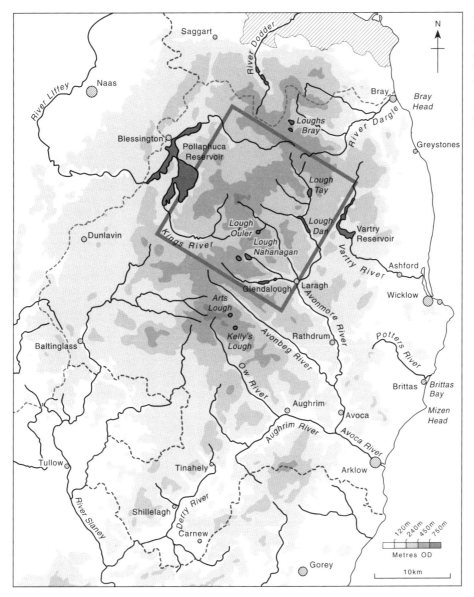

Map 7 Main rivers lakes and reservoirs in County Wicklow. The area within the box includes the headwaters of the Liffey, Vartry, Avonmore and King's rivers which were sampled by Mary Kelly-Quinn and a team from University College Dublin, in a study of the effects of afforestation on the acidification of freshwater.

broad enough to allow confusion with eagles. A major part of the buzzard's diet is rabbit but they will also feed on smaller animals including mice, shrews, frogs and lizards. They like to use tall structures such as pylons or masts for stationary hunting. The main danger for the buzzard comes when it is attracted to carrion, which may be poisoned. As the buzzard makes its slow recovery in Wicklow it will need all the help it can get from sympathetic landowners and farmers. Perhaps the protection of some of the remaining broadleaved woods as nature reserves will help its recovery.

In many parts of the lowlands, especially in the more remote areas of south and west Wicklow, are ruined houses and cottages, some dating from the nineteenth century. These provide good nesting places for barn owls and bats if there is still some shelter from the elements.

In the early 1990s **barn owls** were surveyed in Wicklow in a number of sample areas. The results show that the owls are still fairly widespread in the lowlands but numbers are small. Barn owls prefer to hunt over rough grassland, marshland, and recently planted forestry but they will also use areas of long grass on roadsides, riverbanks and on field headlands (the grassy strips left around a ploughed field). These are the habitats used by their main prey, the small mammals. The typical diet of the barn owl consists of field mice, house mice, brown rats, pygmy shrews and the occasional bird.

Breeding of barn owls is often difficult to prove as the nest is usually well hidden. On a farm near Newtownmountkennedy young owls emerged each summer to sit along the branches of an old rotten tree. Here they called loudly throughout the summer nights for the parents to bring offerings of food. Unfortunately, in some places there are casualties, especially where owls are prone to take poisoned rats. Road traffic casualties are also an increasing feature of some of the busier parts of Wicklow. The tendency for barn owls to feed along roadsides makes them especially vulnerable to dazzling and collision with fast-moving traffic.

The attic spaces of older occupied houses provide good summer roosting places for bats. Six species of bat are recorded from Wicklow, with the **pipistrelle, long-eared, Leisler's** and **whiskered bats** being the most common. Avondale House near Rathdrum, the former home of Charles Stewart Parnell, is known to have a large colony of bats. This includes at least forty whiskered bats, which were recorded emerging from a chimney of the house. This is probably a nursery colony. As the Irish population of this species is only several hundred, all such colonies are of national importance.

Bats are entirely insectivorous. They are at their most active in summer when insects are abundant and they hibernate in winter when food is scarce. The greatest number of insects fly in the hour or two after sunset when the air is still warm and humidity is high. Large beetles such as the **cockchafer,** make a loud buzzing noise as they warm up for flight. Hearing this, the bats may swoop down to catch them on the ground or just after take-off. Slow-flying insects such as **midges, craneflies** or **moths** are tracked down by echo-location and consumed in flight.

Daubenton's bat feeds commonly over water. It may sometimes be seen swooping low along a river or lake shore catching emerging **caddisflies** and other aquatic insects. Unlike the other bats, it regularly roosts under bridges which it may share with nesting dippers. Old stone bridges are ideal because they contain cracks and crevices. The recent practice of spraying liquid concrete under the arches of old bridges may kill bats and destroy their roosting sites. Most of the roosts in old buildings are secure, though, because they have plenty of openings for the bats to use. However, such houses often need treatment of roof timbers against woodworm and fungi and the slow emission of poisonous vapours can be lethal to the bats.

Lowland Wetlands

Wetland sites in the lowlands of Wicklow are generally few and scattered. A typical example is the marsh at Kilmacanogue, just south of Bray. This is a small area of wet woodland dominated by alder and willow, through which flows a stream. In the centre of the woodland is an area of springs which give rise to extensive seepage in the soils. This feeds a small fen and wet grassland dominated by **reed grass** with **meadowsweet, horsetail** and **purple loosestrife** prominent in the vegetation. Along the stream there are areas of rushes, sedges and wet grass with **greater tussock sedge** and flowering plants such as **lady's smock** and **ragged robin.** The vegetation here is seldom grazed as the ground is wet and dangerous for livestock. There are deep pools and streams throughout the marsh and the vegetation in the water includes **fool's watercress, starwort, watermint** and **horsetails.**

These sheltered waterways are important for aquatic insects. On sunny summer days there may be dozens of beautifully coloured **dragonflies** and **damselflies** hovering over the water surface and landing on the vegetation. The soft ground is also an ideal feeding area for **snipe,** which like to probe with their long bills in the peaty soil. The breeding birds of the area are typical of wet woodland with a mixture of tree-nesting species such as **robin, wren** and **blackbird** and those species associated with the wet ground, **sedge warbler, willow warbler** and **chiffchaff.**

It is surprising that sites as rich as the Kilmacanogue Marsh have survived, given their proximity to urban areas. A recent threat to this site comes from the improvement of the main N11 road which will be widened by taking a section of the marsh. Other small wetland sites, such as the Ballynamona Marsh near Arklow, have been irreparably damaged by afforestation and now barely exist at all. In west

Wicklow, close to the border with Kildare, Dunlavin Marshes once contained an extensive area of calcareous fen with a rich flora. However, extensive drainage and reclamation, especially in the southern half of the marsh, has involved new deep drains and clearance of vegetation. All through 1992 there were machines working on the marsh digging drains and attempting to reclaim the area for farmland. Ironically, EU money is now being paid to farmers under the Rural Environment Protection Scheme to protect just this type of wildlife habitat.

Meadows

Environment-friendly farming methods will be required if any of the species-rich meadows, once so common in Wicklow, are to survive. The difficulty of finding today an old pasture with field mushrooms is an indicator of the ecological effects of artificial fertiliser.

The **corncrake** was once widespread in meadows throughout Wicklow and as late as the 1970s the birds were thinly distributed over a wide area, especially in the lowlands. Many older Wicklow residents can remember being kept awake at night by its electric calls echoing through the summer evenings. However, with the modernisation of the 1950s and 1960s, many old meadows were ploughed and reseeded or turned over to silage production, causing the distruction of nests of the corncrake, which breeds quite late in the summer.

Occasionally hay meadows can be found in some of the more remote parts of the lowlands such as around the village of Knockananna. Here some of the meadows are a riot of colour in early summer with many wild flowers including **vetches, yellow rattle** and sometimes wetland plants like **lady's smock** and **ragged robin.** Such meadows are a wonderful habitat for insects and are alive with buzzing sounds during the summer days. They are also a favourite nesting place for the **skylark** which sings its continuous song high above the field.

Long grass in the fields also gives plenty of cover to the **foxes** which are common residents in most of the Wicklow countryside. Foxes usually live a fairly silent, solitary life but the piercing bark in the night air indicates that the mating season is under way. Most vixens have a short season in January when they are receptive to the males and the vast majority of cubs are born in freshly scraped-out holes in March. Foxes are a familiar sight for most Wicklow people, even if it is only as a fleeting glimpse in the glare of the car headlights as the white tip of the tail disappears into the nearest hedge.

The morning after a fresh fall of snow is a good time to look for fox tracks. They are similar to the footprints of a sheepdog but much smaller and with distinctive long claw marks opposite each toe. The tracks are usually left during a regular nightly patrol which the fox will make through its territory, feeding on whatever it chances to encounter. This may be a mouse in the long grass, some worms in freshly dug soil, ground beetles newly-emerged from the soil or a selection of hedgerow fruits such as blackberries when in season.

The fox makes use of all the available habitats in the lowlands feeding in meadows and fields, travelling under the cover of hedgerows and often breeding in badger setts along field margins or in small woods. Despite hunting and regular road casualties, fox populations in the lowlands are strong and widespread. The habitats and feeding opportunities provided in the well-wooded valleys fields and hills are perfectly suited to the needs of the wild fox population. There is plenty of room for us to share the landscape with this wild predator.

Badger Habitats

The life of another large mammal, the **badger,** is intimately linked with the habitats and farming of the lowlands of Wicklow. Most of their underground breeding places or setts are located in hedgerows, though woodland and scrub are also favoured sites. In general, sites which provide the best cover are preferred for setts, but research by Dr Chris Smal has shown that the number of badger social groups is largely dependent on the proportion of good agricultural grassland, especially cattle pasture, and the density of their primary food item — earthworms — in an area. Sheep-grazing areas, especially those at higher altitudes and in poorer land are less favoured by badgers.

Silt and clay soil seem to be avoided, with most setts found in sandy or loamy soils, probably because these soils are easier to dig extensive tunnels through. In general, badgers locate their setts under cover away from human activity, avoiding disturbance from farm machinery.

Loss of hedgerow cover in the farming areas of the coastal plain and near the Kildare border, combined with change from pasture to arable use, has reduced the badger habitat in Wicklow. The mountainous area in the centre of the county has relatively low densities of badgers because of the poor soil quality, absence of improved pasture and hedgerows and general lack of cover. Badgers are not completely absent on the mountains, however, and individual setts can be found even on the slopes of Lugnaquillia.

In general, the best badger habitat is the foothills, where low hills are interspersed with rich valleys containing permanent pasture and small areas of deciduous woodland. This is typical of the plateau area which runs from the Great Sugarloaf south via Roundwood, Ashford and Glenealy to Rathdrum. It is also typical of the southern part of the county around Aughrim, Tinahely and Shillelagh and of parts of the west between Dunlavin and Blessington, where the foothills of the mountains interfinger with the central plain.

117

5.1   *Aerial view of farmland and*
peaty ground near Annamoe
(Cambridge University Collection of Air
Photographs: copyright reserved)

Badger watching

In numerous places in Wicklow you may come across the distinctive bear-like track of the badger on a roadside, by a hedgerow or on the edge of a woodland. These tracks usually follow a well-established route which is used by a family of badgers night after night throughout the year. Unfortunately, where such routes cross busy roads, many badgers end their days as a pile of grey fur and claws, with the distinctive black and white striped head, lying in the road.

Following one of these tracks for a short distance one may find fresh droppings, indicating recent use of the area. Further on there may be the distinctive diggings where the badger has used its powerful snout and claws to excavate beneath the grass for earthworms. The track may eventually lead to a secluded spot, perhaps on the bank of a stream or a quiet field corner, or even in a small woodland. Great piles of soil mark each of the entrances to a sett. The presence of fresh soil and discarded straw or bracken shows that badgers have been busy cleaning out the tunnels and chambers below the ground.

A badger-watcher who finds a convenient vantage point, perhaps in the low branches of a tree overlooking the sett, and is prepared to wait for twilight will gain an insight into the badgers' world. As the last of the roosting blackbirds calls to its neighbour and bats emerge to feed on the evening crop of insects, there is the first glimpse of a black and white head at the main entrance of the sett. One of the older badgers emerges cautiously into the moonlight sniffing the air for the tell-tale signs of danger carried on the wind. If it senses human presence it will be gone in a flash. But if the watcher is correctly positioned downwind of the sett, the entire badger family will emerge and begin its nightly forays into the Wicklow countryside.

Setts

Not all badger setts are equally important to the animals. Dr Chris Smal has classified them as main setts, annexe setts, subsidiary setts and outlier setts. Main setts usually have a large number of entrances, with conspicuous soil heaps outside them and many well-worn tracks leading away into the countryside. These are breeding setts and are normally in continuous use. Annexe setts may be close to a main sett and connected to it by well-worn paths. However, they may only be used at certain times of the year, even if the main sett is very active. Subsidiary setts are usually at least 50m (150ft) from a main sett and may not be connected to it by obvious paths. These are not continuously active and may be used only infrequently. Outlier setts are often difficult to associate with badgers as they may have little soil outside the hole and no obvious path connecting them with another sett. These holes are only used sporadically and when not occupied by their main tenant may be taken over by foxes or rabbits.

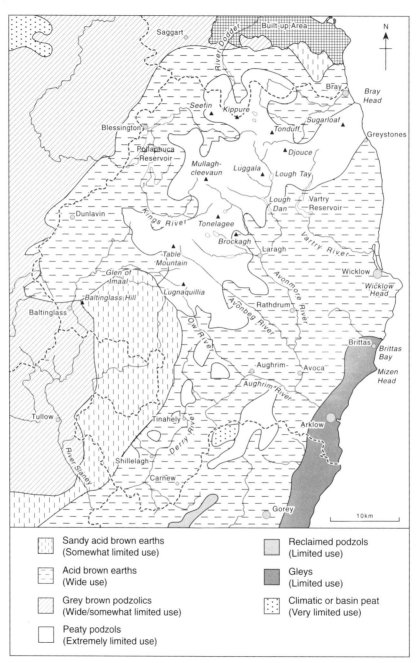

Map 9   Soil types and land use capabilities in County Wicklow. The most fertile lands are on the acid brown earths of the eastern and western lowlands and the river valleys. The peaty soils of the mountain chain are mainly used for sheep grazing. (after Stout in: Hannigan and Nolan 1994)

120

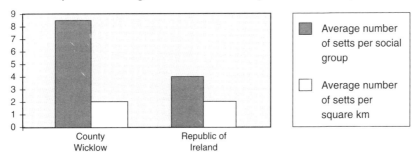

**Density of badger setts in County Wicklow
compared with national averages
(from the Badger and Habitat Survey of Ireland 1995)**

Legend:
■ Average number of setts per social group
□ Average number of setts per square km

Although there are more setts in Wicklow per square kilometre than elsewhere in the country, the proportion of active setts in the county (42%) is very low, compared with the country overall (73%).

Badger setts in Wicklow are frequently disturbed (28% of setts surveyed) by digging, blocking, snaring, land development or other human activities. Some of these are deliberate attempts to remove the badgers, while others are incidental to farming activities or other land use.

Looking to the Future

As the morning sun rises to warm the dew-covered fields of the Wicklow lowlands, a farmer, rounding up his cattle for milking, might disturb a badger out for some late foraging. The local badger sett, which has been on this farmer's land for generations, has seen many changes in the landscape, not least since Ireland's accession to the European Union. Cereal production has already been subject to set-aside policies with some areas of cultivation left fallow. With surpluses of beef and milk in Europe it is likely that the land released from grazing will be turned over to other uses in the short term. The Wicklow–Kildare borderlands already have many stud farms supporting the horse industry around the Curragh.

On both the west Wicklow lowlands and the eastern coastal plain there is already significant pressure for housing development as the conurbation of Dublin stretches its tentacles further south. Towns such as Blessington, Enniskerry, Ashford, Rathnew and Wicklow, which are now surrounded by countryside, will inevitably become suburbanised as road improvements link these areas with the city. A rising population also demands more space for recreation, industry and refuse dumps. However, the wildlife of the lowlands is adaptable and, given time, may adjust to these changes in future. Let us hope that in the process of change we do not lose all of the natural areas which are such an important part of this landscape.

6. ON THE SEASHORE

Compared with the rugged west coast, the coastline of Wicklow is relatively straight and the waters of the Irish Sea are sheltered. A good point to begin exploring this coast is the ruins of the old Black Castle above Wicklow Harbour. As you walk away from the older part of the town, the land rises into a series of rocky headlands and small shingly beaches. The vegetation on the cliff path is a springy turf of plants that thrive in the salt-laden winds. Occasionally the star-shaped blue flowers of the **spring squill** catch the eye, shining out from the clifftop vegetation.

The rocks along the shoreline are a tangled mass, twisted and contorted by successive earth movements and then eroded by the sea to form spectacular arches and caves. Further south, the cliffs become higher and the waves smash against the rocks far below. Fulmars glide about the cliff tops on stiffened wings and an occasional grey seal watches from the water below. Looking down from the cliffs, there is a fierce tidal rip around one of the most exposed shorelines in the county. As the walker rounds the final bend, three lighthouses come into view, for Wicklow Head has long been a landmark for seafarers, marking as it does the most easterly point of land in the Republic of Ireland.

Wicklow Head is about the mid-point of the county's 33-mile coastline. To the north stretches a long, almost straight shingle coast between Wicklow Harbour and Greystones. To the north, the land rises steeply to the broad back of Bray Head, its ancient rocks forming a buttress against the sea. South of Wicklow Head the coast angles away to the south-west with a series of low, boulder-clay cliffs interspersed by long sandy beaches. Here the main sand dunes of Wicklow continue to the county border just south of Arklow. Offshore, the seabed reflects the coastal sediments, becoming progressively more sandy the further south one goes. This sand is built by the offshore currents into a series of shallow sandy banks.

Rocky Headlands

Each of the three rocky headlands in Wicklow has a different character, largely due to the underlying geology. **Bray Head**, at the north of the county is composed of ancient Cambrian rocks. These massive quartzites are resistant to the erosive power of the sea, deflecting wave energy onto neighbouring beaches and coasts.

By contrast, **Wicklow Head** is made of younger metamorphic rocks with a high component of the plate-like mineral mica. These rocks crumble more easily under the power of the waves and have allowed the sea to form caves and small stony beaches at their foot.

122

Arklow Head is made of dolerite, the remnant plug of an ancient volcano, which is being actively quarried and shipped away. Arklow Head is clothed with a mantle of boulder clay which softens its margins and prevents the formation of substantial cliffs, except in the quarry itself.

Seabird cities

Each of these headlands has a small colony of cliff-breeding seabirds, providing birdwatchers with an opportunity to experience the wonderful sights, sounds and smells of a seabird city. Walking along a cliff path in mid-summer the cries of the **kittiwakes** can be heard, as they perch precariously on their nests, which are plastered to vertical cliffs.

Wherever narrow ledges have developed auks are found — the **razorbills** and **guillemots**. These smart, black and white seabirds crowd along the ledges, each with a single egg cradled between its feet. In flight, their short stubby wings move rapidly carrying them in a long descent to the surface of the sea where they are most at home. They feed, often far from the colonies, by diving from the surface waters after shoals of small fish. As evening approaches, large rafts of these birds gather in the sea below the cliffs, waiting to come ashore.

As the small fluffy black chicks hatch on the narrow ledges there is an increase in frequency of feeding trips by the adults. With loud clacking noises, they jostle for position on the ledges, each pair attempting to defend a small space for its growing chick. As the summer days grow shorter, the adults encourage their young to leap from the cliffs and glide down to the sea where they will spend the coming months fattening up ready for migration to the south.

On the lower, more broken rocks at the foot of the cliffs is a third species of auk, the **black guillemot** (a separate species from the guillemot). This distinctive bird, with bright red feet and white wing patches, is most often seen sunning itself on rocky shorelines or swimming in the weedy shallows. The black guillemot is less colonial than the other auks with pairs holding larger territories along the coast.

The larger **shags**, relatives of the cormorants, also nest in pairs among the fallen boulders and crevices at the foot of the cliffs. If a person approaches the nest of one of these birds it will open wide its substantial bill and display the bright yellow inside of its mouth in an attempt to frighten off intruders. Less colourful members of the seabird colony include **herring gulls** and a small numbers of **great black-backed gulls**, which are fierce predators of other seabirds.

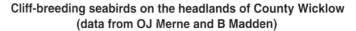

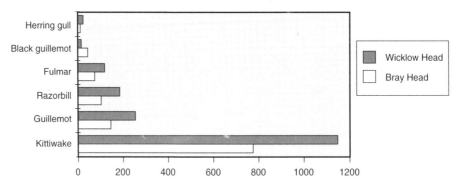

Cliff-breeding seabirds on the headlands of County Wicklow
(data from OJ Merne and B Madden)

The headlands of the Wicklow coast provide a vantage point from which to see passing migrant birds in spring and autumn. Typical early arrivals in late March and April are the **wheatear**, **sand martin** and **sandwich tern**. Occasionally, large movements occur, such as on 25 May 1994 when over a thousand **swifts** were recorded passing Wicklow Head. Relatives of the swifts are the tiny **house martins**, which usually breed below the eaves of modern houses. Their nests are plastered to the wall without any apparent support. House martins occasionally nest on cliffs, and a small colony of up to 30 pairs of house martins breeds on overhanging rock faces on the cliffs at Bride's Head. Another small colony of house martins nests under the roof of two caves at the back of the beach at the Silver Strand.

Seals

There are no regular breeding sites for seals on the Wicklow coast, but small numbers may be seen in the sea at Bray Head and Wicklow Head. At Wicklow Head, occasional **grey seal** pups may be born in the caves or on the cliff-bound beaches. Through the rest of the year individual grey seals are known to have feeding territories, sections of the coast which they will defend against others of their species. Their food consists mainly of non-commercial, rocky shore fish but in late summer and autumn they will often chase migrating salmon, even following them into the river mouths.

Sand Dunes

About 10,000 years ago, the ice was beginning to retreat northwards leaving behind huge spoil heaps of sand and gravel dumped on land and sea. The offshore sand bars of the Arklow Bank were destined to provide a huge sediment supply as sea-level subsequently rose and fell. The wave energy of the sea, newly released from the grip of the ice, gathered up the sand from the seabed and piled it against the coast like plaster applied to walls. Over the millennia which followed, this sand and gravel was worked and reworked by the sea, producing the fine wide sandy beaches that we see today at places like Brittas Bay, Magheramore, Buckroney and the north beach in Arklow. The climate began to warm and there were periods of extremely windy conditions when much of the beach sand was lifted into the air and blown inland across the boulder clay base.

Flint implements made by early human inhabitants of the area have been found in various sand dune sites along the Wicklow coast, usually associated with so-called fossil soils. These suggest long periods of settled conditions. But wild and windy conditions were to return again in medieval times, reworking the old sand dunes and piling up fresh sand to make some of the highest dunes in Wicklow, which we see today at Brittas Bay. Some of the dunes on the Wicklow coast became mobile yet again in the nineteenth century, as great sheets of sand were carried inland during storms, in some cases enveloping whole villages and farms.

Sandy beaches

The Avoca river enters the sea at Arklow Harbour. In the eighteenth century, the river took a completely different course: its original mouth became blocked by mobile sand dunes and it flowed out to sea a mile or two north of its present exit. A hundred years later, the first major engineering works were under way to create the port of Arklow and provide a deep channel for shipping, guided between artificial sea walls. This caused a change in the tidal circulation around the river mouth and led to the deposition of extensive sand bars north of Arklow, forming what were then a fine set of sand dunes backed by coastal marshes. More recently much of this sand dune area has been altered both by the development of caravan parks and by permanent stabilisation with a massive boulder defence system. All that remains intact is a tiny area of sand dunes at Seabank, about a mile north of Arklow. These dunes can be approached on foot across a rocky headland known as Porter's Rocks.

The shelving sandy beach here is normally deserted even in early summer except for the piping calls of a nesting **ringed plover**. To distract an intruder away from its newly hatched young, the bird will feign injury and trail its wings to attract attention. Its nest, a mere shallow scrape in the sand, relies for survival on camouflage, as the eggs resemble the granite pebbles and shells among which they are laid.

Dune plants

On the strand line, where last winter's seaweed debris has been covered by a fresh layer of sand, the new shoots of the pioneer plants of the dunes emerge. These highly specialised, salt-tolerant plants such as **sea sandwort**, **prickly saltwort** and especially **sand couch grass** begin to turn the bare sand into a green sward. These growing shoots also act as fences, trapping the blowing sand and forming the beginning of a line of sand dunes.

Another dividing line occurs slightly further inland, where the tall flowering shoots of the **marram grass** have colonised the first ridge of sand dunes. On the bare sand between the grass stems grow such attractive plants as the **sea bindweed** with its pink trumpet-like flowers and the grey prickly leaves of **sea holly**. A startled young **rabbit** here may bound away inland for cover among the deeper grass.

In the shelter of the first dune ridge is an area of carpet-like vegetation which blossoms in early summer with a colourful array of wild flowers. Most obvious are the yellows of the **bird's-foot trefoil** and the purples of the **seaside pansy**. If one searches closely the deep purple flowering spikes of the **pyramidal orchid** may be found. A very rare but unspectacular plant known as **Moore's horsetail** grows at Seabank. This primitive plant, a sub-species of the common horsetail, is known only from the south-east coast of Ireland, where it clings on precariously to a few remaining sites.

Dune slacks

The zones of vegetation which mark the transition from maritime conditions on the beach to terrestrial habitats inland are typical of most of the sand dunes on the Wicklow coast. At some sites, such as Buckroney dunes just south of Mizen Head, they are even better developed. Here the wind has scooped out hollows in the dunes reaching down to the water table, which rises in winter to form flooded areas known as dune slacks.

Dune slacks are filled with a distinctive vegetation including a creeping form of **willow** and many rushes and sedges. There are also rarer plants here such as the **meadow saxifrage**, **wild asparagus** and **green-flowered helleborine**. In spring **sedge warblers** and **reed buntings** feed mainly on wetland insects.

Older dunes tend not to survive on the inland fringe, because they are turned into either farmland or holiday developments. At Brittas Bay there are extensive areas covered by the prickly stems of **burnet rose**, profusely covered in white flowers in early summer. Many of the back dune slopes are covered with **bracken**, which reaches to up to a metre high, forming a canopy similar to woodland. This shelters such woodland flowers as the **bluebell** and **dog violet**. A solitary **kestrel** is a common sight hovering above these bracken dunes as it quarters the ground below for the slightest movement from a wood mouse or shrew.

One of the commonest mammals on the sand dunes, the **rabbit**, was introduced here by the Normans as a ready source of meat and skins, which were exported in large quantities. So profitable was this trade in the Middle Ages that many sand dunes became valuable properties and were cultivated as warrens, primarily for their rabbit stock. Today these same sand dunes are used either for grazing by cattle or more commonly for recreational use. Lying within easy reach of the capital city, they have attracted the development of caravan parks, holiday housing and the inevitable golf courses. Only those sand dunes that are largely in single ownership, such as Magherabeg, remain relatively intact today.

Inland from the dunes

Coming inland, away from the sea, the flower-rich turf of the sand dunes is gradually shaded by increasing competition from shrubs such as **hawthorn** and **blackthorn**. Overhead the trilling song of the **skylark** fills the air, with **meadow pipits** flitting about in the vegetation below.

At the junction between the sand dunes and the boulder cliffs against which they lie is a thickening of the vegetation with young trees of **sycamore** and **ash** growing on the richer soil. On these steep and well-drained slopes a narrow woodland has developed, whose canopy is filled with the songs of **chaffinch**, **blackbird**, song **thrush** and **wren**. Such wooded slopes are also much favoured by **badgers** who dig their extensive tunnel networks into the soft clays, emerging at night to feed on earthworms and insects grubs in the neighbouring pastures.

The Murrough

On the northern half of the Wicklow coast there are some small sand hills with typical dune vegetation dominated by **marram grass**. However, these thin sandy soils merely form a cap over an extensive area of shingle, made up of gravel and cobble-sized stones. This shingle is now perched above the height of present sea-level and has come to form a long continuous barrier between the Irish Sea and the low-lying marshy land behind it. This remarkable feature, known as the Murrough, stretches a full ten miles from Wicklow Harbour to Ballygannon near Greystones.

The name Murrough comes from the Irish word *murbhach*, meaning a saltmarsh along the sea. The Murrough is situated in the barony of Newcastle. Its most easterly promontory is at Six Mile Point (exactly six miles north of Wicklow town). The railway from Greystones to Wicklow, which runs along the Murrough, has been threatened by coastal erosion at several places and large concrete blocks have been placed at the top of the beach to prevent damage to the track.

When the glaciers of the last Ice Age retreated, about 16,000 years ago, they left behind large amounts of sand and gravel in the shallow depression of what is now the Irish Sea. With the re-adjustment of land and sea-level, quantities of these sediments were deposited along the coast. Shingle is the largest of these sediments and can only be moved by strong currents or storms. Once they reached the coast, the pebbles were moved along parallel to the shore by long-shore drift. The shingle barrier then moved on-shore cutting off the lagoon behind it from the sea. The Vartry was thus forced to flow southwards for two miles behind the Murrough before entering the sea at what is now Wicklow Harbour.

The pebbles on the present beach represent a wide range of rock types which were collected by the glaciers as they moved across the landscape. These include granite, limestone, conglomerates, flint and even a type of granite from Ailsa Craig in Scotland.

The beach is widest at the Breaches where Kilcoole Marshes enter the sea. This opening is regularly blocked by the movement of beach material and then the lagoon floods. A cross-section through the beach and lagoon at Leamore near Newcastle shows that the crest of the shingle ridge is nearly 4m (12ft) above present sea-level. This represents the highest point to which sea-level rose in post-glacial times.

The sediments in the former lagoon are up to 3.5m (10ft) thick and comprise several layers of fen peat (laid down in freshwater conditions) interbedded with layers of marine or estuarine clays. This suggests that the barrier was breached several times since the last Ice Age. The artificially straight lines of many of the channels in the Kilcoole Marshes suggest that the peat here was dug out in previous centuries, possibly during a time when the opening to the sea was blocked for an extended period.

Despite the normally sheltered nature of the Murrough coast, the sea can exert enormous energy here in certain conditions. On rare occasions, the waves can wash across the Murrough. In a great storm in November 1915 the sea deposited huge quantities of sand all along the Murrough wetlands and all the houses along the coast were flooded. After Hurricane Charlie in August 1986, the floodwater from the River Vartry, combined with a high spring tide in Broadlough, flooded large parts of the low-lying area of the Murrough, cutting off a number of houses.

The Murrough is a complex of different habitats such as shingle beach, sand hills, drainage ditches, reed beds, saltmarsh, mudflats, fen and woodland. Each one of these contains a characteristic plant community with species specially adapted to the environmental conditions.

Shingle beach

Few plants can survive on the shingle beach which is occasionally covered by high spring tides. On the upper beach **sea rocket** and **sea purslane** grow on the stones alongside **sea beet** and **sea campion**. Some rarer species such as **yellow horned poppy** and **sea samphire** are found in places.

On the inland side of the railway near Broadlough a band of shingle is now mostly covered with **gorse**, which forms dense thickets. Further north this gorse is

128

5.2   Silage cutting near Hollywood. With high-yielding grass varieties, large fertiliser inputs and modern harvesting machines, several cuts of grass may be taken from the same field each year. The west Wicklow hills in the background are intensively grazed by sheep. (Richard Nairn)

5.3   Kilruddery House, near Bray, set in an estate on the slopes of the Little Sugarloaf mountain. The surrounding landscape is an important component of these historic gardens. The mature woodlands in such estates are rich wildlife habitats. (Richard Nairn)

5.4   Great Sugarloaf mountain. The east Wicklow landscape is a mixture of arable land and pasture on the better soils with rougher grazing on the steep slopes. The tall hedges on the lowlands give way to low hedges and stone walls in the uplands with open land from about 1200 feet above sea level. (Richard Nairn)

5.5

5.6

5.5 Hawthorn in flower in May. Also known as whitethorn or maybush, this thorny plant is the commonest constituent of Wicklow hedges. Its leaves, flowers and fruit provide food for a wide range of insects and other small animals. (Richard Nairn)

5.6 Food for free. Haws and sloes are the fruit of hawthorn and blackthorn respectively. They are usually eaten by flocks of migrant birds such as thrushes, finches and starlings by mid-winter. Some mammals such as foxes and mice also rely heavily on hedgerow fruit during the early winter months. (Richard T. Mills)

5.7 *Barn owl in a churchyard.
Ruined buildings, farmyards and
occasionally hollow trees provide
the nesting places for these
beautiful birds. Areas of long grass
on roadsides and river banks are
favourite hunting areas as they
hold high populations of small
mammal prey. (Frank Doyle)*

5.8 *Swallows prefer to nest
indoors. The mud platform is
often fixed to the rafters in an
outbuilding. Here the growing
chicks await repeated deliveries of
insect food which the adults catch
on the wing. After a winter spent
in southern Africa, the young
birds may return to the same
building to nest the following
summer. (Frank Doyle)*

5.9 *Cuckoo. Once common in
the countryside, the cuckoos call
is now heard only on rough hill
land and along the coastal strip.
This is where the nests of its
principal host, the meadow pipit,
are concentrated. The female
cuckoo will seek out pipit nests,
removing one of the hosts eggs
and laying one of her own in its
place. (Richard T. Mills)*

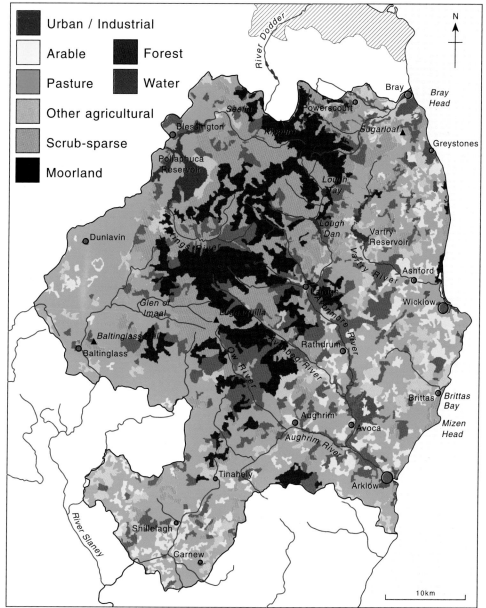

Legend:
- Urban / Industrial
- Arable
- Pasture
- Other agricultural
- Scrub-sparse
- Moorland
- Forest
- Water

Map 10 Land cover classification of County Wicklow based on a satellite image taken in 1989/90. Arable land is mainly concentrated to the east of the mountains. The main areas of moorland are now within the National Park. Some areas classified as industrial lands in the south-east of the county are the spoil from the former Avoca mines. (CORINE data from the European Commission (DGXI) supplied by Natural Resources Development Centre, Trinity College Dublin)

133

5.10   Spraying a cereal field near Ashford. The use of agrochemicals has been implicated in breeding failure in birds of prey and water pollution where the run-off enters rivers. Arable land is among the poorest of wildlife habitats because the soil is constantly disturbed and invertebrate populations are low. (Richard Nairn)

5.11   Fox cub in a summer meadow. Near the breeding den there is usually a network of runs in the vegetation where the young animals play while the adults are away hunting. As they grow stronger and more adventurous, the cubs will venture further from the den. Many are killed on roads at this age. (Frank Doyle)

134

5.12 *Hollywood. The lowlands of west Wicklow are covered with a network of hedgerows dominated by ash, hawthorn and gorse. The mature trees in the hedges give the impression of a wooded landscape. (Richard Nairn)*

5.13 *Ragged robin in a damp meadow. Such species-rich grasslands are alive in summer with the varied sounds of insects. They are becoming increasingly rare in Wicklow due to drainage and more intensive grazing. (Richard Nairn)*

5.13

5.14 Bats roosting in the cellar of an old house. Such places are often chosen for winter roosts because they have a steady temperature and are usually undisturbed. In summer, the bats may move to the attics of houses where single young are born to each female. They are most active at this time emerging at dusk and dawn to feed on flying insects. (Frank Doyle)

5.15 Damselfly. A typical insect of lowland wetlands. The adults fly in fine summer weather, resting frequently on vegetation or on rocks to warm their bodies in the sun. The male is mostly blue, while the female is mainly black. (Richard T. Mills)

6.1 Beach at Wicklow Head. In
the foreground, thrift or sea pink
is in flower. This headland marks
the most easterly point of County
Wicklow. Its cliffs hold a small
seabird colony in summer. The
seabed offshore, which is swept by
strong tidal currents, has an
unusual series of reefs formed by
honeycomb worms. (Richard
Nairn)

6.2 The shag is among the
seabirds which nest in summer on
the rocky cliffs at Bray Head and
Wicklow Head. It is a smaller
relative of the cormorant and is
usually found among the jumble
of boulders near the base of the
cliffs. The rest of the year is spent
at sea where the bird fishes by
plunge-diving from the surface.
(Richard T. Mills)

6.3 Ringed plover. The nest is
only a shallow scrape in the sand
or gravel at the top of the beach.
The four eggs are camouflaged to
look like pebbles. After hatching,
the chicks immediately run into
the cover of vegetation. Breeding
takes place early in the summer
before the beach is too busy with
visitors. (Richard T. Mills)

6.2

6.3

138

6.4   *Brittas Bay. At the southern end where the beach is widest, a new line of sand dunes has built up since the 1960s. Marram grass is the plant which stabilises the sand blown off the beach. On the back dunes near the road, bracken and burnet rose give dense vegetation cover. A few of the higher dunes have large blow-outs formed by wind erosion. (Con Hogan)*

6.5   Little tern. A colony of these tiny seabirds nests on the beach between Newcastle and Kilcoole. Despite full-time wardening each summer for over a decade, the numbers of birds are still small and breeding success is low in some years due to predators and flooding of nests. (Richard T. Mills)

6.6   Shingle beach flora on the Murrough. Sea campion, scurvy grass and kidney vetch are the main flowers at the top of the beach near the railway. (Richard Nairn)

6.7   Sea bindweed among marram grass in the foredunes. Here the sand is annually recycled between the beach and dunes. There are few nutrients in the sand and plant diversity is low. Only a few specialised plants can survive here. (Richard T. Mills)

6.8   Sea holly in the fixed dunes. Here the sand is completely covered by a rich variety of flowering plants including wild thyme, lady's bedstraw and kidney vetch. Rabbits are common grazers and insect life is abundant in summer. (Richard T. Mills)

6.7

6.8

142

6.9   Brittas Bay. Trial planting of marram grass has been used to combat erosion caused by visitor pressure on the sand dunes. This grass can withstand burial of up to a metre a year and its extensive root system binds the mobile sand. (Richard Nairn)

6.10   Shore crab. This crustacean lives below lowwater mark on rocky shores. Underwater boulders, rocky overhangs and kelp forests provide plenty of shelter from predators. Empty shells are often found on the strandline. (Richard T. Mills)

143

6.11   Common blue butterfly. A typical insect of sand dunes, here resting on the food plant of its caterpillar, bird's-foot trefoil. The female butterflies are darker than the males. (Frank Doyle)

6.12   Coastal grassland on the Murrough. Regular inputs of windblown sand and the absence of grazing have produced this species-rich sward along the Murrough near Newcastle. This is the habitat of skylark and numerous butterflies. (Richard Nairn)

replaced by rough pasture which is dominated by grasses, **knapweed** and **chrysanthemum**. As recently as the early 1960s, barley and potatoes were grown at the southern end of the Murrough. By the late 1960s the big field here was lying fallow and the gorse had begun to creep back. Today, the signs of former cultivation can just be detected in the swathes of **poppies**, typical weeds of arable land. Closer to Wicklow town, the dry sandy banks on the edge of the Leitrim river support a unique plant community with several rare clover species. For one species, **subterranean clover**, this is now the only known site in the country.

Sand hills and saltmarshes

In places, the stones of the Murrough are covered with low sand hills on which the typical **marram grass**, and occasionally, the larger **lyme grass** grows. Among the grasses on the seaward edge of the sandhills, **sea holly** and **sea bindweed** are common. Closer to the railway line where the sand is less mobile a wider range of plants occurs. These include **bird's-foot trefoil**, **kidney vetch** and, occasionally, the **pyramidal orchid**. Here the ground is completely covered and mosses carpet the sand. The prickly stems of **burnet rose** are also widespread on the fixed dunes. An introduced plant, the **hottentot fig**, has become established near the railway at the Breaches. Between Kilcoole and Newcastle another introduced species, **sea buckthorn**, has been planted in an attempt to stabilise the blowing sand.

The largest areas of saltmarsh on the Wicklow coast occur near the Breaches, where the tide enters Kilcoole Marshes, and at Broadlough. Here the plants are all salt-tolerant species such as **common scurvy grass**, **sea beet** and **sea aster**. **Sea rush** and a variety of saltmarsh grasses are prominent in the sward. In winter storms the Breaches occasionally becomes blocked with beach material and the marshes can be flooded for days at a time. Much of the saltmarsh at Kilcoole has now been drained to improve the grazing and the vegetation is considerably modified. In Kilcoole Marshes and at the northern end of Broadlough, the tide retreats to expose small areas of mudflats. These are devoid of flowering plants but do support some green seaweeds, including **sea lettuce**, which provides food for the large flocks of wildfowl in winter.

Murrough marshland

Between Broadlough and Kilcoole Marshes are areas of marshland and wet grassland which support a great diversity of wetland plants especially where they are not used for intensive agriculture. In the central area around Blackditch there are some brackish (slightly saline) pools up to 20cm (8 inches) deep. These are surrounded by marshland vegetation dominated by **great fen sedge**, **black bog rush** and **common reed**. Other common wetland plants include **angelica**, **devil's bit scabious**, **purple loosestrife**, **tormentil**, **meadowsweet** and various rushes and sedges. The rare **marsh pea** occurs here well outside its main range in the midlands of Ireland. Low-lying land on the western side of Broadlough and many of the drainage ditches on the Murrough are filled with a dense growth of **reeds**. These can grow up to 3m in height and are so close together that few other plants can survive in their shade.

Wet woodland

In a few places, such as Blackditch south of Newcastle, woodland has developed in the absence of grazing. The typical trees are **willow, alder** and **birch**, all of which can survive occasional flooding. Some of the trees are up to 200 years old and have a profuse growth of lichens. Before the land was farmed, this type of woodland was probably widespread on the Murrough. Woodland such as this is a very important habitat for insects, many of which are hardly visible. More than 600 species of two-winged flies have been found here, including three tiny species which are only known from one or two places in Europe. The only known Irish breeding site for the **gold-tailed moth** also occurs in this area. Striking red and black **burying beetles** roam the drier parts, searching for small dead animals on which to lay their eggs. The network of small creatures such as flies, beetles, moths, snails and spiders forms a basis for the life of birds, mammals and other larger animals. They are locked together in a mutual dependency whose richness we are just beginning to comprehend.

Waterfowl on the Murrough

Published information on waterfowl populations on the Wicklow coast is limited, and the counts shown in the graph opposite did not cover the agricultural area between Kilcoole and Broadlough, which is used by a nationally important flock of greylag geese.

At Kilcoole Marshes, total numbers of wildfowl have increased significantly since the 1980s. This is partly due to embankment of large areas of saltmarsh by local farmers. This has turned the saltmarsh into coastal grassland, which has been improved with the addition of fertiliser. This improved grass has acted as a magnet for wildfowl such as **brent geese**, which have steadily increased to peaks over a thousand birds in winter. The improved grassland has also attracted larger flocks of **whooper swans**. Meanwhile, the exclusion of the tide from most of the channels has almost converted these to freshwater, which is attractive for ducks but is less suitable for waders. A further factor has been the decrease in shooting pressure at this site, perhaps because of an increasing awareness of its value as a refuge on the Wicklow coast.

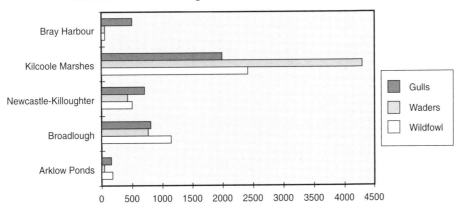

Peak counts of wintering birds on the Wicklow coast 1996/97

Broadlough has a limited amount of intertidal mudflat, which is mainly concentrated in the northern half. This is where the majority of waders, especially the smaller species such as **dunlin** and **ringed plover**, feed at low tide. They search out the tiny marine snail **Hydrobia** and shrimp-like creatures such as **Corophium**.

The southern part of Broadlough, near Wicklow town, is up to 250m wide and is generally filled with seawater except at extreme low water spring tides. The majority of ducks are found in this southern area. The principal high-tide roosts for **teal**, **mallard**, **curlew** and **redshank** are on the western shoreline around the edge of the saltmarsh and reedbeds of Knockrobin. This makes them difficult to see without the aid of a telescope. **Wigeon** and mallard may be found in small groups in most parts of the estuary during winter months although they prefer the wider sections with the greatest feeding opportunities.

The central, narrow part of Broadlough near the outlet of the Vartry river is favoured by certain species such as **goldeneye**, **greenshank** and **grey plover**. This section is also used by a large flock of **black-headed gull**s, which prefers the freshwater for washing their plumage at low tide. We regularly see a **kingfisher** on this section of the estuary near the river mouth, especially in winter. The flash of vivid blue and orange which darts by in a few seconds is reward enough for a morning's birdwatching.

The narrow point of the estuary was used as a ford in previous centuries to bring grazing animals to and from the Murrough. There was once a wooden footbridge across the estuary near here (to allow ladies to walk to the beach and 'take the air') and, at low tide, the stakes which supported it are still visible.

A flock of **mute swans** normally builds up at Broadlough in late summer. These are non-breeding birds, which are mature but unable to occupy breeding territories, such is the density of the swan population in the east coast area. The flock generally remains at Broadlough until mid-winter, feeding throughout the estuary. During recent winters numbers have been lower as the majority of the flock moved to the Grand Canal at Inchicore, Dublin. The remaining smaller flock has changed to feeding principally on bread supplied willingly by the people of Wicklow town.

Songbirds

The heathland on the southern part of the Murrough is used by a range of common breeding songbirds including **blackbird**, **wren** and **robin**. The areas of scattered gorse scrub also provide territories for **stonechat**, **whitethroat**, **grasshopper warbler** and **linnet**. The continuous rattling calls of the grasshopper warbler are easily confused with the sound of a fishing reel. The wetland habitats around Broadlough are used by a typical range of breeding birds, including **sedge warbler**, **reed bunting** and **water rail**.

Two nationally rare species, the **bearded reedling** and **reed warbler**, have also occurred here. Bearded reedling bred in small numbers in various reedbeds on the Murrough between 1975 and 1985 but has not been recorded since then. One factor has been the almost continuous harvesting of reeds for thatching at Broadlough, which has reduced the density of reeds and the piles of reed litter which are found in a natural reedbed. Reed warbler has been recorded breeding at Broadlough since 1982, with up to six males in song in some years, and it is probably also breeding now at Kilcoole Marshes and Arklow Ponds.

Rare birds

Broadlough is well known as a location for rare bird sightings. Species reported at Broadlough within the past few years include **Slavonian grebe**, **garganey**, **long-tailed duck**, **Baird's sandpiper**, **ruff** and **spotted redshank**.

Broadlough also has a reputation as a good location for **ospreys** with an increasing number of spring sightings since 1991. A single osprey stayed at Broadlough for at least two weeks in October 1994 where it fed on mullet in the shallow estuary. Known also as the fish eagle, the osprey has a wing span of five feet and hunts by snatching fish from the surface of the water. Ospreys do not breed in Ireland, but they migrate in spring from their wintering areas in west Africa to their Scottish and Scandinavian nesting grounds, and the east coast of Ireland is on the route. Perhaps one day they may stay here to breed.

The **little tern** is the smallest of the breeding seabirds on the Wicklow coast. In May, these attractive birds arrive back from their wintering grounds in Africa to nest at the traditional site near the Breaches between Kilcoole and Newcastle. Laying beautifully camouflaged eggs among the stones on the beach, they flitter and hover above the shallow coastal waters, like delicate moths, hunting for the fish fry and sand eels that form their main food source.

The birds feed along the entire length of the Murrough in the shallow coastal waters. Breeding numbers fluctuate considerably from year to year but are rarely less than 30 pairs. This represents about 10–20% of the Irish population of the species and is thus of national importance. The colony is only successful about one year in every three. Natural predators such as foxes and kestrels seem to be a major part of the problem.

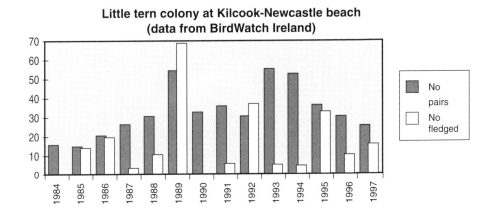

Little tern colony at Kilcook-Newcastle beach (data from BirdWatch Ireland)

Coastal Waters

About six miles from the coast is an area of offshore sandbanks where, at low tide, it is possible to climb out of the boat and stand in water less than a metre deep. This line of sand banks runs parallel to the coast all the way from the south of Dublin Bay past the Codling Bank to the Arklow Bank. These banks have been a hazard to shipping over the centuries and for many years the Arklow light ship was moored at the southern end of the banks to warn seafarers of the danger of running aground here.

Birds all at sea

The keepers who manned this light ship were an important source of information on birds and they regularly reported their sightings to the nineteenth-century Wicklow naturalist, R M Barrington, who was a pioneer of the study of bird migration. From the records submitted by light-keepers all over the country he was able to establish the time of year, the parts of the coast and the relative numbers of each species.

In the shallow water off the coast of Wicklow a coastal current runs, mostly in a band about 10–12 miles (16–19km) wide. It extends south beyond Dublin Bay and picks up the enriched plumes of water coming out of the bays and estuaries. This is one of the most consistently rich areas of the Irish Sea, occurring where the Western Irish Sea Current meets the coastal current off the Kish Bank. Seabirds, especially **razorbills** and **guillemots**, move into these sheltered waters to moult and tend their young after the breeding season. They rely on these rich feeding grounds to build up body weight for the harsh winter ahead.

At the end of the 1969 moulting season, an estimated 10,000 guillemots were washed up dead or dying on the Irish Sea shores. Most of the birds, which had failed to complete the moult, were emaciated and had substantial levels of polychlorinated biphenyls (PCB) in their tissues. At the time, the importance of the seabird moulting area off the south-east coast of Ireland was unknown.

The shellfish in the shallow sandy waters also attract a small black diving duck called the **common scoter**. They concentrate here between August and April feeding on bottom-living molluscs and crustaceans, usually in depths of 5m to 15m (15ft to 45ft) but sometimes up to 20m (60ft) deep. Their numbers are very dependent on the fluctuations in populations of their food items. Numbers of these birds off County Wicklow are quite variable. These birds are also very vulnerable to oil pollution and they were the main casualties of the *Sea Empress* disaster of 1996 in South Wales.

During the late 1960s and early 1970s, Major Robin Ruttledge, who watched for seabirds from Six Mile Point near Newcastle, recorded considerable numbers of **skuas**, larger relatives of our gulls, migrating along the coast. These are arctic breeding birds which move south every autumn and return in the spring. Of all the seabirds recorded here, the **manx shearwater** makes up the most spectacular flocks. At times, thousands of these birds are seen moving along the coast.

The wintering population of the **little gull** in the Irish Sea is the largest regular concentration in north-west Europe. The size of this population, which does not breed in Ireland, fluctuates considerably between winters, varying from 10 to 600 birds. They are mostly seen close to the Wicklow coast in winter.

Of fish and fisheries

The shallow waters off County Wicklow are also an important resource for fisheries. Among the most valuable resources are the **Dublin Bay prawn** and the **scallop**, which are trawled from the sea bottom. The western Irish Sea is also an important nursery area for **herring** and **plaice**. In the mid 1980s fishing boats from Arklow and Wicklow began extensively fishing for **whelks** using baited pots on the seabed of Wicklow and Arklow Bays. Each boat could work up to 500 pots with average landings of 40kg per 100 pots per day. This fishery is carried on throughout the year as weather permits and it is not regulated. Local fishermen report that whelk catches in the immediate area of Wicklow Harbour are low relative to catches further north off Six Mile Point and there is concern about overfishing of this precious resource.

There are **seed mussel** beds also in these waters, which are dredged by boats from Wexford. These tiny shellfish are transported to Wexford where they are laid out for ongrowing to commercial size. Seed mussel beds are highly mobile, and entire stocks can be dispersed by winter storms.

A small number of local boats in Wicklow Harbour engage in lobster fishing on the Murrough coast. This is mainly concentrated on the rocky substrates and **lobsters** are regularly caught among the boulders on top of the outfall pipe from the Murrough pumping station at Wicklow. Several local boats use ground nets for fishing **plaice** and **codling** in the area between Wicklow Harbour and Six Mile Point. Bycatches included **bass** and **mullet**.

Seabed creatures

The seabed off Wicklow Harbour is fairly flat and featureless, with sand close to the coast and beyond this cobbles, gravel and occasional small boulders compacted in a muddy sand. The boulders and some of the stones provide a stable attachment for large brown **seaweeds**, **red algae**, **bryozoans** and **barnacles** giving shelter for **crabs**, **shrimp** and fish such as **ballan wrasse**. Other marine animals on the seabed include **sun stars**, **starfish**, **feather stars** and a small red **sea squirt**. Crusts of **coraline algae** and zones of erosion on the sides of some of the boulders reflect the rocking action caused by the strong water currents.

In the more open areas, where little shelter exists, **hermit crabs** and a small bony fish called **pogge** have been observed. The sand mason worm, which builds sandy tubes in the seabed, is common throughout this area. This marine community is typical of an exposed seabed in a fast-moving current. The only unusual species recorded here was a colony of the **sea squirt** *Distomus variolosus*. This is the first record of this species occurring north of southern England.

Reefs are usually thought to be formed by corals in tropical waters, but there are similar structures in the sea off Wicklow Head. These have been found in depths of between 12 and 30 metres (about 35 to 100 feet). The 'reefs' are constructed by the **honeycomb worm**, which forms numerous hard tubes from the surrounding sandy sea bed. The reefs are colonised by a whole range of other animal species — sponges, bryozoans, mussels, starfish, barnacles, crabs and many others. Up to 53 species have been recorded from these high-rise seabed habitats.

The seabed sediments off the coast of Arklow are typically clean coarse sand on the lower beach, changing to finer sands with increasing depth and muddy sand with shell debris at between 10m and 20m deep. The seabed community here is dominated by a single bivalve mollusc known as *Abra alba*. Other prominent species are the **carpet shell**, the **common nut shell** and the **sand gaper**, which can grow up to 15cm (6 inches) long. There are also many species of small **bristle worms** and beds of **seed mussels**, which provide physical cover for a number of other marine organisms.

The highest numbers of species at Arklow occur in muddy sand and mud-shell gravel areas. This rich fauna provides a food source for juvenile **plaice** and other fish species. There is a clear gap in the rich community, however, directly off the mouth of the Avoca river. This is almost certainly due to the effect of the freshwater outflow and its highly contaminated load — the Avoca river has a history of heavy metal pollution due to copper mining activities in the Woodenbridge area. Among seven Irish estuaries which were assessed for their pollution status in 1991, the Avoca estuary was by far the most heavily contaminated.

Creatures of the ocean

Little is known of marine mammals off the Wicklow coast but almost certainly a range of dolphins, porpoises and small whales (collectively known as *cetaceans*) migrate through these waters every year. The evidence comes from the stranding of dead animals whose records have been published in the Irish Naturalists Journal. The three **white-sided dolphins** which were reported in April 1984 on a strand near Porter's Rocks, Arklow, are the only recent records from Wicklow. A picture of these animals, which were undoubtedly part of a small related group, appeared in the local *Wicklow People* newspaper.

However, the commonest species is almost certainly the **harbour porpoise**, the smallest European cetacean, which rarely exceeds 2m in length. The harbour porpoise seems to prefer shallow waters less than about 50m in depth. Sightings of these marine mammals in the Irish Sea have been linked to the fronts between stratified and mixed water bodies. Both **common** and **bottlenose dolphin** are also seen regularly in the Irish Sea, although their numbers are completely unknown.

Historical accounts suggest that several of the larger whales used to be much more common in the Irish Sea than today. **Humpback whales**, **fin whales** and **bottlenose whales** were reported frequently in the Irish Sea in the nineteenth century. There are old records of **blue whale** (stranded at Arklow in 1802) and bottlenose whale (captured off the Wicklow coast in 1888). All these species have been hunted extensively and are now very rarely recorded in Irish waters. There is a record from the National Museum of Ireland of a **leathery turtle** stranded at Greystones in October 1960. These large and impressive marine reptiles almost certainly swim into the coastal waters of Wicklow in the summer months.

BOTTLENOSE DOLPHIN

6.13 *Aerial view of the Murrough (Cambridge University Collection of Air Photographs: copyright reserved)*

Map 11   Main coastal features of County Wicklow. The northern half of the coast is dominated by the shingle barrier of the Murrough while the southern coastline is sandy with a series of rocky headlands.

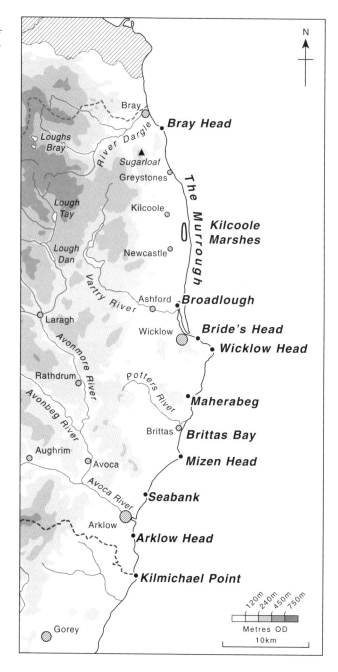

Caring for the Coastline

Buckroney dunes

Just south of Mizen Head, there is a sand dune system known as Buckroney. In the 1970s and 1980s it provided a complete contrast to the crowded and eroded dunes of nearby Brittas Bay. It had all the elements of a natural dune system — a long sandy beach with nesting ringed plovers, high foredunes covered with marram grass and echoing with the song of skylarks, and wet dune slacks with orchids and reed buntings. The distance from the road to the beach, at nearly half a mile, was too great for most day-trippers to walk, burdened with picnics, iceboxes and windbreaks. So the beach remained virtually deserted except for the occasional walker and a flock of terns fishing in the shallow waters offshore.

On the inland side of the road is an extensive marsh or fen which has long been known for its rare plants. J P Brunker wrote in his *Flora of the County Wicklow* (1950) that it probably contained more than half the plants of the rare **marsh fern** in the whole of Ireland. In winter, the water table rises and this peatland, which was once a lake cut off from the sea by blowing sand, attracts flocks of ducks and herons to feed in the shallow water among the reeds. In 1980, the Forest and Wildlife Service carried out a comprehensive survey of Buckroney marsh and dunes. Involving botanists, zoologists and engineers in a fine piece of interdisciplinary work, they concluded that the entire marsh and adjacent sand dunes (which are all part of the same natural system) should be acquired by the state as a matter of urgency and managed as a nature reserve. The whole area was considered to be of national importance and immediately vulnerable to drainage and reclamation.

However, in the spring of 1990 a large section of reeds was cut from the marsh, and diggers began to excavate peat from the southern end, loading it into muck spreaders and spraying it all over the nearby dunes. Bulldozers worked unceasingly in the dunes, flattening the steeper slopes, scraping away the natural vegetation and carving great runways through the landscape. This was a new golf links in the making. The County Council was powerless to act, because golf course development (with the exception of buildings) was then exempt from any requirement for planning permission. Thankfully, since the opening of this golf course the law has been changed so that golf courses are now required to apply for planning permission. This came too late for part of the Buckroney dunes. The remaining southern portion of the dunes at Buckroney has been purchased by the state and will ultimately be declared a nature reserve.

Controlling erosion at Brittas Bay

Immediately north of Buckroney lies the popular beach of Brittas Bay. In the winter of 1995–6 a series of easterly storms cut away the foot of the dunes at the top of the beach. The traditional response to winter erosion on dune fronts has been the use of rock armouring to 'prevent further erosion'. But this can be counter-productive in a dynamic system which depends on free movement of sediment between beach and dunes. At Brittas Bay the scale of the perceived problem was addressed by setting up a series of profiles across the beach and dunes. Historical data from maps and aerial photographs was digitised, allowing comparison of shoreline changes from 1838 to the present. The conclusion was that Brittas Bay has achieved equilibrium in sediment balance and that seasonal erosion and accretion will occur naturally in the central and narrowest part of the beach. The new management strategy has focused on visitor management to prevent damage to the foredunes and allow the beach and dunes to recover naturally from marine erosion.

Managing the Murrough

Further north, the coastal feature of the Murrough has been a testing ground for a number of conservation issues. Coastal erosion has long been a problem here and the traditional solution of rock armoury was still being used here in the late 1990s. This long shingle ridge protects the low-lying north Wicklow coast from the sea but its natural barrier function is often overlooked. Various developments have been proposed for this long flat area. In the 1970s a proposed airstrip opposite Broadlough was defeated in a planning appeal when the threat to the bird sanctuary became a serious issue. In the 1980s a sand and gravel quarry in the same location took half of the barrier away, almost before it was noticed. In the 1990s the new threat was industrialisation.

Meanwhile, in 1991, a bird park for Wicklow was proposed, and eventually, in 1996, a detailed feasibility study for the proposal was carried out. The report also assessed the nature conservation requirements of the area around the estuary of Broadlough. The growing value of this undeveloped green space to the people of Wicklow was clear. The recommended strategy for the future was for a nature park development, combining nature conservation and public access, with the main emphasis on outdoor recreation and the appreciation of nature.

Shared shorelines

The marine and coastal resources of the Irish Sea are a shared heritage which must be valued and protected. The coastline of Wicklow is one of the less well-studied sections of the Irish coast, and it still holds many secrets, which makes it a fascinating place for the naturalist to visit. The coast is quite vulnerable to the pressures of human use and misuse but, as a dynamic and changing landscape, given time, it has the capacity to recover.

7. THROUGH THE AGES

There is almost nowhere in Wicklow, or indeed in Ireland, which has escaped the effects of human activity. This makes the concept of naturalness somewhat meaningless, as there is nothing in nature which is wild in the sense that it is completely untouched by humans. If we consider human evolution as part of nature too then we get a better understanding of our role in the changing landscape.

In 1932, a naturalist called Charles Martin was walking on the coast just south of Wicklow town when he was forced to take shelter in a nearby cave at Bride's Head. The entrance was just over a metre (3 ft) high and the floor of the cave was covered in broken flints and flint pebbles, which he recognised as similar to those found on raised beaches in other parts of the country. These were later identified as the remains of tools used by hunter–gathers who lived here between 7500 and 5500 years ago. These mesolithic (middle Stone Age) people left little evidence and probably had little impact on the primeval landscape.

Early Farmers

The beginning of the farming way of life in Ireland is usually associated with the appearance of the great megalithic tombs which, in Wicklow, are concentrated in the north-west of the county along the present border with Dublin and Kildare, in small clusters south of Rathdrum and east along the coast at Brittas Bay. However, archaeological evidence now suggests that agriculture in Ireland may actually have predated court tombs by some centuries and passage graves by up to a millennium.

The wealth of passage and portal tombs in north-west Wicklow suggests a thriving farming community on the rich soils at the edge of the central plain with elaborate grave sites on the summits of hills such as Seefin, Seefingan and Baltinglass Hill. A saddle quern (or grinding stone) discovered on Baltinglass Hill strongly suggests that cereal cultivation was carried on in the vicinity of this settlement during the neolithic (late Stone Age) period.

The archaeologist Geraldine Stout believes that the passage tombs of north-west Wicklow and south Dublin demarcate a sacred and political territory. She suggests that their builders were the first to clear large tracts of the forest and impose an artificial structure on the Wicklow landscape. This, she believes, was achieved by a major communal enterprise in a community integrated by religious unity and shared burial customs, expressed in tomb architecture and symbolism. The tombs are mainly located on hilltops, which suggests that, like border posts of today, they had a territorial marking function. Stout also believes that north-west Wicklow was a core area of settlement in neolithic times and that there may have been intensive agriculture here, including the making of fields with dividing walls. She emphasises the importance of preserving not only the monuments themselves but the landscape context around them in order that we may understand a little of how these communities may have lived.

Stories from the pollen record

A major breakthrough in understanding of the vegetation changes associated with early farming was made by a Danish scientist, Knud Jessen, who made a series of studies of Irish bogs in the 1930s. Jessen was a pioneer in the study of vegetation history using the pollen remains which are preserved in peat. These microscopic remains can be removed from a core through the bog layers and the relative amounts of different pollen-producing plants may be calculated for each of the phases of pre-history represented in the bog.

One of the sites where Jessen worked was at Ballybetagh bog close to the Scalp on the Dublin–Wicklow border. This was a site that had long been famous because of the large number of bones of giant deer and reindeer which had been excavated during turf-cutting. It seems that these mammals were trapped in the mud of a late glacial lake which has been dated at between 11,000 and 12,000 years ago.

Pollen remains in the bogs between Seefin and Seefingan suggest an early clearance of **elm** and **pine** woods and their replacement with pastures of grass and heath. At Seefin the early farming phase was followed by a heath community and there is some evidence to suggest the burning of this heath, as heather is burnt on the mountains today. This was followed by the spread of blanket bog, which may have resulted partly from the impact of grazing on the vegetation and soils of the hills, combined with a change to a wetter climate about this time. However, recent evidence from Liffey Head bog indicates that blanket bog was already forming there before the post-glacial immigration of trees, at least as early as 8000 years ago. Perhaps the bogs advanced and retreated several times over a period of some thousands of years.

The pollen record showed that at certain times in pre-history there were significant reductions in the amount of tree pollen in the air and this usually coincided with the appearance of pollen from other plants such as grasses, plantains, nettles and docks. Such plants are associated with farming and these changes must indicate the clearance of forest followed by farming activity. It is now known that a major phase of forest clearance took place around 5000 years ago. This increased human activity coincided with a widespread disease in elm trees, probably similar to the present-day Dutch elm disease, which must have accelerated the clearance of trees from some of the more fertile soils.

158

The pollen record shows that periods of intensive agriculture, often lasting only a few hundred years, were sometimes followed by regeneration of woodland, suggesting that the soil was exhausted and the people moved on to colonise other areas. Several centuries later the farming peoples could have returned to the abandoned site and cleared away the secondary woodland, once again exposing a fertile soil to further cultivation.

The woodland clearances were primarily to provide grazing areas rather than cultivation. It is quite likely that, as in other parts of Europe, a form of wood pasture was practised. We can imagine early herdsmen living with their cattle in the clearings in the forest. The cattle would have readily grazed the young trees regenerating around the woodland edge, as well as browsing the understorey beneath the mature trees. Wherever these cleared areas of forest were abandoned they were immediately colonised by **hazel** scrub, which produces abundant pollen grains and is thus quite prominent in the pollen record. The hazel itself was a valuable resource for the early people, not only for the nutritious nut crop produced in the autumn but also for its timber, which was extensively used in house building and construction of stockades and fences. It would have been necessary for these early herdsmen to protect their cattle, goats and pigs at night from native predators including wolf and brown bear.

Plants and animals coming and going

The successive waves of human settlers arriving in Wicklow over the millennia which followed the retreat of the Ice Age almost certainly brought with them many plants and animals that had not previously been found on Irish soil. The apparent absence of **red deer** during the mesolithic suggests that they may have been introduced in later times. In the neolithic period, archaeological evidence suggests that at least **fox, badger** and **wild cat** were present in the Irish environment.

The **wild boar** disappeared in the neolithic or in the Bronze Age, possibly owing to a combination of hunting, deforestation and competition with the domestic pig. Woodland clearances in pre-historic times may also have sealed the fate of some specialist woodland birds such as **goshawks** and **woodpeckers,** of which there are none in Ireland today.

The Age of Metal

Scattered finds of copper or bronze axeheads indicate the coming of the Bronze Age in Wicklow, but the stone monuments of Bronze Age people are a more obvious legacy. Although many of these monuments have been destroyed by farming activity, a great concentration of stone circles and standing stones still survives on the Wicklow–Kildare border in the west of the county.

These stone circles and standing stones may be interpreted as evidence of highly sophisticated ritual practices, as markers of territorial boundaries between clans or as grave markers. The burials were generally in single graves (or cists) and their distribution in the lower, more fertile fringes of Wicklow is the best evidence of settlement in the period 2000–1500 BC. The upper valleys of the Liffey, Slaney and Avoca rivers were important areas to these people, who also colonised the coastal strip north of Wicklow town. Perhaps the rich mineral ores of the county were a focus for this metal-based civilization; the gold ores of Avoca would have been especially prized.

Iron Age hillforts

A massive stone-built rampart or wall enclosing the entire summit of Brusselstown and Spinans Hill, near Baltinglass, was discovered by an archaeologist, Tom Condit, when he was examining aerial photographs of the landscape. This huge wall, which is now partly collapsed, measures between 5m and 12m in width and parts of it have survived up to 2m in height. The total area enclosed by this wall has been estimated at around 130ha, making it by far the largest hillfort in Ireland. It is remarkable that a structure of this kind had gone relatively unnoticed for so many years.

The original entrance to the enclosure has not been located, but there is some slight evidence for hut sites (level areas on which small houses were constructed). These hut sites vary in diameter from about 6m to 10m and suggest a small cluster of houses or settlement within the hillfort. We can only speculate on the lifestyle of the people who lived here in the Iron Age. Undoubtedly these great stone enclosures must have had some defensive role but they may also have enclosed a significant area of farmland. The hill itself overlooks the fertile Glen of Imaal which today contains a mixture of pasture and cereal fields grouped around the headwaters of the River Slaney. Perhaps the fortified camp on the hill provided a place of retreat from the rich farmland in the glen during times of war or attack by outsiders. The all-round view from the summit of the hill would have allowed a sentry to warn of any approaching trouble. To the east lies the sheltered Glen of Imaal, encircled by some of the highest mountains in Wicklow. To the west lie the fertile lands of the upper Slaney valley.

These lands around Baltinglass must have been a very important centre of power in the early Iron Age, as there are no fewer than seven hilltop fortifications here. The cluster of defences is the greatest concentration of multivallate hillforts (with two or more concentric ring ramparts) in the country. Most of these enclosures were large (up to 500m or 1500ft in diameter) and settlement in these strategic locations may have stretched from late Bronze Age into the early centuries AD. At Rathgall, there are over 7 hectares (17 acres) enclosed by earthen ramparts and the finding of clay moulds for swords and spears on the site suggest that these centres of power had to be heavily defended.

160

Fulachta fiadh

In the north-east of Wicklow on the slopes of the Sugarloaf mountain a group of Bronze Age cooking sites (*fulachta fiadh*) has been found. These were associated with a series of ring barrows (or circular mounds) and house sites. These ancient cooking places, which have often been overlooked in the Irish landscape, are now known to have been widespread and common in many parts of the country. Today they normally survive as small semi-circular mounds of stones, usually situated close to a small stream or marsh. Nearby a rectangular pit would have been dug in the ground and lined with wooden planks or stone slabs to form a trough. This would have been filled with water which was then heated using stones from a nearby fire. It has been shown by practical experiment that water can be kept boiling in this way sufficiently long to cook a large haunch of meat such as venison. The red hot stones would have shattered on contact with the cold water and after the cooking was finished the broken stones would have been cleared from the pit and thrown into the semi-circular mound we see today.

This primitive method of cooking is thought to have been used extensively in Wicklow from the Bronze Age to historic times, when the methods of using them are described in early texts. Again, they are associated with settled farming people and they were probably abandoned only when the use of clay vessels for heating water became widespread.

Swords and ploughshares

According to the late Professor Frank Mitchell, at about 2650 years ago there was a period of intensive agricultural activity which coincided with the introduction of a primitive type of plough into Ireland, allowing much more efficient tillage. This is demonstrated by the high values in the pollen record for cereals and weeds such as **dock, thistle, sage** and **goosefoot,** which are thought to indicate tillage.

From about 300 BC there are dramatic changes again in the pollen record with increases in **hazel, elm** and **ash,** suggesting disruption to the previous farming activity in the lowlands. This coincides with the appearance of large hillforts such as that at Brusselstown in west Wicklow. We might imagine that a period of warfare disrupted farming activity around this time.

At about AD 300 the pollen record shows that there was renewed active clearance of hazel scrub, with a corresponding increase in grassland and tillage. This coincided with the spread of Christianity in Ireland and the large monasteries, such as that at Glendalough, may well have brought improved agricultural efficiency.

The Coming of Christianity

Cill Mhantáin, the Irish name for Wicklow, commemorates the church of St Mantan who is thought to have come to Ireland to support St Patrick in AD 432. He is said to have landed at Travilhawk Strand near Wicklow Head to a hostile reception from the local population. In the fight which ensued Mantan had his teeth knocked out and became known as 'The Toothless One'. Despite this unpleasant introduction, Mantan eventually returned to the area and established several churches in and around Wicklow.

The mountain barrier which divides the east of Wicklow from the fertile plain to the west was a major obstacle to early travellers. The passes through the mountains at Sally Gap, Wicklow Gap and the mountain road between Glenmalure and Glen of Imaal, must have been important routes for trade between the coastal ports (with good sea access to Britain) and the inland centres of power. Barriers to early travel were also formed by the rivers, such as the Avonmore which flowed south-eastwards from the mountains to the sea through what was then a poorly drained and heavily wooded lowland area. There were a number of key river crossings such as that at Annamoe (*Áth na mBó* — ford of the cattle).

Glendalough monastic site

The strategic location of the monastery of Glendalough at the junction of two valleys and on the road to one of these mountain passes is no coincidence. It signals the importance of control over the medieval trade routes between the coast and the richer hinterland. Its founder, St Kevin, crossed the mountains from Kildare in the sixth century AD. A paved road, now known as St Kevin's Road, was later built from Glendalough over the Wicklow Gap some time between the eighth and twelfth centuries.

St Kevin's rapport with the wildlife around him was legendary. It is said that he held a blackbird in the palm of his hand for so long that she laid eggs and reared a family. St Kevin is also said to have gained the trust of wild animals from the woods. A deer visited him daily to leave milk in a small hollow on the top of a large boulder for a child in his care. This boulder or 'bullaun stone', thought to have been used as a pestle and mortar for grinding medicinal herbs, can be seen today on the path near the monastic ruins.

The advanced farming practices accompanying the arrival of Christianity fuelled an expansion of the Wicklow population, which spread even into the higher mountains. The monastery was supported by this large population, which was living in raths and cashels.

The monastery St Kevin founded became a centre of learning and wealth and was much exploited by powerful local warlords. The monastic city was burned in AD 775, possibly as a result of an attack by local tribes hostile to the ecclesiastical rulers.

Animal life in early Christian times

While the glensides were probably still largely wooded at this time, the valley floors around the monastery were under tillage and pasture (mainly cattle and pigs). Occasional records from then until the eighteenth century indicate that black cattle were grazed in the uplands in the summer. This is supported by the surviving placenames, such as Boleynass, near Ashford, containing the Irish word *buaile*, meaning a summer milking place. The pigs were mainly kept in the woods where they foraged for roots and acorns and would have occasionally fallen prey to wolves, which were present in the Wicklow mountains at this time.

By the early Christian period two more carnivores, the **pine martin** and the **stoat** are recorded from archaeological excavations in Ireland. To these native or indigenous mammals can be added the typical introductions which follow human activity. These include the **house mouse, black rat** and **brown rat,** which might easily have arrived among boat loads of fodder for domestic animals. The introduction of domestic livestock such as cattle, sheep, goats and pigs almost certainly hastened the disappearance of some wild mammals such as the **wild boar** and the **wolf.**

The fish which would have been found by the early Christians in Wicklow's rivers and lakes would have differed considerably from those we find today. **Salmon** and **sea trout** were certainly present as shown in archaeological excavations. So too was the **arctic charr,** which is thought to have survived the Ice Age, living in waters near the edge of the ice sheet.

Eels and **lampreys** were almost certainly present but, as Giraldus Cambrensis noted in the twelfth century, most of the coarse fish such as **pike, perch, roach, minnow** and **loach** that we know today were absent in prehistoric times. At least seven coarse fish species were introduced into Ireland within the last few centuries.

Viking raids

Around the early years of the ninth century AD, raids on churches and battles between Irish tribes and raiding parties of Scandinavians were becoming increasingly frequent. The raids intensified during the 830s and the Vikings began to stay over the winter at coastal strongholds. Glendalough was plundered in 834 and there were other raids in Clonmore, Co Carlow, and Ferns, Co Wexford, around this time, suggest a Viking base in Arklow.

The establishment of a Viking stronghold in Dublin in 841 seems to have eclipsed any smaller Wicklow bases, although there are a few finds of Scandinavian artifacts which suggest small settlements on the coastal fringe about this time. The Norse origin of the names of Arklow and Wicklow is well established. The second element in each case comes from the Scandinavian *lo* meaning a low-lying meadow near water. The possible Scandinavian origin of other placenames such as Cooladoyle and Trudder is less certain.

Medieval Wars

Before its establishment as a separate county in 1606, Wicklow was theoretically administered from Dublin but the rugged nature of the landscape meant that it was effectively outside the control of the Dublin government. The lower lands to the east and west of the mountains were settled in the Anglo-Norman invasion. To defend these fertile lands there were strong manor houses guarded by stone castles such as that of Newcastle, midway between Wicklow and Greystones. The mountain strongholds were dominated by two Irish families — the O'Byrnes in the east and the O'Tooles in the west. To the south of the county in the fertile valleys were the MacMurroughs who, in time, were to become the dominant political force in this part of Leinster.

A Norman traveller using one of the great passes through the mountains would have had to be heavily protected from ambush by Irish bandits. Raids into the lowlands by the 'Irish of the Mountains' became common, especially at harvest time. Bad winter weather, famine and general food shortage in the mountains must have made the well-stocked manors near by seem like easy targets. By the late thirteenth century the Crown was dispatching troops to 'deal vigorously with the Irish and the King's enemies'.

Improved weapons also allowed the occupants of Wicklow to decimate many of the surviving large mammals and birds. In 1611 the heads of a bill in the Irish Parliment concerned 'an Act for killing wolves and other vermin' and in 1653 a system of bounties was introduced to encourage **wolf**-hunting. It has been suggested by O'Donovan in the *Ordnance Survey Letters* (1838) that the last wolf in Wicklow was killed at Glendalough in 1710. There is good historical evidence that a large woodland game bird, the **capercaillie** or 'cock of the wood', also survived in Ireland up to the seventeenth century but was probably hunted to extinction in the eighteenth century. The rapid decline of the last native woods in Wicklow would have left these species with fewer and fewer refuges.

Recent Centuries

Even in prehistoric times, the human imprint on the Wicklow landscape was substantial, although it was still constrained by the limits of muscle power. Into the last few centuries, we find a landscape which was already supporting a significant human population but still with areas of wild country which were beginning to be heavily exploited for their timber, game and minerals.

Exploiting the woods

The English settlers in Wicklow in the sixteenth and seventeenth centuries quickly realised the rich natural wealth offered by the land and they established timber and iron industries to maximise their profits. The extraction of timber from the extensive forests of south Wicklow began well before 1600, when great quantities of ship-building planks and pipe staves were exported to Spain. The famous Shillelagh woods were later to supply hugh amounts of timber, which was rafted down the River Derry and via the River Slaney, to the sea at Wexford. In 1671 the Shillelagh woods were reported to be 'nine or ten miles long and contained a large quantity of "great" timber'. The total area of wood then consisted of 6326 statute acres (about 2560 hectares) — a reduction of almost a third on the preceding fifteen years.

In the same area were the tanneries which developed to process local cattle hides, especially for shoe leather. Large amounts of bark were stripped from oak trees leaving the rest of the timber to be used for barrel staves.

Iron works and forges also became established all over Wicklow in the seventeenth and eighteenth centuries. The smelting of pig iron, which was imported from England, required large quantities of cheap timber for charcoal and this was produced in the forests close to where the timber was felled. Around the Upper Lake at Glendalough there are numerous charcoal burning platforms probably dating from the late seventeenth and early eighteenth centuries. Some may date from the late Middle Ages as thirteenth-to-fourteenth-century iron working on an extensive scale has been revealed in excavations at the entrance to the Glendalough Visitor Centre car-park.

In the mid-seventeenth century there were numerous ironworks in the valleys of south Wicklow. Woodcutters and sawyers would have worked in the forests, water course-keepers looked after the supply of water power to the mills and colliers made the charcoal in smoking bonfires. This was then carted into the furnace where gangs of labourers would have kept the great fires burning and hammered the metal into iron bars. Irish charcoal was also exported to supply the iron industry in England.

Reafforestation

While both timber and iron production led to a major reduction in the wooded area in Wicklow, reafforestation had already become common by 1640, with cultivation of trees on the large estates. By the early 1700s coppice management, or the rotational cutting of trees to produce a regular crop, had become a regular practice on the Shillelagh estate with the construction of ditches and banks to protect the new growth from grazing animals.

The great estates

It is estimated, using the Civil Surveys of 1654–6, that about 3–4% of Wicklow was wooded at that time. This was about double the national average for woodland cover in the mid-seventeenth century. **Oak, elm** and **beech** were the main timbers used in shipbuilding. In the eighteenth century, the best surviving woodland in Wicklow was found in the valleys of the Avonmore, Vartry and Dargle and these soon began to be incorporated into the landscapes of the great estates.

The question of ownership of land in Wicklow was largely settled by 1700. The main 'plantations' (with English families, not with trees) were in the sixteenth and seventeenth centuries when large blocks of Wicklow land were granted as rewards for military or church service. The local families of O'Byrne and O'Toole were dispossessed of their lands and the people became tenants of (mainly) absentee landlords.

The landed gentry split up the county among them, with ten of the largest estates each measuring over 10,000 acres (4046 hectares). The largest of these, covering almost 80,000 acres in 1838, was owned by Fitzwilliam of Coolatin. He governed almost one-fifth of the area of the county including virtually the entire south-west corner and large tracts on the east coast between Wicklow and Greystones. The second largest estate in the county was that of the Archbishop of Dublin, who owned large tracts of mountain land in north-west Wicklow.

This was an age of contrasts between the abject poverty of the ordinary people and the wealth and affluence of the landlord class. In Wicklow it was also the time of 'creation' of landscapes for the pleasure of their owners. 'Nowhere else,' wrote W H Bartlett in *The Scenery and Antiquities of Ireland*, 'is to be found assembled such a variety of natural beauties heightened and improved by the hand of art.'

Deer parks

In the seventeenth century deer hunting was a common pastime among the landed gentry and this led to the creation of deer parks where the animals could be 'protected' for the pleasure of the landlord. Several large deerparks were created in the heavily wooded valleys of south Wicklow at the same time as the timber from here was being heavily exploited for shipbuilding and iron-smelting. The Lord Deputy, Sir Thomas Wentworth, who owned some 10,000 acres (4046 hectares) at Fairwood Park near Shillelagh, wrote how on some evenings he saw as many as five hundred deer feeding near his hunting lodge. In the north of the county, the Earl of Meath laid out a deerpark surrounded by 12 miles (19km) of fencing at Kilruddery, south of Bray, while Sir Adam Loftus established a deerpark at Knockrath between Laragh and Clara in the Avonmore valley.

Perhaps the best known deer park, still called Deerpark today, was that created by Lord Powerscourt in the deep valley of the Dargle just south of Enniskerry. As a young man in 1857, Powerscourt 'had a fancy to try to acclimatize various kinds of deer and other animals'. In an enclosure of about 100 acres (405 hectares) on the estate, he introduced Indian Sambur deer, South African eland, Wapiti deer and several colour varieties of **red deer.** Then, in 1860, he introduced Japanese **sika deer,** for the first time to either Ireland or Britain. These bred very successfully, interbreeding freely with the red and Sambur deer, and by 1884 Powerscourt wrote that he had 'upwards of 100 of them, besides having shot two or three yearly and also having given away a great many others'. Inevitably, some deer escaped and naturalised in the wild from where they spread throughout Wicklow.

The Great Famine

In the census of 1841 the population of County Wicklow had reached 126,143 people, the highest level it has ever been at. The vast majority of the people lived in dispersed houses throughout the countryside with only 15% in settlements numbering more than twenty houses. Even so, the population density, at 151 persons per square mile, was the second lowest of all the counties in Ireland at that time, because of the largely uninhabited mountainous centre of the county. Only 56% of Wicklow's land was arable and most of the low-lying land was then tilled for potatoes with comparatively little meadow or pasture.

The upper limit of cultivation was reached at this time as the evidence of nineteenth-century lazy beds (or cultivation ridges) may be seen today high on the mountain slopes in most of the valleys from Glencree to Glenmalure. Lazy beds are also visible up to altitudes of 365m (500ft) above Powerscourt waterfall. The occurrence of potato blight in 1845 and 1846 was not as devastating in Wicklow as in some other parts of Ireland; nevertheless, it had dramatic effects on the landscape. By the winter of 1846–7, starvation, death and desertion of the land were well under way, especially in the hills and isolated glens. Emigration in the 1840s and 1850s also contributed to the rapid replacement of tillage land by pasture especially in the less fertile uplands.

Sheep farming

In 1812 a report to the RDS on agriculture in Wicklow calculated that there were 20,000 ewes in the mountains all year. These were an old breed known as Cottagh sheep, which in general received no supplementary feeding. The collapse of the woollen industry in the mid-nineteenth century made it necessary to produce more sheep meat at an earlier age and new breeds, especially the Cheviot, were introduced.

Traditionally the mountain grazing in Wicklow has been organised on a townland basis. Under this system the landholders in a particular townland have the right of grazing a certain number of *collops* on the open hill commonage in proportion to their holdings in the enclosed land of the townland. A *collop* is the term used for a unit of grazing which is taken as equivalent to one adult cow or steer. However, there is now variation locally in the number of sheep regarded as equivalent to a *collop,* possibly originally reflecting size differences between the breeds of livestock kept in separate districts. In the Glendalough area, one *collop* is equivalent to ten sheep; in Ballynabrocky (Coronation Plantation) a collop equals five sheep. The unenclosed mountain part of an individual townland usually comprises a single commonage, but sometimes there may be more than one commonage plot in a townland or landholders in a group of townlands may have rights on the same commonage.

The Land Acts of the late nineteenth and early twentieth centuries usually left the ownership of the actual land of the mountain commonages in the hands of the old landlords. However, the grazing rights and sometimes also turbary rights (to cut turf) and rights to cut heather and fern (bracken) for litter on the commonages adjacent to individual enclosed holdings were handed over to the former tenants.

Up to the 1950s the practice of grazing wethers (male lambs) on heather throughout the year must have had a significant impact on the mountain vegetation. Throughout the 1960s and 1970s sheep numbers in Wicklow continued to increase but wethers declined in importance and the ewes were generally removed from the mountain pastures in winter. Between 1980 and 1990 the number of ewes in Wicklow doubled, although the expansion of lowland flocks was greater that that in the uplands. Based on the payment of ewe premia it was estimated that there were 25,784 sheep in the central area of the mountains in 1990. This represents an increase of 70% over the preceding decade. Over the same period cattle numbers in the mountain area decreased by 7%.

Forestry

While the rapid rise in population in the first half of the nineteenth century caused increased pressure on the mountain landscape it coincided with the beginnings of reafforestation on the larger estates. The Powerscourt estate in the Dargle valley was the site of large-scale plantings of both broadleaved and coniferous trees. The Coronation Plantation, a mixture of **Scots pine** and **oak,** was laid out in the 1830s over some 200 hectares (500 acres) in the upper Liffey valley. By this time the upper Glendalough valley was relatively treeless but in 1857 the mining company which operated near the Upper Lake planted about a quarter of a million trees. Mainly Scots pine, these were to be used as pit props but, because of the closure of the mines, many have survived to this day on the north side of the valley.

By the end of the nineteenth century modern forestry practices were already emerging in Wicklow with some of the first large coniferous plantations in the country. A number of experimental plots containing a variety of new North

7.1

7.1   *Glen of the Downs and the Great Sugarloaf. Oak woodland covers most of the valley sides with ash and hazel on the valley floor. The main Dublin to Rosslare road passes through the centre of this national nature reserve. A proposal to widen the single carriageway in the northern part of the glen met with sustained opposition from protesters. (Richard Nairn)*

7.2   *Miners' village at Glendalough. There is still a special atmosphere among the ruined buildings, where the miners lived and worked in the late nineteenth century. A cable railway brought the ore from the mine shaft down the slope on the right. The tall building on the left was a stamping mill, where the ore was crushed to a fine sand using water-powered hammers. The stream was diverted through the village so that the heavy lead ore could be washed out of the sand. (Richard Nairn)*

7.3   *Sheep in Glencree. Up to the 1950s, the practice of all-year-round grazing had a significant impact on mountain heather. Flock sizes continued to increase up to the 1990s but the ewes were generally removed from the hills to lamb in the lowlands. In the background is a former British Army Barracks, now the Glencree Centre for Peace and Reconciliation. (Frank Doyle)*

7.2

7.3

170

7.4 Brusselstown Ring from the air. This massive hillfort encloses an area of around 130 hectares. It was constructed in the Iron Age and guards the entrance to the fertile farmland of the Glen of Imaal. It went unnoticed for many years but was discovered by examination of aerial photographs. (Dúchas, The Heritage Service)

7.5 St Kevin's Church and graveyard at Glendalough. Surrounded by dense woodland in an isolated valley, this was the ideal location for a reclusive churchman to found his monastery. It later became a major centre of learning and a base for control of the medieval trade routes between the coast and the central plain to the west of the mountains. (Richard Nairn)

7.6 Turf cutting in the Sally Gap. Improved access to the mountains provided by the building of Military Road in the early 1800s allowed the transport of turf to supply fuel for the growing city of Dublin. Turf-cutting accelerated again in World War II with restrictions on imported coal. There are still significant turbary rights in the hills but their use is declining as the National Park takes over management of the blanket bogs. (Frank Doyle)

7.7 *Sitka spruce plantations in Glendasan have reduced the area of heather moorland. This land is now part of the Wicklow Mountains National Park and the area will revert to natural vegetation when the trees have been harvested. (Richard Nairn)*

7.8 *Wicklow has the highest proportion of forest cover of all counties in Ireland. Many of these plantations are now mature and are being harvested. The replanted areas provide new habitats with dense scrub for a few years before the canopy closes over again and the ground vegetation is shaded out. (Richard T. Mills)*

7.9   The Murrough and the estuary of Broadlough form a green lung for the fast developing town of Wicklow. Urban sprawl is quickly absorbing a number of coastal landscapes (Richard Nairn)

7.10   Sand quarry in west Wicklow. Large resources of glacial sands and gravels have led to countless sandpits throughout the county. As with opencast mining, the resulting scars on the landscape can be significant. (Richard Nairn)

174

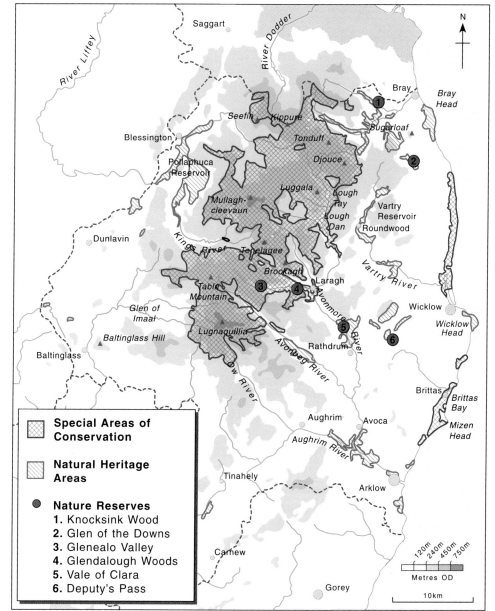

Map 12 Protected areas in County Wicklow in 1998. The proposed Special Areas of Conservation include the Wicklow Mountains National Park and the Murrough. Most of the statutory nature reserves are small areas of native woodland.

Special Areas of Conservation

Natural Heritage Areas

● **Nature Reserves**
1. Knocksink Wood
2. Glen of the Downs
3. Glenealo Valley
4. Glendalough Woods
5. Vale of Clara
6. Deputy's Pass

120m 240m 450m 750m
Metres OD

10km

7.11 Vartry reservoir. The original dam was built in the 1860s and a second higher reservoir was created in 1924. Most of the water in Wicklow's reservoirs is now piped to the Greater Dublin area. Demand regularly exceeds supply, leading to low flows in both the Liffey and Vartry rivers. (Richard Nairn)

7.12 Ballycullen near Ashford. Buildings in the countryside can blend in well with the existing hedgerows or they can stick out like a sore thumb. The spread of residential development in the lowlands puts pressure on all the natural resources of the land. (Richard Nairn)

American tree species were laid out in the Avondale estate, which had been acquired by the new government from the Parnell family.

State afforestation in many of the valleys such as Glencree, Glendalough and Glenmalure began in the 1920s and accelerated in the 1950s with mountain areas up to 500m (1500ft) being planted for the first time. Many semi-natural woodlands acquired by the Land Commission were transferred to the State Forest Service and some of these were underplanted with conifers before their conservation value was realised. By the 1980s state planting in the mountains had declined but, as the incentives improved, the rate of afforestation of private land increased again in the 1990s, especially on the west side of the mountains.

Mining

At various times in the past Wicklow has been famous for its minerals and its mines, but this activity has completely ceased today. The mines at Avoca in the south of the county have a long history and have been exploited for different minerals: iron in the seventeenth and eighteenth centuries, lead and zinc in the nineteenth century, copper in the nineteenth and twentieth centuries and sulphur from 1840 to 1865. The ores here are found in volcanic rocks and analyses indicate the presence of lead, zinc, iron, silver and antimony. The early miners stopped their activities at the base level of the old valley, possibly prevented from deeper mining by the limitations of pumping equipment.

With the exception of the Avoca mines all the lead deposits in Wicklow occur along the eastern margin of the Leinster granite in a band stretching from Glenmalure to the Dublin border. The main centre of lead mining was at Glendalough and Glendasan. Mining began in this region in the period 1807 to 1812 and up to ten separate veins were worked, each having its own name such as Luganure, Rupalagh, Hawk Rock, Old Hero, Moll Doyle, Fox Rock, Glendalough and Van Diemen's. This last name was given to the mine in the Glenealo Valley above the Upper Lake at Glendalough, as it represented the very last place that people wished to be.

By walking up the miners' track past the Upper Lake, it is still possible to visit the old mining village at Glendalough and to imagine what life must have been like there during the last century. The heaps of white mine spoil are still unvegetated because they contain high concentrations of metals which are toxic to plant growth. Each of these heaps represents waste from a single shaft which, in some cases, was driven for as much as 1.5km (about a mile) into the mountain. Hundreds of people would have worked here, extracting the ore from the mine tunnels and processing it before it was taken away by horse and cart. All through the nineteenth century the mining village at Glendalough was a busy place with up to 100 people living and working there throughout the year. Most of the trees in the area were cut to make pit props, supporting the roof of the mine shafts. The people, probably including children, worked underground by the light of candles only. Gun powder was used to blast out the rock and the noise of underground explosions must have filled the valley. The ore was loaded onto wooden sleds or rail trucks and dragged or rolled to the outside.

At the foot of the cable railway a small square building with a sloped floor was the place where the rock was unloaded and hammered into small pieces by old men, women and children. They picked out the valuable pieces of lead ore by hand and this was then taken to the mill. This tall building is still visible alongside the river and once contained a water wheel which powered a hammer to pulverise the lead ore and crush it to a fine sand. The crushed rock was washed through stone-lined troughs and the heavy grains of lead ore were trapped while the lighter minerals were washed away. The concentrated lead ore was then loaded onto carts and taken away either to the port of Wicklow or to a smelter at Ballycorus in the south Dublin mountains.

The mine at Glendalough was abandoned in 1880 but opened again for a short time in 1919. The lead mines of the Wicklow valleys have left their mark, not alone in the bare spoil heaps which litter the upper slopes, but also in the leaching of heavy metals over many years into the lakes below. The content of lead in the marshes at the head of Glendalough Upper Lake is many thousands of times higher than normal and there have been cases of swans dying of lead poisoning in this area.

By the twentieth century, mining had passed its peak in Wicklow, but in the 1930s gold was discovered on the slopes of Croghan Kinsella near the Wexford border. Gold had in fact been discovered here in the mid-nineteenth century, by panning in the Gold Mines River. Later efforts to discover a rich vein of gold in this area completely failed and it appears that the metal was widely distributed in a very thin band which is now exhausted.

A wartime shortage of sulphur led to a search in the 1940s by a semi-state mining company in the Avoca district. Ore was produced from Avoca from 1958 to 1962, when the mine was closed. In 1971 copper concentrate was again mined from here and shipped from Arklow to Spain.

Quarrying

The famous Wicklow granites which have been used in many Dublin buildings were mostly quarried from the Ballyknockan area east of the Blessington reservoir. There are several quarries still in operation near this village today and a tradition of stone working here goes back over several generations. There were many other old granite workings throughout Wicklow but these were often shallow and usually developed in weathered granite, producing a low-grade stone.

Slate has also been quarried in some areas but was rarely thin enough to be suitable for roofing. The slate quarries were generally small and found to the east of the granite centre of Wicklow. Near Ashford there were several small quarries from which the stone was said to resemble Welsh slates. Near Rathdrum a quarry produced black slates which had an additional use as writing slates for use in schools.

Today, a major quarry has been developed in intrusive diorite rocks just east of the Avonmore River at Rathdrum. At Arklow building stone is quarried from the dolerite deposits of Arklow Rock. There are numerous sand and gravel pits located on the eastern and western flanks of the Wicklow mountains in glacial till. Large workings can be seen beside the N11 road just south of Rathnew and at a number of places around Blessington. Unfortunately, a number of abandoned quarries have been used as local dumps and have become an unsightly element in the Wicklow countryside.

Turf cutting

Another important land use in the Wicklow mountains over the centuries has been the cutting of turf for fuel. The parallel banks of old cutover blanket bog are especially evident in the Sally Gap area. The improved access provided by the building of the Military Road in 1800–03 probably caused an increase in turf-cutting in the higher regions. In the northern parts of the mountains much of the turf was used to provide fuel for the growing population of Dublin city.

By the 1930s the greatest turf-cutting activity was in the central mountain districts of Lacken and Glendalough. During World War II, with restrictions on the importation of coal, turf-cutting accelerated again with up to 25,000 tons being removed from the Wicklow mountains in some years. This activity declined in the 1950s but there are still turbary rights over large parts of the Wicklow mountains and some are exercised on a small scale.

In the mid-1980s the offer of grant aid for commercial exploitation of peat on the Liffey Head bog caused a national controversy which resulted in state purchase of the most important parts of this peatland. Commercial harvesting of peat was carried out in the upper Liffey valley, west of the Military Road, but this land was purchased by the state from the Powerscourt estate and now forms part of the Wicklow Mountains National Park.

Like any landscape, the Wicklow landscape is dynamic, ever-changing in response to both climatic changes and the pressures of use by humans. Today, we are left with just the remnants of a wild landscape. To ensure the survival of the best of this natural heritage, we need a plan for conservation of the remaining fragments of wild Wicklow.

Conserving Habitats

Nature reserves

There are a number of statutory nature reserves in Wicklow. Most of these are quite small areas and could be regarded as islands of semi-natural woodland in a sea of intensive farmland. The reserves of Glendalough and Glenealo Valley are now incorporated in the Wicklow Mountains National Park, which covers over 20,000 hectares (50,000 acres) in the upland area.

Statutory nature reserves in Co Wicklow

Name	Area (ha)	Habitats
Glen of the Downs	59	Deciduous woodland
Deputy's Pass	47	Deciduous woodland
Vale of Clara	221	Deciduous woodland
Glendalough	157	Deciduous woodland
Glenealo valley	1,958	Blanket bog, heath, mountain grassland
Knocksink wood	52	Deciduous woodland

Natural Heritage Areas

The National Parks & Wildlife Service proposed a list of sites for designation as Natural Heritage Areas (NHAs) in the mid-1990s, replacing the previous list of Areas of Scientific Interest. Unfortunately, the whole NHA designation process got off to a bad start in Wicklow, with confusion about the rights of farmers and landowners. Despite a major investment by the state and the EU in surveying these areas and publicising the need for their conservation, the necessary legislation was not in place to enforce the designation.

One incentive that had been put in place for the management of NHAs was the Rural Environment Protection Scheme (REPS), introduced in 1992. This offered a system of grants to farmers to manage the land in environment-friendly ways, and those who owned land within a proposed NHA were eligible for a premium payment on top of the basic REPS grant. However, there was a slow uptake of the scheme in Wicklow and lack of monitoring made it impossible to assess the environmental benefits of the scheme.

EU Directive on Habitats, Flora and Fauna

In the meantime, the government implemented the EU Directive on Habitats, by passing a new set of regulations in 1997. This allows for the designation of sites of European significance as Special Areas of Conservation, and a number of these have been proposed in Wicklow. The most significant area is the entire central mountain region.

Habitat types have been categorised according to their importance in a European context. Most of the significant habitats of European importance in Wicklow are found along the coast and in the mountains. Two of these stand out as having the most urgent conservation requirements: blanket bog, which is still actively forming in parts of the Wicklow mountains (for example at the Liffey Head bog), and fixed dunes (such as occur at a number of sites between Wicklow town and Arklow).

Species under Threat

Plants and animals do not recognise our national or county boundaries. Wicklow's flora and fauna are part of the biogeographical island of Ireland and the status of many of the rarer species is now established in a series of government-published Irish Red Data Books, which list the most threatened and vulnerable species of plants and animals.

Rare plants

The mountains, woodlands, grasslands and the coast have the greatest number of threatened plant species in Wicklow. One species, the **alpine lady's mantle,** is known in Ireland only from mountain cliffs in Kerry and Wicklow.

On the coast there are several protected plant species, including the **wild asparagus.** Recently, this plant has been seen in only eight sites in Ireland, including one on the Wicklow coast. Its habitat is under threat from amenity, agricultural and development pressure on sand dune systems. At its Wicklow site it is uncomfortably close to a newly developed golf course. Similar pressures have threatened the future of the **meadow saxifrage** which is also known from only two sites in Ireland, including one north of Arklow town.

Perhaps the rarest plant in Wicklow is an unassuming grassland species called **subterranean clover.** This plant is confined in Ireland to two sites in Wicklow. The main site occurs along a 30m (150ft) stretch of sandy river bank near the coast. This plant is really native to the Mediterranean region, but grows here because of the frost-free conditions on the coast and the absence of competition from more vigorous plants. This species is so rare that its seed has been collected by staff of Trinity College Botanic Gardens and it is being grown in artificial conditions for the sake of preserving the genetic material, in case the last remaining site in Ireland should be wiped out. If this happened, the stored seed could be used to reintroduce the plants into suitable habitats elsewhere.

Vulnerable birds

Rare bird species associated with the mountains are of the greatest importance. The birds of prey, including **peregrine, merlin** and **hen harrier,** require the

7.13 *Castleruddery Lower*
stone circle from the air; the two
quartz boulders which form the
entrance are clearly visible
(Dúchas, The Heritage Service)

strictest protection to ensure their survival in Wicklow. Of these, the hen harrier has a very tenuous foothold with possibly only a single pair surviving in Wicklow. Other rare mountain birds include the **golden plover, ring ousel** and **nightjar.** The nightjar is found in dry heathland areas, where it is rarely seen and is thought to be declining. It is considered to be endangered at national level. The **goosander** is a new colonist in Wicklow river systems but is still extremely rare nationally. On the coast, the colony of **little terns** at Kilcoole, Newcastle, is certainly of national importance and vulnerable to a number of pressures.

Important mammals

Among the Red Data Book mammals found in Wicklow are six species of **bats**, all of which are of international importance and are listed for protection in the EU Habitats Directive. Little is known of their distribution, but several are under threat internationally owing to loss of roosting sites and feeding habitats.

The **hedgehog** is, amazingly, regarded as intenationally important because it is threatened in Europe as a whole. The **otter** is another internationally important mammal which occurs widely across Wicklow but is more common in the lowland river systems where there is an abundance of fish.

Climate Change

In the longer term, the changes to the landscape of Wicklow will be increasingly affected by climatic factors. Since the mid-1950s the trend has been a general warming of climate in north-west Europe and much of the evidence now suggests that this trend has been accelerated with the effects of greenhouse gas emissions to the atmosphere. Current predictions are that the average air temperature in these latitudes will increase by approximately 2°C by the year AD 2030.

Rising sea-levels

This general warming is predicted to cause some melting of the world's ice caps and a consequent rise in sea-level throughout the globe. In Irish waters the rise is expected to be in the region of 18cm (about 7 inches) over the next thirty-five years. Linking this with the expected increase in storminess of the North Atlantic climate, we may predict a period of increasing pressure on Irish coasts as we enter the twenty-first century.

The late Professor Bill Carter, a leading authority on the coast of Ireland predicted that the most vulnerable areas of Wicklow were the low-lying wetlands behind the barrier coast of the Murrough. These post-glacial shingle ridges lie less than 4m (12ft) above present sea-level, and we can envisage increasing amounts of storm damage to the lower parts, possibly causing the closure of the present

railway line which runs from Greystones to Wicklow. At the worst, there could be breaches of the Murrough and major flooding of farmland, housing developments, golf courses and a complex of semi-natural habitats.

If this situation does develop there is very little we can do to stop the advancing sea. Instead, we should plan to accommodate rising sea-level, restricting development in vulnerable areas and establishing a 'set-back line' which will prevent new developments coming under threat. We should accept that natural systems such as shingle beaches, sand dunes and saltmarsh can act to absorb the energy of the waves, thus dissipating damaging storms before they create havoc with coastal developments. For this reason the embankment and attempted reclamation of saltmarsh in the Kilcoole–Newcastle area during the 1980s now seems very misguided.

Changing habitats and species

Small changes in global climate over the coming decades may also have impacts on inland vegetation. Warmer temperatures, for example, could increase the prospects for faster woodland regeneration on the high mountain areas if the pressures of grazing can be controlled. However, drier summers and increased average temperatures could cause an increase in decay rates on the mountain blanket bogs, some of which are of international importance. This would probably lead to shrinkage of the peat surface and an increase in the extent of heather cover.

Wetter winters, coupled with an increased frequency of heavy rainfall episodes, could cause an increase in acidification in streams and rivers running off the upland blanket bog, with consequent effects on the mountain lakes and reservoirs. In wetland areas increased summer drying and warmer temperatures are likely to accelerate invasion of fens and other wetlands by scrub and, ultimately, trees.

Individual species of plants and animals may well respond to small changes in climate. For example some mountain species are here at the southern limit of their range in Europe. The **merlin,** a small falcon which nests in heather moorland, may well disappear from Wicklow as summer temperatures rise. Similarly, some insect species such as the **glaucous shears moth,** which is at the southern limit of its European range in Wicklow, may disappear with a slight warming of climate.

On the other hand, we might expect that some species which are currently limited to southern England may spread across the Irish Sea into a slightly warmer south-east Ireland. This could include some presently rare birds such as the **little egret, nightingale** and **hobby.** With milder winters we could also expect some of the warblers which currently winter here in small numbers, such as the **chiffchaff** and **blackcap,** to survive in larger numbers. Other migrants which currently come to Ireland for the summer months only include the **red admiral, clouded yellow** and **painted lady** butterflies, all of which may in future survive

185

the winter here by hibernation. On the other hand, the **arctic charr,** a rare fish which still hangs on Lough Dan, may be unable to survive a slight warming of temperature in future. Nature is dynamic, always adjusting itself in response to the changing environment.

A Symbol for the Future

Despite the mistakes of the past in exploiting and managing the wild parts of Wicklow, much has been learned over the years. Wicklow has been a testing ground for many national and international conservation issues: forestry and landscape, mountain bog development, acidification of waterways, woodland conservation, coastal protection and national park management. One of the most encouraging signs is the increasing involvement of local people in influencing decisions about the future of the Wicklow landscape.

As we walked in the hills thinking about the future for Wicklow's wild places, a solitary **peregrine** rose ahead of us on the moorland, soaring on the rising air from the cliffs below. This bird must surely be a symbol for the conservation of Wicklow's wildlife and natural habitats. It is the largest falcon in Ireland and occurs throughout the county, but especially in areas of mountain and coast where it chooses the more remote cliffs and crags to nest. Its nesting places are traditional and from these lofty crags generations of peregrines have watched the changing landscape below over the centuries. Each pair requires a large hunting territory which contains a variety of prey, each in turn depending on a variety of habitat types.

So these birds are at the top of the food chain, intimately dependent on all other elements of their natural environment. In winter, the peregrine leaves its upland territory and wanders widely in the lowlands and along the coast in search of suitable prey. In the 1960s the peregrine itself came very close to disaster. The use of persistent agriculture chemicals led to a population crash and only a few pairs remained in the county. Since then, with the resilience of wildlife in its natural surroundings, the peregrine population has recovered to its former levels and now the birds can be seen in almost any part of Wicklow. Soaring high above us, the clarion call of the peregrine was like a beacon in the darkness. Its remarkable recovery from near extinction gives us hope for the future.

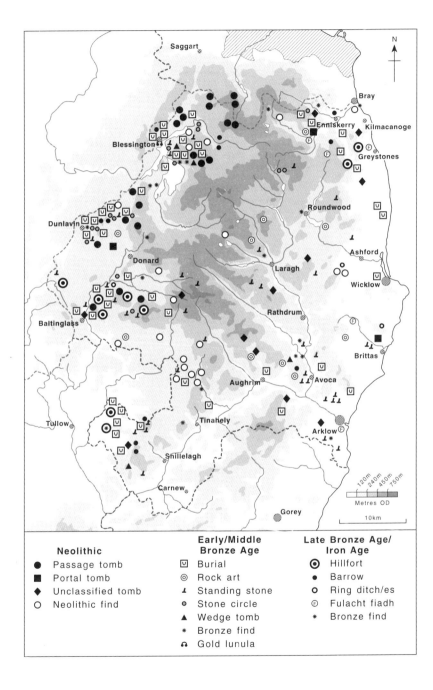

Map 13 Archaeological sites in County Wicklow. The concerntration of monuments and burial sites in the western foothills and lowland areas marks the importance of the fertile central plain to the early farmers. The central mountain area was less attractive to early settlers. (after Stout in: Hannigan and Nolan 1994)

Neolithic
- ● Passage tomb
- ■ Portal tomb
- ◆ Unclassified tomb
- ○ Neolithic find

Early/Middle Bronze Age
- Ụ Burial
- ◎ Rock art
- ⌇ Standing stone
- ⊙ Stone circle
- ▲ Wedge tomb
- ✳ Bronze find
- ∩ Gold lunula

Late Bronze Age/Iron Age
- ◉ Hillfort
- ● Barrow
- ○ Ring ditch/es
- Ⓕ Fulacht fiadh
- ✳ Bronze find

GAZETTEER

This gazetteer covers a selection of the best sites for wildlife in Wicklow. Many of these sites are listed as proposed Natural Heritage Areas but few are owned by the state. In some cases permission from the owners is required before entering the land. In all instances, great care should be taken with regard to safety, especially where there are cliffs and steep slopes.

*Map 14
Location of
sites to visit*

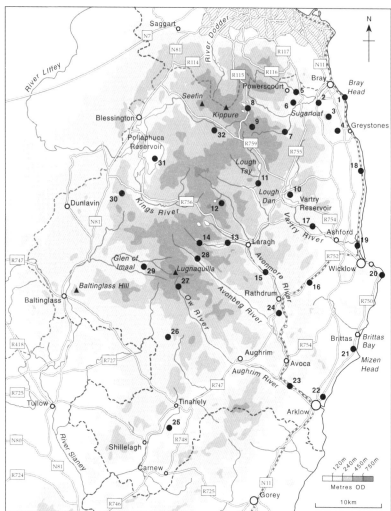

1. Bray Head
2. Dargle Glen
3. Great Sugarloaf
4. Glen of the Downs
5. Knocksink Wood
6. Powerscourt Demesne
7. Powerscourt Waterfall
8. Lough Bray
9. Liffey Head bog
10. Vartry Reservoir
11. Lough Dan and Lough Tay
12. Lough Ouler
13. Glendalough
14. Glenealo Valley
15. Vale of Clara
16. Deputy's Pass
17. Devil's Glen
18. Kilcoole Marshes
19. Broadlough
20. Wicklow Head
21. Brittas Bay/Buckroney Marsh
22. Arklow Pond and Dunes
23. Avoca River Valley
24. Avondale
25. Tomnafinnoge Wood
26. Knockananna Bog
27. Lugnaquillia/Ow Valley
28. Glenmalure
29. Glen of Imaal
30. Hollywood Glen
31. Blessington Lakes (Pollaphuca)
32. Coronation Plantation

188

1. Bray Head

Map reference: O2816 Nearest town: Bray

A walk around the cliff path from Greystones to Bray is best on a summer's morning as the sun rises over the sea to the east. The sea pinks are flowering all around the cliffs and from below comes the noisy clamour of seabirds in their nesting colony.

Landscape: Bray Head is one of the most prominent headlands on the east coast of Ireland. Its summit reaches 240 metres (787 feet) above sea-level and forms a low ridge in line with the Sugarloaf mountains inland. It gives its name to the Bray group of rocks which are among the oldest in the region (at least 500 million years). These are mainly quartzites and the area is an important locality for Cambrian fossils.

Habitats: The light, sandy soils on the south-facing slopes of Bray Head support extensive heathland dominated by ling and bell heather with large patches of gorse. The heather and gorse are often burnt in summer but they quickly recover after a fire. An uncommon annual species, yellow fumitory, grows here in abundance, as its seeds remain dormant in the soil. Both burning and grazing maintain the area as heathland and prevent the re-establishment of woodland. However, there is a small area of oak woodland on the northern side of the headland and some ash scrub near the Cable Rock. The glacial boulder clay which clothes the south side of the headland has a rich grassland vegetation with many species of grasses and herbs including three species of orchids. The rare bloody cranesbill is also found here. The sea cliffs are affected by salt spray and have a maritime vegetation including sea pink, sea campion and white stonecrop.

Wildlife: A small herd of feral goats grazes on the slopes above the cliff path. The heathland and scrub on the upper slopes of Bray Head hold a variety of songbirds which do not normally occur in gardens. These include cuckoo, skylark, meadow pipit, stonechat, wheatear, whitethroat, linnet, yellowhammer and reed bunting. A small colony of seabirds nests on the cliffs below the railway between April and July. Most obvious are the herring gulls with a few great black-backed gulls. The smaller, more delicate kittiwakes nest on the steepest rock faces, each nest built on a narrow ledge. Fulmars nest around the tops of the cliffs, preferring the boulder clay to bare rock. Low down, near the water's edge, some shags nest and their larger relatives, cormorants, are sometimes seen. Razorbills and guillemots nest in small colonies on the cliff ledges while the black guillemot is present in scattered pairs right around the headland. Butterflies such as wall brown, small heath and small copper are common on sunny days and in late summer they are often joined by migrants such as peacock, red admiral and painted lady.

Access: Leave the N11 at Bray and follow signs for the seafront. The best access to Bray Head is on the cliff path which runs from the south end of the promenade in Bray to Greystones harbour 6 miles (3.5km) to the south. Parts of the path are unfenced so great care is required especially with children and dogs. The path is relatively level and dry and takes about 2 hours to walk at a steady pace. Binoculars are useful to see the seabirds but do not go near the cliff edge, which is dangerous in places. A walk to the summit of Bray Head and back to the promenade takes about one hour.

189

2. Dargle Glen

Map reference: O2416 Nearest town: Enniskerry

The river rushing through a wooded ravine creates a wonderful atmosphere of wilderness within a mile or two of suburbia. Some of the glen is inaccessible but there are fine views from the high path on the south side.

Landscape: This is a deep glacial valley through which the River Dargle flows in a series of rocky gorges. The Dargle is a typical 'spate' river which falls steeply over a short distance from highland to lowland causing flood conditions in the lower reaches after heavy rainfall in the mountains. The glen is well hidden in the surrounding wooded landscape and its depth and wildness are quite surprising, given its proximity to Bray and Enniskerry. Along the river there is a well-exposed contact between the Cambrian rocks similar to those on Bray Head and the younger volcanic rocks of the Ordovician period.

Habitats: The steep sides of the valley are clothed in broad-leaved woodland which is dominated by oak and hazel. Some of the higher areas contain birch and beech and many introduced trees, especially laurel, have escaped from nearby gardens. Laurel casts a dense shade which prevents regeneration of other trees. Common plants of the ground layer include woodrush and bramble. The spray from the river produces constantly damp air which creates ideal conditions for the growth of mosses and ferns. Water moss covers the rocks in the river and on the banks are found red campion, wood pimpernel, creeping willowherb and many species of hawkweed.

Wildlife: The water in the Dargle river is generally acidic but of high quality due to the absence of any significant sources of pollution upstream. As a result the invertebrate life in the river is varied, with mayfly, stonefly and caddis fly present in all suitable areas of stream bed. These provide food throughout the year for the dipper which perches on stones in mid-stream and swims underwater when feeding. Grey wagtails also use the lower reaches of the river, preferring to nest near fast-moving water at the many waterfalls and rapids. Signs of otters are often found on the river bank but the animals themselves are nocturnal and difficult to see. Typical woodland songbirds such as blue tit, robin, chaffinch and wren breed here and these are joined in summer by migrants such as chiffchaff, blackcap and willow warbler. The raucous cries of the jay can be heard here throughout the year and a fleeting glimpse of a sparrowhawk is not unusual.

Access: Turn west off the N11 dual carriageway about 2km (a mile and a quarter) south of Bray at the signs for Enniskerry. Passing by the gates of Dargle Gardens on the left, take the next minor road to the left and stop at an old gateway on the left about 200 metres (yards) from the junction. From here a high level path leads along the north side of the Glen passing a prominent viewing rock after about 1km (half a mile). There is no easy access to the riverbank and the south side of the glen is privately owned.

3. Great Sugarloaf Mountain

Heath, woodland, marsh

Map reference: O2313 Nearest town: Bray

The prominent location of this mountain makes it an exciting place to start an exploration of the Wicklow hills. The view from the summit includes the northern part of the mountain range and the Dublin coastline to the north-east.

Landscape: This steep, cone-shaped mountain is visible from many parts of north-east Wicklow. Its summit is made of Cambrian quartzite which has weathered to form a collar of boulder scree (hence the 'sugarloaf' appearance). During the last Ice Age the summit stood above the ice cap while the surrounding hills, including Bray Head, were overridden by ice, giving them a rounded appearance. The sides of the mountain were scoured by glaciers and the Glen of the Downs, to the south, was formed as a meltwater spillway near the ice margin. The view to the south-west gives a good panorama of the Wicklow mountains.

Habitats: The scree slopes are relatively mobile and the upper parts are bare of vegetation. The lower slopes have heather moorland with ling heather, bilberry and gorse providing both the main cover and the brightest colours in summer. Some areas are covered with dense stands of bracken which turns a golden colour in autumn. In a small depression on the north-east side of the mountain, known as the Quill, there is an area of broadleaved woodland dominated by oak, birch and holly. The ground layer contains woodrush, ivy, hard fern and various mosses. At the base of the mountain, near Kilmacanogue village, there is a small marsh with alder–willow woodland, which formed where drainage of a small stream is blocked by a stone weir. The wettest part of the marsh is dominated by greater tussock sedge, reed canary grass and various other sedges and grasses. There are deep pools and the vegetation in places is floating on water. Other colourful plants include marsh marigold, meadowsweet, ragged robin and purple loosestrife.

Wildlife: Few birds breed on the summit due to the high winds but wrens are usually present among the boulders. Meadow pipits and cuckoos are present in the moorland vegetation and grouse are occasionally recorded here. The Quill woodland, though small in area, has a typical woodland bird community with robin, chaffinch, blackbird, blue tit and wren. In the spring woodcock can be heard making their strange 'roding' call as they fly around their territory. In the marsh near Kilmacanogue there are breeding sedge warbler, whitethroat and willow warbler with a few wintering snipe. Otters use the stream through the marsh as a regular route.

Access: Leave the N11 dual carriageway at Kilmacanogue and park in the car-park in front of the pub. Walking up the Rocky Valley road take the first minor road to the left, opposite St Mochonog's Church, which leads to the Quill wood. This road passes above the Kilmacanogue marsh, giving good views of the Little Sugarloaf across the valley. The road eventually becomes a track which leads up the south-eastern side of the Great Sugarloaf. A clockwise circuit of the mountain, sometimes on sheep tracks, takes you back to Kilmacanogue village.

4. Glen of the Downs

Glacial valley, woodland, stream

Map reference: T2611 Nearest town: Delgany

Landscape: This deep glacial valley formed as a meltwater channel near the margin of an ice sheet. The water may have been forced out under pressure with the great weight of ice above. The rocks are ancient Cambrian quartzites of the Bray group, similar to those on the Great Sugarloaf mountain to the north-west. The valley sides rise over 100 metres (300 feet) from the road which runs alongside a small stream. The valley is filled with broadleaved woodland, although there are some conifer plantations at the southern end and on higher ground to the east. In Victorian times the view from the rectangular room of the nearby Bellevue House was described as 'a scene of luxurious softness, combined with grandeur and significance'.

Habitats: Most of the woodland on the steeper slopes is oak with some birch, cherry and rowan. The understorey is composed of holly, honeysuckle and bramble in the more open areas. The luxuriant ground flora includes woodrush, wood sage, ivy and bilberry. On the valley floor to the east of the road a small stream flows south towards Delgany. This is surrounded by ash and hazel woodland although there is a lot of introduced laurel. Wild garlic is especially abundant on the damp soils here with wood anemone, wood sorrel and lesser celandine in spring. There is a fine stand of planted beech trees to the west of the road. They cast a dense shade in summer, which reduces the ground flora but provides good conditions for fungi in the autumn.

Wildlife: The woodlands are filled with birdsong in spring with the main sound coming from wren, robin, blue tit, chaffinch, great tit and blackbird. Watch out for treecreepers working their way up the trunks of trees. A few pairs of jays nest in the woodlands and their loud cries are very obvious in spring. Sparrowhawks fly through the trees using the element of surprise to hunt down small bird prey. Blackcaps breed near the roadside edge and in some springs the rare migrant wood warbler sings in the glen. Grey wagtails nest along the stream feeding their young on aquatic insects. Resident birds like robin, wren and blackbird remain on in autumn and winter but they are less obvious.

Red squirrels are the most likely mammals to be seen as they scavenge at picnic sites around the car-park. A few sika deer venture into the woodlands on the west of the road. Fox and badger are present in the woods but they are not likely to be seen during daylight. Several species of bats feed in the woods at dusk and long-eared owls hunt here. Watch out for woodcock flying around the edge of the trees at dusk in spring, making their strange 'roding' call. A number of insect groups have been well studied at the Glen of the Downs and it is the only known site in Ireland for several species. Common butterflies include speckled wood and ringlet.

Access: The car-park entrance is on the east side of the N11 road, about 8km (5 miles) south of Bray. Good dry paths lead up the east side of the glen giving a steep circular walk, returning along the stream to the south of the car-park. Access is difficult on the west side of the road and there are no marked paths here. Most of the Glen of the Downs is a National Nature Reserve owned by the Heritage Service. Management of the reserve includes the removal of exotic species such as laurel.

5. Knocksink Wood

River and woodland

Landscape: The wood survives on the steeply sloping banks of the Glencullen River which is a tributary of the River Dargle. The river passes through a series of gorges with steep rocky outcrops on either side.

Habitats: The area contains a mixture of old broadleaved woodland and more recent coniferous plantation along the banks of the Glencullen River. Parts of the woodland are dominated by oak with birch around the edges and an understorey of holly and hazel. The ground flora includes wood rush, bracken, bramble, wood sanicle and primrose. In the more open patches, where there is more light, gorse and ling heather grow. Much of the ground on the banks of the river is wet and supports a mixture of ash and willow trees with herbs such as horsetail, great willowherb, hemp agrimony and wood rush. On the steeper slopes above, hazel scrub grows with a scattering of ash and sycamore trees. Some beech woodland has been planted in this area and, while the ground layer here is sparse, it is a good place for fungi in the autumn. Parts of the wood were underplanted with conifers during the 1960s but the present management policy is to remove these.

Wildlife: The woodlands hold a variety of mammals including badger, fox and red squirrel. Deer are occasionally seen but they do not like disturbance. There is a good variety of songbirds in the woodland with the commonest being blue tit, great tit, robin, blackbird and wren. Repeated visits should be rewarded with views of long-tailed tit, jay and treecreeper, although the latter is quite secretive. Blackcaps usually sing here in May. The stony riverbed has a good variety of freshwater life including caddisflies whose larvae make a little case of pebbles to protect their soft bodies. Some rare insects have been recorded here and there are probably many more species awaiting discovery. Common woodland butterflies in summer include speckled wood and meadow brown.

Access: Located on the trunk road from Dublin, Knocksink Wood is less than 1km (half a mile) from the centre of Enniskerry village. Dublin Bus route 44 passes the gate and the terminus is in the centre of the village. The woodland is a National Nature Reserve owned by the Heritage Service. It is open to pedestrian access. A National Conservation Education Centre has been established here but it is not open to the public except by prior arrangement. A brochure on the centre is available from the National Conservation Education Centre, Knocksink Wood, Enniskerry (Telephone: 01-2866609).

6. Powerscourt Demesne

Map reference: O2216 Nearest town: Enniskerry

Landscape: This is an old estate which is world-famous for its magnificent gardens, exotic trees and semi-natural woodland. The estate is situated on south-facing slopes of glacial moraines between the Dargle and Glencullen rivers with spectacular views of the Great Sugarloaf mountain to the south.

Habitats: The best areas of woodland are on the lower slopes between the formal gardens and the river. These include some oak woodland and wet alder woods on the river bank. There are also extensive areas of mixed amenity woodland with a mixture of broadleaved and conifer trees in the canopy and much laurel and rhododendron in the understorey. The entrance driveways have groves of mature beech and lime trees which were planted for amenity purposes and are mostly surrounded by mown grass. The damp hazel and alder woodlands on the banks of the river have a dense undergrowth of wild garlic, woodrush, bramble and various sedges. In some places the twayblade and early purple orchids may be found. On parts of the riverbank there are dense stands of the introduced plant, giant hogweed, whose large umbrella-shaped flowers form a canopy like that of woodland. The sap from this plant can burn the skin.

Wildlife: In the nineteenth century, this estate held a captive herd of deer with many exotic species from all parts of the world. The most successful was the Japanese sika deer which bred here for the first time in Ireland or Britain. Some animals escaped and interbred with the native red deer on the surrounding mountains. Hybrid deer are common today in the woodlands around the estate but they only emerge at night to graze on the parkland and farmland. There are several large badger setts in different parts of the estate, especially on steep ground under old woodland. Large mounds of freshly dug soil at the entrances and well trampled tracks through the undergrowth are evidence of their nocturnal activities.

Some of the fine old trees in the estate are used by nesting kestrels and long-eared owls which often breed in old crows' nests. The woodlands are rich in breeding birds with blackcap, jay, woodcock and sparrowhawk often seen along with the commoner species. Crossbills have been recorded here in winter. The river is fast-flowing with a gravelly bed and has breeding dipper and grey wagtail, especially near the bridges at the gateways. There are also signs of both otter and mink using the river banks as a corridor. Sand martins breed in old sand pits around the estate and they feed by catching insects in flight over the river and lake.

The lake is an ornamental one in the formal gardens in front of the house. It is used by breeding coot and moorhen and in winter by mallard and teal. A flock of pied wagtail feeds around the gardens and, at dusk, they roost communally in the ruins of the main house. Either side of the main door of the house are several yew trees whose red fruits attract flocks of wintering thrushes such as fieldfare and redwing.

Access: The main entrance to Powerscourt is on the southern edge of Enniskerry village and the estate is well signposted from nearby roads. Public access is available to many parts of the estate but restricted in areas of the farm and private land. An entrance charge is payable at the main gate and parking is restricted to the official car-park beside the formal gardens. A garden centre, restaurant, shop and toilets are available for visitors.

7. Powerscourt Waterfall and Deerpark *River, woodland*

Map reference: O1912 Nearest town: Enniskerry

Climb among the old oaks up the steep slope beside of the waterfall and soak up the view. Below you is the Deerpark with the Dargle snaking away into the woods in the valley. Then the shining cone of the Great Sugarloaf rises out of the forest to capture your attention while away in the background the blue of the Irish Sea is visible.

Landscape: The Deerpark is a deeply incised glacial valley now occupied by the River Dargle with a spectacular waterfall nearly 100 metres (300 feet) high at the western end. The steep cliff over which the waterfall plunges is formed at the contact between two rock types, granite and mica schist. At the base of the waterfall is a small corrie (glacial depression) and associated mounds of sand and gravel (moraines). The river meanders across the valley floor forming small cliffs where it cuts through the moraines. The deerpark is part of the Powerscourt estate and formerly held a herd of enclosed deer. It has been a popular amenity area for centuries.

Habitats: The rocky area within the spray zone of the waterfall contains many interesting mosses and liverworts with ferns such as the filmy fern and hart's tongue. Grassland is predominant on the gentler slopes with woodrush and bracken invading some areas. Broadleaved woodland occurs around the upper slopes on both sides of the waterfall. This is mainly oak woodland with some rowan and holly, although there are substantial plantations of beech and conifer on the northern slopes. On the valley floor there are scattered oak and Scots pine trees and extensive areas have recently been planted with hardwoods.

Wildlife: Sika deer can be seen on the higher slopes near the waterfall but they are shy animals and retreat into cover of woodland or forestry if disturbed. They graze on the lower grassland at night when most of the visitors have gone. Badgers are common in the more wooded areas and their tracks may be seen in soft ground on some paths. Red squirrels breed in the woodlands and they scavenge leftovers from picnic sites in the valley. There are signs that otters use the river as their droppings (spraints) may be found at various points.

Kestrels breed on cliff ledges near the waterfall and are a regular sight hunting over rough grassland and heather. Peregrines also nest here and they prey on wood pigeons as well as on the small number of stock doves that breed near the waterfall. The woodlands have a number of migrant songbirds in summer including chiffchaff, willow warbler, blackcap, and occasionally, wood warbler. Both sparrowhawk and long-eared owl hunt small birds among the trees. The distinctive call of the rare nightjar has been heard here at dusk on summer evenings.

Access: From Enniskerry take the R760 road and follow signs for the waterfall about 5km (3 miles) to the south. Alternatively, leave the N11 road at Kilmacanogue and take the R755 road to the west following signs for the waterfall. There is a charge for cars entering the Deerpark. Parking, picnic tables, toilets and shop are available in summer, close to the waterfall area.

8. Lough Bray (Upper and Lower)

Corrie lakes, heathland

Map reference: O1315 Nearest town: Enniskerry

Sitting on the rugged crags above the brown, peat-stained waters of the twin lakes, it is easy to imagine a pair of eagles soaring on great wide wings as they did here a century and a half ago. Although the eagles are gone, the wilderness feeling of water, rock and sky remains for those who take the time to stand and stare.

Landscape: These are two of the finest glacial corries in the Wicklow mountains. During the last Ice Age snow and ice built up in these north-facing hollows and the subsequent movement of ice down the Glencree valley plucked rocks away from the granite cliffs behind. The corries both have lakes that are dammed by piles of glacial sand and gravel (moraines). The water is deep and, although they may be connected below ground, there is no apparent surface connection between the two lakes. Below the lower lake, an isolated house known as Lough Bray Cottage stands on the shore among a garden and scattered trees. The rounded summit of Kippure (757 metres or 2482 feet high) rises to the west topped by two television masts.

Habitats: The lake water is very acidic with several rare aquatic plant species including an unusual form of quillwort. The lakes are surrounded by blanket bog with a vegetation dominated by ling and cross-leaved heath with bilberry, deer grass, woodrush and various mosses. Bell heather and cowberry grow on the moraine ridges around the lakes. There are scattered groups of birch and rowan trees on the steep ground near the lake shores and some planted Scots pine around the north and west side of the lower lake.

Wildlife: Fox and mountain hare range widely over the blanket bog but their droppings are usually the only evidence to be seen. The steep cliffs behind the lakes are a good nesting place for peregrine, kestrel and raven. Their calls are often the best indication of their presence. The Eagles' Crag, which towers above the two lakes, once held breeding eagles but they disappeared in the nineteenth century due to persecution. Red grouse can be seen and heard among the heather at any time of year. A rare migrant, the ring ousel or mountain blackbird, breeds high above the lakes. Resident songbirds include wren and meadow pipit with wheatear on the rocky outcrops in spring and summer. Few birds use the lakes because of the impoverished aquatic life but wild whooper swans occasionally visit in winter. Occasional dipper and grey wagtails can be seen feeding on some of the shorelines.

Access: Leave the N11 south of Bray and follow the signs for Enniskerry. Through the village, follow the signs for Glencree Reconciliation Centre. Turn left at the junction with the R115 (the old military road from Dublin). About 3km (less than 2 miles) to the south (in the direction of Sally Gap) there is a small roadside quarry on the left which is used as a car-park. From here a well-worn path descends through the heather to the shore of the Upper Lake. Several paths lead between the lakes and return to the road. Take great care, as the cliffs are dangerous, especially in wet conditions. Beware of deep pools due to rehabilitation work.

9. Liffey Head Bog

Blanket bog

Map reference: O1313 Nearest town: Enniskerry

Despite the apparently endless miles of high-level bog in Wicklow, this particular patch has a special magical quality. Not only is it the source of three of Wicklow's main rivers, but it is of international significance because of its very wet bog surface.

Landscape: This is rolling wet moorland between 500 and 550 metres (1500 to 1800 feet) above sea-level in the saddle between Tonduff and Kippure mountains. The television mast on the summit of Kippure dominates the skyline to the north-west while the upper reaches of the River Liffey cut deep into the peatland flowing westwards towards Blessington lakes. The source of the Dargle is here too, flowing eastwards out of the bog between Tonduff and War Hill. There are extensive peat workings especially near the road from Glencree to Sally Gap. Most of the peat cuttings are rented by people from Dublin who come to cut turf in the traditional way every summer. To the west of the road on the lower slopes of Kippure, an extensive area has been developed for commercial peat production

Habitats: This is almost entirely high-altitude blanket bog with no trees or shrubs. In many places the drainage is below the surface of the bog, forming natural tunnels in the peat. There are numerous deep pools on the surface of the bog where it is still intact. The wetter parts contain luxuriant growth of bog cotton, bog mosses and the club moss, which is not a moss at all. The flowers of bog asphodel and bog rosemary add a splash of colour to the bog vegetation. Drier moorland on the higher slopes is dominated by ling heather with bilberry and crowberry in places. Purple moor grass is common in the wetter peat among the heather.

Wildlife: Quite large herds of hybrid red–sika deer are often seen in the upper Dargle valley and occasionally feed in the bog. Mountain hare, fox and badger all use the trails through the bog but sometimes their droppings are the only evidence of their presence.

Meadow pipits are the commonest nesting birds but the song of the skylark is also heard high over the bog in spring and summer. Wheatears arrive in March and set up their territories using rocky areas as song posts. You may be startled by the explosive calls of red grouse which fly low across the bog. Peregrine and merlin also nest near by and hunt over the bog. Dippers feed along the upper reaches of the river and ravens often fly overhead, their deep croaking calls carrying far across the bog.

Peatland insects include the day-flying emperor moth whose large green caterpillar feeds among the heather. In summer, dragonflies fly around the pools from which the larvae have emerged. There is aquatic life in abundance with pond skaters, whirligig beetles and caddisfly larvae being the most obvious.

Access: The R115 road from Glencree (8km or 5 miles west of Enniskerry) to Sally Gap passes through the centre of the area. There are few safe parking places except at the entrance gates to the Kippure television mast. The area of bog immediately to the left hand side of the Kippure entrance as you face the transmitter is the most accessible. Beware of very soft ground and old peat workings, which often have deep drains and pools. The bog is part of the Wicklow Mountains National Park.

10. Vartry Reservoir

Lake, woodland, grassland

Map reference: O2101 Nearest town: Roundwood

Although little over a century old, this artificial water body has developed a series of semi-natural habitats which give it a wild atmosphere. This is especially true in winter as the wind carries the calls of ducks and geese across the freezing waters.

Landscape: This reservoir is the largest area of freshwater in the east of the county with a total area of 283 hectares (700 acres). The original embankment across the valley of the River Vartry was constructed in the 1860s while the second dam, 3.5km (2 miles) upstream, was completed in 1924. The reservoir supplies drinking water to Dublin city and parts of County Dublin and County Wicklow. In recent years demand has increased rapidly and the reservoir rarely fills to capacity.

Habitats: Marsh, woodland and grassland habitats all occur around the edges of the reservoir. Over the last century extensive tree-planting (mainly Scots pine) has been supplemented by natural colonisation of willow and alder near the water's edge and ash, sycamore, birch and rowan on drier ground. When water levels are low the shoreline is carpeted by shoreweed with spike-rush, sneezewort and reed canary grass. At the foot of the upper embankment there is a large area of wet woodland dominated by willow with many channels and pools. On the embankment itself is an area of species-rich grassland, which is managed as a hay meadow. The wild flowers here are at their best in June before the mowing.

Wildlife: Badger and fox both breed in the woodlands around the reservoir and often feed along the shoreline. Both otter and mink fish in the waters and their signs may be seen at various points around the lake.

Herons nest in a colony on the top of tall trees near the upper embankment and are a common sight feeding around the water's edge. Both herons and cormorants feed on a variety of fish in the reservoir including trout, minnow, stickleback and eel. Great crested grebes have recently nested here, which is an indication of the increasingly natural habitats around the reservoir. Moorhens are plentiful wherever there is cover on the banks and some mallard ducks breed each year. The distinctive drumming sound of snipe is often heard in the marshes and damp pastures around the reservoir. In winter the water levels rise and flocks of waterfowl gather on the reservoir. These include mallard, wigeon, teal and tufted duck with the occasional small flock of pochard and goldeneye. Little grebe are usually present in winter and spend much of their time diving for food. The flock of greylag geese here is of national importance. Observations of ringed birds have shown that they move between the reservoir and the wetlands on the coast.

The unimproved grasslands and more sheltered pathways are good places to look out for butterflies such as red admiral, peacock and meadow brown in summer.

Access: Turn left at the south end of Roundwood village street and follow the road for about 3km (less than 2 miles) to the entrance to the Vartry Waterworks. Starting on the left of the road there is a circular walk around the southern half of the reservoir on a good track. While access to this path is permitted by the owners, Dublin Corporation, visitors should note that there are some steep cliffs near sections of the path which are unsuitable for children. In late summer the shoreline is accessible but take care of soft marsh areas which can be dangerous.

11. Lough Dan and Lough Tay
Lake, river, woodland

Map reference: O1503 Nearest town: Roundwood

A very special atmosphere pervades this valley which is steeped in history. In the 1798 uprising the valley provided a stronghold for rebels and witnessed a massacre of its inhabitants and burning of houses. Today, one can stand among the ruined cottages and imagine how it may have looked a century or two ago.

Landscape: The Cloghoge is a typical U-shaped valley, formed by a glacier during the last Ice Age. It is now occupied by the Cloghoge River which flows out of Lough Tay at the northern end and into Lough Dan at the southern end where it forms a small delta. The Inchavore river flows in another glacial valley from the west to enter Lough Dan where it forms a sandy beach. The contact between granite and mica schist can be seen in the cliffs to the north-west of Lough Dan. The valley floor, at about 230 metres (750 feet) above sea-level, is surprisingly fertile and there is evidence of past farming activities in the cultivation ridges (or lazy beds) which cover the valley sides.

Habitats: Lake, river, fen, cliffs, scree, woodland and heathland all occur close together in one of the richest areas for nature in Wicklow. The lake water is acidic but supports several rare plant species and a rare fish, the Arctic charr, which is isolated here from other small populations in the west of Ireland. Floating bur-reed and white water lily also grow in the lake water. At the north-west corner of the lake where it is joined by the Inchavore river, an extensive fen occurs although this has been partly reclaimed for agriculture.

Steep cliffs of mica schist overhang the northern edge of the lake and the scree at their foot is clothed in gorse scrub down to the water's edge. To the east and south-east of the lake extensive areas of broadleaved woodland survive. These are mostly oak and birch woodlands with an understorey of holly. Typical spring flowers include bluebell, wood sorrel and wood anemone. The valley sides have extensive areas of heather moorland with purple moor grass on the wetter soils.

Wildlife: The lake and river systems are used by otters, while badgers breed in the woodlands and on open moorland. Sika deer are common on the higher slopes, especially on Knocknacloghoge mountain to the north of the lake and red squirrels are common in the woodlands.

The river and its tributaries are rich in invertebrate life and support breeding dippers and grey wagtails with common sandpipers on rocky shores around the lake. Herons and cormorants roost in the tall trees along the shore of the lake near the mouth of the Cloghoge River and small numbers of whooper swans winter in the lake. Meadow pipits, skylarks and wheatears breed on open moorland and there is also a chance of seeing a merlin or hen harrier. Kestrels, peregrines, ring ousels and ravens breed on the high cliffs and the ravens are almost constantly present in the valleys on either side of the lake. The woodlands hold a typical breeding bird community with chaffinch, wren, robin, blackbird and blue tit the most obvious. Redstarts and wood warblers occasionally breed in the woodlands near the lake. Willow warblers are common in summer in the scrub areas.

Access: Leave the N11 at Kilmacanogue and follow the R755 in the direction of Roundwood. Turn west on to the R759 at the signpost for Sally Gap and follow the road uphill for about 3km (less than 2 miles) until the valley becomes obvious to the left. A few parking places are available in forestry plantations or on the roadside at the 'Pier Gates'. Enter the valley on foot between stone pillars and follow the tarred road down into the valley and downstream along the Cloghoge River to Lough Dan. Take care crossing the river especially when it is in flood. Alternatively, enter from the south by Oldbridge (3km or less than 2 miles south-west of Roundwood) and park where the tarred road ends along the west side of Lough Dan.

12. Lough Ouler

Lake, moorland, cliffs

Map reference: O0902 Nearest town: Laragh

After a steep climb up the little stream from the Glenmacnass waterfall, you can sit for a while on one of the boulders that fringe the shore of the lake, and absorb the stillness and beauty of the surroundings. In snowy weather when the water surface may be frozen, the deep call of the raven echoes from the cliffs behind the lake.

Landscape: This is a glacial corrie on the side of Tonelagee which, at 817 metres (2680 feet), is one of Wicklow's highest peaks. The corrie was scoured out by a glacier during the last Ice Age leaving a steep rocky cliff up to 200 metres (600 feet) high on the north-east side of the summit. Part of the cliffs are formed of granite, which is in contact here with the older mica schist. The corrie is filled by a deep, heart-shaped lake which is enclosed on the east side by a series of moraines. The blanket bog on the northern slopes of Tonelagee above the cliffs is severely eroded, forming a series of rugged peat haggs. A small stream flows out of the lake to join the Glenmacnass river. There are numerous deep pools and banks of granite sand on the bends of this picturesque mountain river.

Habitats: Most of the area around the lake is covered with blanket bog which is dominated by heather and purple moor grass. Ling heather is the most abundant but bell heather also grows here and cross-leaved heath in the wetter areas. There are many wet flushes on the hillside below the lake with mosses, bog cotton and soft rush. Bilberry and woodrush are plentiful among the heather but heavy grazing by sheep and deer reduces the amount of flowering. Burning of the heather allows grasses such as sheep's fescue, creeping bent and purple moor grass to colonise the open areas. The lake shore is rocky and sparsely vegetated but shoreweed and quillwort grow here in the shallow water areas. The steep cliffs behind the lake have some alpine plants such as golden saxifrage and starry saxifrage, growing mainly in the small streams which flow down the cliff. The lake water itself is acidic with few nutrients.

Wildlife: Dippers are usually present on the main Glenmacnass river in both summer and winter. Watch out for them perching on large stones in the middle of the river or flying low and fast upstream. Red grouse feed in the longer heather areas around the lake and on the banks of the small stream which flows from it to the Glenmacnass river. They stay in the area throughout the winter, even when deep snow covers the ground. Ravens soar widely over the area searching for carrion. Peregrine falcons breed here in some years and can often be seen hunting for small bird prey in the surrounding moorland. The lake holds some brown trout which breed when still quite small — a survival strategy in low-nutrient areas.

Access: Leave the R755 at Laragh and take the Military Road to the north for Sally Gap. Travel north-west for about 8km (5 miles) to the top of Glenmacnass where a spectacular waterfall plunges into the valley below the road. Park in the large roadside car-park just above the waterfall and walk upstream for about 1km (half a mile) along the banks of the Glenmacnass river. Take care crossing the river on the large boulders and follow the first main tributary uphill in a south-westerly direction. The ground is very wet and slippery in places and requires strong and waterproof footwear. After a climb of nearly 200 metres (600 feet) and a distance of 1.5km (about a mile), the ground levels out around the shore of the lake. Heed warning signs around waterfall.

8.1 Glendalough (valley of two lakes) is a classic glaciated valley. Its U-shaped profile was carved by a moving glacier over 10,000 years ago, while the rounded shape of the surrounding hills was worn down by the overlying ice sheet. A river entering the centre of the valley later created a delta which separates the two lakes. (Slidefile)

8.2 Lough Ouler on the slopes of Tonelagee mountain. This is a classic corrie, scraped out by a mountain glacier, which plucked rocks from the back wall. The deep basin was later filled with a dark, heart-shaped lake, whose acid waters now contain a few small trout. (Richard Nairn)

8.3 Wild asparagus at Buckroney dunes. This is a very rare and legally protected plant which is limited to the south-east coast of Ireland. Its habitat is under pressure for agriculture and amenity uses. (Richard Nairn)

8.2

8.3

8.4 Steep cliffs above the Glendalough valley are difficult terrain even for the mountain goats. In the absence of grazing, a variety of native trees including rowan, oak and holly survive here. (Richard Nairn)

8.5   Six-spot burnet moth. A day-flying insect, which is typical of coastal grassland, such as that on the Murrough, where its larval food plant, birds foot trefoil, occurs. As in butterflies, the antennae are clubbed. (Richard Nairn)

8.6   The skylark is the commonest bird on sand dunes. Its continuous stream of song is delivered from the sky above its breeding territory. It nests in the grass and uses an occasional gorse bush as a convenient perch to watch for predators. The feathers on the head form a distinctive crest. (Richard T. Mills)

13. Glendalough

Woodland, lakes, fen and moorland

Map reference: T1296 Nearest town: Laragh

One of the best ways of approaching Glendalough is on foot, as the early Christians probably did, approaching the monastic ruins from the east through Derrybawn Wood. The ancient track is overhung by gnarled trees and, through gaps in the woodland, the spectacular scenery begins to unfold before your eyes.

Landscape: This is one of the most beautiful and best-known sites in Wicklow and, as well as being of archaeological and historical interest, it is rich in plants and animals. The original Irish name *Gleann dá Locha* means the valley of two lakes and these are still the main natural features which dominate the area. The valley is deep and narrow with the typical U-shape showing that it was carved out by a glacier during the last Ice Age. In retreating, the glacier left a moraine across the mouth of the valley, on which the present Glendalough Hotel is built. A tributary, the Poulanass river which plunges into the valley from the south, created a delta which eventually divided the original lake in two. The valley is surrounded by high mountains with summits rising over 650 metres (2132 feet).

Habitats: Glendalough contains some of the best surviving examples of native broadleaved woodland in Wicklow. While they have all the appearances of ancient woodland most of the trees are less than 150 years old, as substantial clearances took place in the nineteenth century. The present woodland is dominated by sessile oak with an understorey of holly and birch with rowan around the margins. There are groups of introduced trees, including beech and Scots pine, near the lakeshore and on the northern slopes. The ground flora includes woodrush, bilberry, sweet vernal grass, a number of ferns and many typical spring flowers such as wood anemone and lesser celandine. Grazing by sheep, goats and deer has restricted natural regeneration on all but the steepest slopes. The Lower Lake, close to the monastic ruins, is fringed by a marsh and fen containing articulated rush, horsetail and marsh violet. The acidic water of the Upper Lake is deep and contains only a few plant species such as white water lily, pondweed and bulbous rush. At the upper end, near the mining village, the lake is shallower owing to large deposits of granite sand. A marsh has formed here with common reed, bottle sedge, articulated rush and horsetail. The Poulanass river forms a deep gorge with rich growths of mosses and bryophytes in the moist conditions.

Wildlife: Deer and badgers are common in the woodlands and otters feed in the lakes and river. Bats are common in the valley. Red squirrels are regularly seen in the trees and stoats use the area for hunting prey such as rabbits. The oak woodlands are rich in breeding birds, especially wren, chaffinch, blackbird, blue and great tits.

The birch and willow woodland around the Lower Lake holds reed bunting and willow warbler. Jay, treecreeper, blackcap and sparrowhawk are scarcer but regular members of the bird community. Wood warbler and redstart breed in most years in the oakwoods. Woodland butterflies include silver-washed fritillary, holly blue and speckled wood. Raven and peregrine breed on the cliffs above the Upper Lake and ring ousel can be seen on the higher ground in spring and summer. Herons and cormorants feed in the river and lakes which contain small brown trout. Whooper swans are present on the Upper Lake in some winters.

Access: Leave the R755 at Laragh and follow the signs for Glendalough. Park at the lower car-park beside the visitor centre, 2km (a little over a mile) west of Laragh village, or in the upper car-park (1km or half a mile further on), for which there is a small entry charge. The entire area is a National Nature Reserve and part of the Wicklow Mountains National Park. Maps and guidebooks are available in the visitor centre in the lower car-park or in the National Park information centre near the upper car-park.

14. Glenealo Valley

Moorland, blanket bog and cliffs

Map reference: T0796 Nearest town: Laragh

After climbing through history in the confines of the mining village, the open vistas of the Glenealo valley are a revelation. Its vastness and the absence of buildings or forestry make it a very special wild place. Large herds of wild deer and the occasional sighting of peregrine falcon add to the feeling of wilderness.

Landscape: This is a broad open hanging valley in the upper catchment of the Glenealo river which flows into the lower Glendalough valley. It is surrounded by a ring of granite mountains with summits reaching 700m. There is much evidence of former mining in the valley with spoil heaps on both sides of the river and ruined houses of the mining village below the waterfall. The mine waste appears white because it is composed mainly of the mineral quartz and has traces of lead, arsenic and zinc, which are toxic to plants. This was the residue left after the lead ore had been extracted. Hundreds of people lived and worked here between 1800 and 1920 and the Glenealo valley became known as 'Van Diemen's Land' because of its remoteness and harsh conditions. During this period most of the remaining trees in Glenealo and Glendalough valleys were cleared for use as pit props and for the charcoal-fired smelting furnace.

Habitats: This is a high-level river valley with blanket bog, moorland, cliffs and scree. The better drained slopes support grass and heather (mainly ling and bell heather). Crowberry and bilberry are common on the higher parts especially where grazing by deer, sheep and goats is limited by cliffs. Wetter areas have a high proportion of mosses (especially the bog mosses *Rhacomitrium* and *Sphagnum*). Purple moor grass covers large areas with patches of bracken, heather and gorse. Cliffs and scree slopes have small patches of remnant woodland with oak, ash, birch, holly and rowan trees, especially around the waterfall on the Glenealo river.

Wildlife: Hybrid red–sika deer are common in the valley sometimes in quite large herds. Feral goats, which graze around the mining village and the waterfall, may be descendants of domestic goats which supplied milk to the mining village. Foxes and mountain hares are frequent throughout the valley. Typical mountain birds in spring and summer include meadow pipit, wren, wheatear and skylark. There are occasional red grouse in the valley but breeding habitat is limited by the overgrazing of heather. The river holds breeding dipper and grey wagtail with feeding herons in summer. The cliffs and scree have nesting ring ousel, kestrel and peregrine. Ravens are common residents, their croaking calls a constant feature of the valley. Typical mountain and peatland insects are plentiful especially in the wetter areas and along the river banks. In summer these include dragonflies and the day-flying emperor moth.

Access: Leave the R755 road at Laragh and follow the signs for Glendalough. Pass the monastic ruins and park in the upper car-park (for which there is a small entry charge) at the end of the road. Walk 2.5km (a mile and a half) along the northern shore of the Upper Lake to the ruined mining village. Follow the steep zig-zag track by the waterfall to the higher level valley. Walking becomes progressively more difficult and the ground is often very wet. The entire area is part of the Wicklow Mountains National Park.

15. Vale of Clara

River and woodland

Map reference: T1891 Nearest town: Rathdrum

The old church at Clara is surrounded by oak woodland as it must have been for centuries. A walk along the riverbank from here to Rathdrum leads down ancient cart tracks, long forgotten except by the deer and the badgers which shelter among the deep foliage of bilberry.

Landscape: The picturesque valley of the Avonmore river cuts through Ordovician rocks which rise on either side to about 300 metres (600 feet) above sea-level. The river is wide and fast-flowing with a gravelly bed. The river is flanked by old woodland which is much more extensive on the eastern side and includes a tributary at Cronybyrne (O'Byrne's hollow with the stream). The old stone bridge and Clara church in the centre of the valley date from the eighteenth century.

Habitats: This is one of the largest surviving areas of semi-natural woodland in Wicklow, located mainly on the eastern side of the Avonmore river between Clara and Rathdrum. It is mainly oak woodland with holly, birch and some hazel. Some parts have been underplanted with conifers. Gorse and broom are plentiful along the river bank and on forest tracks. The understorey is largely ungrazed and contains all the common woodland flowers such as woodrush, bluebell, wild garlic, wood sorrel, bilberry, bracken and bramble with ling heather in places. Wood avens and wood sanicle are indicators of old, long-established woodland. In some open areas, there are patches of heather moorland which thrives in the absence of grazing.

Wildlife: Deer are occasional but not as common as in some other higher woodlands. There are a number of old badger setts in the woodland and the undergrowth is criss-crossed with their tracks and other signs. Typical woodland breeding birds include sparrowhawk, blackcap and jay. This is a good place to see woodcock in spring as the males perform their remarkable 'roding' display flight around the territories at dusk. Both grey wagtail and dipper feed along the river with the latter species breeding in the stonework of various bridges. Woodland butterflies include holly blue, speckled wood, hedge brown and the large silver-washed fritillary which emerges in late summer. The other invertebrates are probably equally diverse because of the absence of grazing and plentiful amounts of old and rotten timber.

Access: Take either the R752 road from Rathnew to Rathdrum or the R755 from Laragh to Clara. There are various access points via forestry tracks off the road between Clara and Cronybyrne or between Garryduff cross-roads and Rathdrum. Most of the woodlands are part of a National Nature Reserve owned by the Heritage Service (Dúchas).

16. Deputy's Pass

Map reference: T2390 Nearest town: Glenealy

This small woodland is a good place for a quiet walk beneath the leafy canopy in spring or summer. The pass was the scene of an ambush of British troops when the Potter's river is said to have 'run red with blood'.

Landscape: This narrow valley through the ridge south of Glenealy is a glacial feature formed by the overflow of meltwater after the last Ice Age. The small Potter's river, which now flows through the valley, eventually reaches the sea at Brittas Bay. Surviving woodland is mainly on the northern side of the valley. Just south of the car-park there is an old ford across the river.

Habitats: A mixture of old broadleaved woodland and more recent coniferous plantations dominate the valley. Oak predominates in the older woodland with an understorey of holly, rowan and hazel. There are some pure stands of hazel which were probably coppiced for poles in past years. A stand of beech trees near the western edge casts a dense shade in summer producing little undergrowth. Look out for interesting fungi here in autumn. In more open patches, heather, bramble, gorse and broom cover the ground. Bilberry and woodrush are plentiful on the woodland floor which is little grazed. There are a number of old tracks and walls within the woodland, which themselves provide an interesting shady habitat. The river that flows through the centre of the valley is small but contains some interesting plants.

Wildlife: Although relatively small, this woodland has a good range of mammals including badger, fox and red squirrel. Bats roost in the older trees and feed along the tracks and over the river at dusk and dawn.

Typical woodland birds such as wren, chaffinch and robin are most abundant but there are also a few jays and sparrowhawks. Blackcap breeds around the woodland edge near the road. Mixed flocks of tits, including long-tailed tit, are often seen moving through the canopy in late summer and autumn. Ravens sometimes fly overhead giving their deep croaking call. They breed on the crags of nearby Carrick mountain.

Access: Turn off the N11 just south of Rathnew and take the R752 to Rathdrum. Turn left 3km (less than 2 miles) after the village of Glenealy and follow the brown signs for Deputy's Pass. Shortly after the road enters the woodland there is a car-park with picnic tables on the left. Most of the woodlands are part of a National Nature Reserve owned by the Heritage Service (Dúchas). Management includes the removal of exotic trees such as conifers. The woodland tracks are also used for horse-riding.

17. Devil's Glen

River and woodland

Stand for a moment on the muddy track and listen to the roar of water in the river as it plunges between the boulders, filling the valley with damp spray. High overhead, the rocky crags seem to hang suspended among the trees.

Landscape: Formed as a meltwater channel at the end of the last Ice Age, this is now a deep gorge through which the Vartry flows. The rocks are from the ancient Cambrian era and are mainly grey and purple slates, best exposed in crags on the northern side of the valley. At the western end the river flows through damp grassland and gorse scrub before plunging over a small waterfall into the glen. In the 1798 rebellion the glen was used as a safe gathering place for the insurgents. A nineteenth-century traveller described the Devil's Glen as 'inconceivably grand and beautiful'. The south side of the glen was formerly part of the Glanmore estate owned by the family of the writer JM Synge.

Habitats: The steep valley sides are clothed in woodland which is mainly oak, hazel and holly on the north side with a mixture of other trees on the south. There is evidence that the ancient oaks here were coppiced in the nineteenth century for making charcoal. The south side of the glen was planted with a mixture of exotic trees such as Scots pine and Spanish chestnut with shrubs such as laurel and rhododendron which have since spread out of control, especially at the eastern end. These evergreen shrubs shade the ground and prevent natural regeneration. However, in places near the river the ground flora is luxuriant with wild garlic, woodrush, wood anemone, lesser celandine and bluebells in spring. Bilberry is also common in dryer parts of the woodland while wet ground has some interesting mosses and liverworts. A variety of fungi can be found throughout the woodlands in autumn. An old millpond on the north side of the river near Nun's Cross Bridge has white water lilies with a fringe of fen vegetation including bulrush and yellow flags.

Wildlife: Sika and fallow deer are frequent but hard to see in the undergrowth. There is a herd of feral goats near the waterfall and they have damaged many trees by stripping their bark. Badgers are plentiful in the woods and there are some ancient setts on the upper slopes where they have good access to the surrounding farmland for feeding. Red squirrels are common and the remains of cones and nuts on which they have been feeding are easily found on the ground. Otters use the river as a corridor but they are rarely seen because they only move about after dark.

Dippers breed under the bridges and fly rapidly close to the water surface. Grey wagtails also feed along the river, flitting from stone to stone in pursuit of aquatic insects. Herons occasionally feed along the river but breed elsewhere. The woodlands have a typical breeding bird community with chaffinch, robin, wren, blackbird and blue tit among the most numerous species. The summer migrants, chiffchaff, blackcap, whitethroat and wood warbler all nest in the vegetation near the river. Jays are common and noisy residents throughout the woodlands. Raven and peregrine nest on the cliffs in the glen and are most easily seen in summer when the young are flying. The woodlands are rich in invertebrates including the scarce butterflies holly blue and silver-washed fritillary. A number of dragonflies are found in mid-summer in pools along the river.

Access: Leave the N11 at Ashford and travel west following the signs for Glendalough for about 4km (2.5 miles). A forestry entrance on the right side of the road gives access along a 2km road to a car-park near the nineteenth-century Glanmore Castle. From here a short walk leads to the edge of the glen and a longer path leads to the waterfall. The south side of the glen is owned by Coillte, the state forestry board. The north side is privately owned and access is not permitted.

18. Kilcoole Marshes

Saltmarsh and shingle beach

Map reference: T3106 Nearest town: Kilcoole

An evening walk in summer along the sandy track beside the railway gives wide views as the sun sinks to the west behind the Wicklow hills. Breeding waders call from the saltmarshes and, over the stony beach, groups of little terns flit backwards and forwards with their fairy-like flight pattern.

Landscape: A flat coastal plain is bordered by a long straight barrier beach which was formed when sea-level was higher after the last Ice Age. Alternate layers of marine and freshwater sediments in the marshes show that the sea has breached the barrier several times in the past. At present the sea enters the marshes through a narrow channel beneath the railway bridge at the Breaches. The channel occasionally blocks with beach material in winter and the marshes flood extensively. Much of the original saltmarsh has been drained and claimed for agriculture.

Habitats: The area holds a complex of saltmarsh, reedbed, and tidal channels which are separated from the sea by a shingle ridge, low sand hills and a wide stony beach. The top of the beach has a rich flora in summer with sea beet, sea campion and sea sandwort. The sandhills are dominated by marram grass with kidney vetch, sea bindweed and sea holly on the more open areas. In mid-summer it is possible to find some scarcer plants such as pyramidal orchid and yellow horned poppy. There are some thickets of the thorny shrub sea buckthorn and another introduced plant, hottentot fig, has become established near the Breaches. Some drainage channels are filled with a dense growth of reeds while the few areas of undrained saltmarsh contain common scurvy grass, sea aster and sea lavender.

Wildlife: Rabbits are common on the sand and shingle and they are regularly hunted by fox and stoat.

Skylark, meadow pipit and stonechat are common breeding birds on the sand hills in summer. The open beach near the Breaches holds nesting ringed plover and oystercatcher and a small but important colony of little terns. These graceful seabirds can be seen fishing in the shallow offshore waters and in tidal channels in the marshes. The saltmarsh has nesting redshank, shelduck and mute swan. Wintering wildfowl including whooper and Bewick's swans; greylag and brent geese are usually seen on grassland around the edge of the marshes. Ducks such as wigeon, teal, mallard and shelduck are common in winter. Pintail, shoveler, pochard, goldeneye and gadwall are occasional. Common waders on the marshes in winter include redshank, curlew and golden plover. The beach has regular small flocks of oystercatcher, ringed plover, turnstone and dunlin in autumn and winter. Kestrel and merlin are frequently seen hunting on the marshes and beach with occasional peregrine and hen harrier in winter. Look out for terns offshore in summer with occasional red-throated divers and little gulls in winter.

Access: Turn off the N11 dual carriageway for Delgany and follow signs for Kilcoole (Glenroe). Follow signs from village to beach (approx. 2km or one mile). Park at the end of the road and take care on the railway crossing. Walk south along the track at the top of the beach parallel to the railway. The Breaches are about 2km from the road. Access to the saltmarsh is prevented by deep channels inland of the railway track.

19. Broadlough
Estuary, reedbeds and shingle beach

Map reference: T3095 Nearest town: Wicklow

In winter, flocks of wigeon whistle their lonely calls across the water, redshanks pipe from around the saltmarsh and flocks of curlew circle in to the edge of the reedbed. With a dazzling flash of blue and orange, a kingfisher may fly past.

Landscape: Broadlough is the tidal estuary of the River Vartry separated from the sea by a long straight shingle ridge and stony beach (The Murrough). The river enters the estuary near the northern end and meets the sea at Wicklow harbour. The landscape is flat but there are good views of the hills of Carrick and Dunran to the west and Wicklow Head to the south. A railway bridge crosses the estuary north of the town.

Habitats: The area contains a complex of shingle, grassland, scrub, saltmarsh, reedbeds and mudflats. The beach has a typical strandline flora with plants such as sea sandwort and yellow horned poppy. Sandy grassland on the seaward side of the railway has marram grass, sea bindweed and sea holly. The shingle ridges inland of the railway are dominated by gorse and bramble scrub with some dry grassland containing milkwort and burnet rose. Saltmarsh fringes the seaward side of the estuary with thrift and scurvy grass flowering in summer. Reedbeds around the mouth of the Vartry and north of the railway bridge contain dense stands of common reed and some willow. A small area of mudflats at the northern end of Broadlough is exposed at low tide. There is some wet grassland and willow carr around Killoughter station at the north end of Broadlough.

Wildlife: Rabbits are very common among the sand and shingle with the occasional fox seen in daylight.

Gorse and bramble scrub holds breeding wren, blackbird, stonechat, whitethroat and linnet. Kestrels hunt regularly over open grassland which contains a high density of small mammals. Reedbeds hold large populations of sedge warbler, reed bunting and occasionally the rarer reed warbler and bearded tit. There is a small heronry on the inland side of the reedbeds with herons feeding widely around the shore. Large numbers of migrating swallow, swift, sand martin and house martin move through in autumn. The estuary is best in winter with large flocks of mute swan, wigeon, teal and waders including redshank, lapwing, golden plover, curlew and greenshank. Goldeneye, little glebe and kingfisher are frequently seen in the southern part near the railway bridge. Small numbers of brent geese and whooper swan occur regularly. Greylag geese move between here and Kilcoole Marshes to the north. In late winter and spring pairs of shelduck are seen displaying on the estuary prior to breeding. Hen harrier often hunt over the reedbeds in winter.

There is rich insect life in all habitats. Day-flying cinnabar and burnet moths can be seen in summer on shingle and sandy grassland.

Access: Follow signs for the beach from the main street of Wickow town. Cross the bridge near the quays and turn north. There is a car-park 1km (half a mile) north near railway crossing and factories. Follow the beach in a northerly direction for 1km and cross railway by gates if the track is clear. Cross the shingle ridge to the narrow part of estuary and continue north along the eastern shoreline. No access to the north or west of Broadlough. Return by the same route.

211

20. Wicklow Head

Sea cliffs and heathland

Map reference: T3492 Nearest town: Wicklow

Lean on the old stone wall around the lighthouse compound and listen to the echoing calls of seabirds as they come and go from their cliff ledges. The views from here stretch to Dublin and Arklow Head.

Landscape: This is the most easterly point of land in the Republic of Ireland and a strong tidal current passes the headland. The present lighthouse is the most recent of three towers which stand on the head. The distinctive outline of Wicklow Head is visible from most other parts of the Wicklow coast. The rock is mainly mica schist which is highly folded and contorted forming sea arches and caves. North of the lighthouse two small storm beaches face in opposite directions at Bride's Head.

Habitats: Sea cliffs, storm beaches, maritime grassland and heathland are the main habitats. Typical clifftop vegetation of the spray zone is dominated by cushions of thrift, sea campion and common scurvy grass. On the flatter parts, maritime grassland is maintained by light grazing and plants such as red fescue and spring squill are common. Away from the salt spray, rough grassland and heathland predominate, with heather, gorse, bramble and bracken forming the main vegetation in areas which are not intensively farmed. At intervals on the clifftop small wet flushes occur. These contain many wetland plants including lady's smock.

Wildlife: Grey seals are a common sight in the water around the base of the cliffs but they rarely come ashore. The nearest regular breeding site for seals is on Lambay Island, over 50km (30 miles) north. Rabbits graze the clifftop vegetation and are most active at dusk and dawn,.

The seabird colony, which is mainly concentrated south of the lighthouse, includes (in order of abundance) kittiwakes, guillemots, razorbills, herring gulls, fulmars and a few black guillemots, shags and great black-backed gulls. The kittiwakes make the most distinctive calls during the nesting season, May to July. In spring the fulmars are most obvious flying around the clifftops while in autumn and winter there are few seabirds present. Songbirds such as rock pipit, meadow pipit and skylark are most numerous on the clifftops with stonechat, yellowhammer, whitethroat, linnet and wren breeding in the gorse scrub. Partridges once bred regularly here but have not been seen in recent years. Kestrels nest nearby and hunt small mammals among the rough grassland. Ravens and peregrines occasionally nest on the cliffs and both are regularly seen in spring and summer months. During periods of onshore winds, it can also be good for watching passing seabirds such as shearwaters and skuas.

All the common migrant butterflies, such as peacock, red admiral and clouded yellow, may be seen on the headland in suitable weather conditions in summer.

Access: Approach via the R750 from Wicklow town. Past the golf club, 1km (half a mile) south-east of the town, there is a car-park on the seaward side of the road. Follow the steps down to the Glen Cove, a small shingle beach, and from here along the cliff path towards the lighthouse. Take care, as the path is unfenced and can be slippery. Access to the remainder of the head is limited by fencing of private land but pedestrian access is permitted along the road to the lighthouse. There are steep cliffs around the lighthouse. These are dangerous and great care should be taken.

21. Brittas Bay/Buckroney

Sand dunes and marsh

Map reference: T3081 Nearest town: Arklow

Landscape: Two large sand dune systems, divided by the rocky Mizen Head, are backed by an extensive marsh and fen. The northern dune system at Brittas Bay is relatively dry and fairly heavily eroded in places, as it gives access to one of the most popular beaches on the east coast. The dunes at Buckroney have been partly developed as a golf links but the southern half is still relatively intact and contains an extensive wet slack area in the centre.

Habitats: The strandline flora is quite rich at the northern end of Buckroney (immediately south of Mizen Head) with large swathes of yellow horned poppy in flower in July. Pioneer dunes are very limited as the overall trend is one of erosion. Marram grass dominates on the front dune ridges with sea holly, sea bindweed, sea rocket and sea purslane. Further back towards the road marram grass becomes less frequent and a rich carpet of dune plants takes over. Predominant in summer are bird's-foot trefoil, wild thyme, seaside pansy, lady's bedstraw and various mosses and lichens. In the dune slacks, creeping willow is abundant with great sea rush and common reed in the wetter parts. Rare species found here include wild asparagus, green-flowered helleborine and meadow saxifrage. At the back of the dunes nearest the road, the vegetation is dominated by bracken, burnet rose and patches of gorse. Inland of the road the fen contains a lot of common reed and willow and is flanked at its eastern edge by rough grazing with gorse scrub. The wetter parts are dominated by tussock sedge with purple loosestrife, bottle sedge, horsetail, bogbean, marsh bedstraw and many other species. A large stand of the rare marsh fern also occurs here.

Wildlife: On the sand dunes rabbits are much in evidence and their grazing and burrowing contribute to the open nature of the vegetation.

The northern end of Buckroney beach has a small colony of little tern and ringed plover, both of which nest on unvegetated shingle. Breeding bird species are relatively few in the sand dune grassland where skylark and meadow pipit predominate. Cuckoos can be seen and heard especially in May and June. Linnet, wren, blackbird and stonechat breed in the bracken and gorse scrub near the inland edge of the dunes and a kestrel may be seen hovering over the dunes and marsh area scanning the ground for insects, frogs or small rodents. The reedswamps in the dune slack and marsh have nesting sedge warbler and reed bunting as well as large flocks of migrating swallows and martins in autumn. In autumn watch out for small parties of migrating waders including dunlin, sanderling and turnstone on the beach.

On a warm summer day many different insect species can be seen on the more sheltered parts of the dunes. Most obvious are the common blue butterfly and the six-spotted burnet moth, but these may be joined by a range of migrant species such as red admiral, painted lady and peacock butterflies.

Access: Turn off the N11 between Rathnew and Arklow at Jack White's pub and follow the minor road for about 1.5 km (a mile) to the coast. There are two public car-parks (with toilets) near the centre of Brittas Bay. The dunes south of the river will eventually be declared a nature reserve but there are no visitor facilities available yet. Buckroney Marsh is best viewed from the road, as access is not yet available to the public.

22. Arklow Pond and Sand Dunes   *Sand dunes and lagoon*

Map reference: T2675 Nearest town: Arklow

Although close to the town, the pond attracts much wildlife and is a pleasant place for a morning or evening walk. The sound of wind in the reeds, combined with the breaking waves on the beach, give a natural atmosphere.

Landscape: The mouth of the Avoca river has changed course many times over previous centuries with the movement of sand dunes that blocked the estuary. The building of harbour walls at Arklow caused the beach north of the town to stabilise and a brackish water lake (Arklow Pond) was formed. Storms have breached the sand dunes at intervals causing serious flooding of the low land behind. A modern sea wall has covered most of the original dune area but some undeveloped sand dunes survive at Seabank, north of the caravan park.

Habitats: The ponds which survive from the original dune area are fringed by a narrow reedbed on the inland side. The gently shelving sandy beach at Seabank has a covering of shingle and seashells near high-tide mark. Pioneer dune vegetation including sand couch grass and sea holly forms a thin fringe along the top of the beach. Behind this the dune ridges are covered with marram grass, which binds the sand and provides a stable base for other common plants such as the seaside pansy and bird's-foot trefoil. Less common plants such as pyramidal orchid flower on the dune ridges for a short time in summer and a rare species of horsetail is found at the northern end where the dunes are narrowest.
On the most stable dunes there is natural scrub, mostly hawthorn and gorse with some bramble and burnet rose. The steep slopes behind the dunes are covered in bracken with a ground flora including bluebells. This grades into a fringe of woodland and scrub around the edge of the farmland behind.

Wildlife: Arklow Pond holds a small number of wintering mallard, teal, wigeon and coot with a few mute swans. Whooper swans and pochard are occasionally recorded. Moorhens and sedge warblers breed here in summer and there is a good chance of the scarce reed warbler. Small flocks of oystercatchers and gulls feed and roost on the beach in winter. One or two pairs of ringed plover breed here in spring but their nest sites at the top of the beach are vulnerable to disturbance. Few birds apart from meadow pipit breed on the open dune ridges although the scrub towards the back of the dunes holds a typical community including willow warbler, chaffinch, linnet, greenfinch, wren and stonechat.
   The dune grassland is rich in insect life especially in warm summer weather. Common blue butterflies and six-spotted burnet moths are among the most colourful insects although there are many smaller bees, hoverflies and beetles among the vegetation. In late summer, migrant butterflies such as red admiral, peacock, painted lady and clouded yellow arrive to join the resident species.

Access: Take the N11 road north of Arklow and turn off towards the beach at the sign for the sports centre. Park just before the sea wall and walk along the path by the ponds. Cross the sea wall to the beach and follow it for about 2 kilometres (a little over a mile) to the north, crossing a small stream and passing a rocky headland known as Porter's Rocks. The most natural sand dunes are behind the beach north of the headland.

214

23. Avoca River Valley

River and woodland

Map reference: T2076 Nearest town: Arklow

Standing on the banks of the river, whose tributaries drain most of the eastern side of Wicklow, you can enjoy the tranquil flow of a mature waterway. The surrounding woodland adds to the sense of peace and naturalness.

Landscape: This is a deeply-incised river valley winding through the south-eastern edge of the Wicklow hills from Rathdrum to the sea at Arklow. Surrounding hills are all less than 300 metres (almost 1000 feet) and well-rounded. The Avonmore and Avonbeg rivers join to form the Avoca River at the Meeting of the Waters, a beauty spot made famous by the poet Thomas Moore. The main channel is joined by the Aughrim river at Woodenbridge, creating a wide and slow-flowing river with an extensive floodplain. In the upper valley the spoilheaps from former copper mines dominate the landscape although many of these have now been planted with conifers. Fragments of old broadleaved woodland survive in the lower valley around Shelton Abbey to the north of the river and Glenart Castle to the south.

Habitats: The river bank is gravelly and well vegetated with broom and gorse. Young birch woodland is widespread on the low ground near the river and on the steep slopes of the mine waste. More mature woodlands in the lower parts of the valley are predominantly oak and birch with some beech although they are limited to a fringe on the steeply sloping sides of the valley. Most have a well-developed understorey of hazel and holly, although evergreen laurel and rhododendron are widespread, especially around the old estate gardens, from which they have escaped. Some areas of pure hazel woodland near Ballyraine House were coppiced for poles in previous centuries. The ground flora in these woodlands is rich in spring flowers such as bluebell, wood violet and wood sanicle.

Wildlife: The woodlands are rich in bird life with typical songbird communities including wren, robin, chaffinch, blackbird and tits among the commonest species. Summer visitors include chiffchaff, willow warbler, blackcap and whitethroat. Jay, sparrowhawk and long-eared owl are all present in the older broadleaved woods. The upper river holds trout and salmon, but is lacking in aquatic life downstream of the Avoca mines.

Access: From Arklow, the road to Avoca runs along the western bank of the river giving good access to many of the woodland areas on this side of the valley. The eastern side of the valley is less accessible except near Woodenbridge and Avoca where bridges cross the main river.

Map reference: T 1985 Nearest town: Rathdrum

Autumn is a favourite time of year at Avondale. The old beech trees are dressed in their finest colours and, after heavy rainfall, the river becomes a raging torrent full of power and action. The riverside walk is a memorable experience.

Landscape: Avondale is best known as the historic home of Charles Stewart Parnell as well as the cradle of Irish forestry. The house was built in 1779 by Samuel Hayes who represented Wicklow in the Irish House of Commons. It is surrounded by a wooded estate situated on the banks of the Avonmore (*Abha Mhór* — big river) river at a point where it enters a deep gorge through high land to east and west. The local rocks are mainly Ordovician slates although the eastern bank of the river is composed of a volcanic intrusion of dolerite which is being quarried for building material. The main Dublin–Rosslare railway also follows a spectacular route along the eastern side of the river on a high embankment. The river here is fast-flowing as it traverses a series of rapids.

Habitats: Although the woodland is mainly dominated by exotic trees, the river itself is still in a fairly natural state. The bed of the river is rocky, with some small gravel beaches downstream of Avondale House. The woodland floor and large boulders in the riverbed are covered with a thick carpet of mosses. The river banks are steep and rocky with woodrush, wood sorrel, bramble and ferns but, where laurel overhangs the water's edge, the shading is too dense even for these plants. On the edge of the plantations occasional mature trees of ash, sycamore, oak, holly and beech have colonised the river bank.

Wildlife: The river is home to breeding dippers which bob about on rocks in the middle of the flow. Grey wagtails prefer to feed on the gravel areas where insect life is abundant. Otters are present on the river but the best you can hope to see are tracks in muddy ground or the distinctive dropping. The Avonmore is an important trout angling river and the fish also attract herons which stand motionless in the shallow areas awaiting their prey.

Woodland birds are abundant and at the height of their song in April and May. Summer visitors such as blackcap sing from the woodland edges in June. Autumn and winter sees mixed flocks of small birds in the woodland and there is a good chance of seeing a flight of long-tailed tits bouncing from one tree to the next. There is a large and very noisy rookery in the trees around the car-park. Ravens often fly overhead betrayed only by their deep, croaking calls. Sparrowhawks are common in the woods and occasionally a peregrine hunts pigeons in the river valley.

Near the entrance to the estate there is an enclosure with a herd of captive sika deer. Avondale House has a colony of whiskered bat, a threatened species in Ireland. They can be seen on warm evenings feeding over the pond and among the trees.

Access: Take the T7 road or the railway to Rathdrum. The entrance to Avondale is 3.5km (2 miles) south of Rathdrum on the R752 road to Arklow. There is a small charge per car entering the car-park. The start of the river walk is across the entrance road near a small pond.

25. Tomnafinnoge Wood *River and woodland*

Map reference: T 0169 Nearest town: Shillelagh

Walking beneath the mighty oak and beech trees, shafts of sunlight pierce the canopy of bare twigs and sparkle on the surface of a slow-moving river. A rustle in the deep foliage of bilberry might reveal some grazing deer.

Landscape: Tomafinnoge is the last surviving fragment of the great Shillelagh woods which once clothed the hills and valleys of south Wicklow. As early as 1444 these woods supplied timber for the construction of Kings College, Cambridge, and later for Westminster Abbey, St Patrick's Cathedral and Trinity College Dublin. In 1634, the woods were estimated to cover 'more than many thousand acres', but from then on they were heavily exploited especially for shipbuilding. In 1670, the woods were reported to be still extensive, 'being nine or ten miles in length' and a valuation in 1671 found a total of 3905 acres (1579 hectares) of woodland here.

The present oaks were planted within an existing coppiced wood in the mid-1700s when there were still extensive native woods in the locality so it provides an important link between the ancient forest of Shillelagh and the woodland of today. It occupies the valley of the Derry river which flows in a south-west direction to join the Slaney. Unlike many other Wicklow woodlands, Tomafinnoge is growing on deep, fertile soils, the lowest of which are liable to winter flooding.

Habitats: This is mature deciduous forest with a relatively open canopy dominated by oak and beech with some Scots pine and a few other exotic conifers such as western hemlock. The standard trees are widely-spaced so that the crowns are well developed and still allow plenty of light to penetrate to the woodland floor. As a result, the understorey of holly, hazel with young oak and beech is extensive. In some areas, the evergreen rhododendron threatens to shade out the natural regeneration but grazing is light and the ground layer of bilberry, woodrush and brambles is luxuriant in places. Under the dense shade of beech, the ground is naturally bare but supports some interesting fungi in autumn.

The river that flows through the woodland is braided in places into a series of streams with much marshy ground and an interesting mixture of wetland and woodland plants. The river bank has willow, alder, birch and dogwood in addition to hazel, holly and birch and the undergrowth here is quite impenetrable. The dampness of the woods has produced a heavy growth of epiphytes such as mosses and polypody fern growing on the branches of the trees. Clean air has also encouraged the growth of lichens such as *Usnea* and *Evernia*.

Wildlife: The age and varied structure of these woodlands and their continuity with former more extensive forest has left a rich animal community. A few sika deer graze in the woods but their effects are limited. In autumn the wet ground near the river is attractive to the stags for wallowing in their own mud baths. Badgers are common in the drier parts of the wood and foxes regularly move between the woodland and surrounding farmland. The river provides an ideal secluded habitat for otter and their signs can be seen under the old stone bridge near the southern entrance.

Breeding birds are typical of high deciduous forest and include some scarce species such as jay, long-eared owl and sparrowhawk. Ravens nest in the area and often fly over the wood searching for carrion.

Access: Tomnafinnoge Wood has only recently been placed in public ownership after a long campaign to save it from destruction. It is now the responsibility of Wicklow County Council but is owned jointly by five parties. At present there are no visitor facilities but access to the woodland is not restricted. Park outside the old stone lodge on the road between Tinahely and Shillelagh (but don't block access), cross the stone bridge on foot and follow the woodland tracks to the north. Some of these paths are very wet and difficult to walk in winter.

26. Knockananna Bog

Raised bog

Map reference: T0182 Nearest town: Hacketstown

This is one of the few places in Wicklow that can be described as raised bog. It has developed in a hollow which was once a shallow lake. It contains a record of landscape change over thousands of years.

Landscape: Within sight of the summit of Lugnaquillia, this bog is situated in the upper valley of the Derreen river, a tributary of the Slaney. Most of the bogs in Wicklow are mountain blanket bogs and it is unusual to find raised bogs away from the midlands in Ireland. The typical domed shape developed as the bog grew from a lake which existed here in the last Ice Age. Stumps of burnt pine in the bog indicate an early clearance of forest on the bog using fire.

Habitats: Vegetation is dominated by ling and bell heather with deer grass in the wetter parts, The yellow spikes of bog asphodel are widespread over the centre of the bog. Rushes, *Sphagnum* mosses and bog cotton grow in the pools formed in old peat cuttings. Gorse, bilberry and a few birch trees grow around the fringes of the bog, especially on the south side which has been subject to some recent peat cutting.

Wildlife: Typical mammals on the bog include fox and hare, whose tracks through the vegetation are everywhere to be seen. Songbirds are few because of the absence of trees but meadow pipits nest in the bog and cuckoos appear in spring for a few weeks. On warm summer days the vegetation of the bog is full of buzzing insects especially bees and hoverflies which are attracted to the abundance of wild flowers. Butterflies are common including the small heath and migrants such as peacock and red admiral. The large green caterpillars and the brown cocoons of the emperor moth are common on the heather. Around the pools there is a great variety of insect life including diving beetles and dragonflies.

Access: Leave the L19 road at Hacketstown and travel east for about 4km (2.5 miles) to the village of Knockananna. At the eastern end of the village, beside Jacob's Lounge Bar, take the road to the north, signposted Rathdangan. About 1km (half a mile) from the village, near the crest of a hill, there is a small lane to the left beside a modern bungalow with a wooden fence. This old track, which is surfaced with stones and suitable for walking, leads out onto the bog; in places it is overgrown by gorse. Take care around the edges of the bog as there are deep pools and drains from the old peat cutting.

27. Lugnaquillia/ Ow Valley
Moorland, blanket bog and forestry

Map reference: T0391 Nearest town: Aughrim

This is a vast and apparently empty place but it is rich in wild plants and animals. The absence of human disturbance must be an important reason for the richness of wildlife in this lonely valley.

Landscape: The Ow river (the Irish word *abha*, pronounced owa, means river) is a tributary of the Aughrim river, which eventually joins the Avoca at Woodenbridge. The Ow valley stretches for 16km (10 miles) from Aughrim back to Lugnaquillia which, at 925 metres (3034 feet), is the highest peak in Wicklow. The upper part of the valley is cut through granite although the river passes through a mica schist zone at Aghavannagh. The eastern side of the valley, as well as Aghavannagh itself, is filled with conifer plantations. However, the western side is still unplanted and provides good dry walking conditions. The sheer cliffs of the South Prison form an impressive amphitheatre at the head of the valley.

Habitats: Open moorland and blanket bog. The lower slopes are mainly covered with heather and purple moor grass. Higher parts, such as the saddle between Slievemaan and Lugnaquillia, have a covering of blanket bog and can be quite wet and difficult walking after rainy weather. The summit of Lugnaquillia is a plateau with a closely grazed sward of bilberry, grasses and mosses. The Ow cuts through some small gorges on its middle reaches.

Wildlife: Hybrid red–sika deer are usually found grazing in small groups in the upper part of the valley. Foxes range widely over the area in daylight due to the relative lack of disturbance. Signs of badgers are plentiful and there is a badger sett high on the slopes of Lybagh, which forms the western arm of the valley.

Dippers and grey wagtails breed along the river, which plunges over several small ravines in its course to Aghavannagh. Ravens are a common sight throughout the valley and peregrines breed intermittently on the cliffs of the South Prison.

Access: Follow the brown signs for the Military Road from Laragh or Aughrim. Park on the roadside near the new youth hostel in Aghavannagh. Best access to the western side of the valley is by a farm gate at Fearbreaga, 1km (half a mile) west of the youth hostel. Follow well-marked farm tracks for about 2km (a mile) to the north-west and then use sheep tracks to reach the ridge of Lybagh. From here it is a relatively easy walk to Lugnaquillia and the views are superb to the west into the Glen of Imaal.

28. Glenmalure
Glaciated valley, forestry, moorland, lakes

Map reference: T0694 Nearest town: Rathdrum

The sheer size of this glen is quite stunning. Viewed from the head of the valley, great fields of boulder scree catch the morning sun as its low light penetrates from the south-east. In the early years of the eighteenth century, the rebel Michael Dwyer fought a guerrilla campaign against the British forces from this valley.

Landscape: Glenmalure is the largest of a series of glaciated valleys in east Wicklow, extending for over ten kilometres (six miles) in a north-west to south-east direction. The valley does not cut across the granite boundary but runs parallel to its margin. During the Ice Age the glen was filled with a slow-moving glacier which left its distinctive marks on the hillside up to 1400 feet (450m) above sea-level. The valley has a narrow constriction in the centre between Carriglinneen and Fananierin. The Avonbeg river snakes its way down the floor of the valley, which is surprisingly fertile. High on the western side of the valley on the flanks of Lugnaquillia are two dramatic corrie lakes, Art's Lough and Kelly's Lough.

Habitats: Many of the valley slopes are afforested mainly with mature larch, spruce and Douglas fir, some of which have been recently clear-felled. Above this there is much heather moorland and some blanket bog. The scree slopes are largely bare but in between the giant granite boulders can be found many interesting ferns and mosses. In wet flush areas, sedges predominate and there may be flowering bog asphodel and bog cotton. The mountain lakes are deep and dark with little plant life due to the natural lack of nutrients.

Wildlife: Deer are common in the forests and on the open moorland but they keep well away from disturbed areas. Glenmalure is well know as a site for rare woodland breeding birds such as wood warbler, garden warbler, grasshopper warbler, redstart and ring ousel, which are all summer visitors. Buzzard are occasionally seen here in summer and may breed in future, as the Irish population recovers from persecution. Peregrine falcon breed in the glen and on the cliffs below the summit of Lugnaquillia. Large flocks of ravens are sometimes seen here in late summer and autumn. The river has breeding dipper and grey wagtail with occasional feeding herons. The high altitude streams which form tributaries of the Avonbeg have an unusual combination of aquatic life which provides feeding for both dipper and grey wagtail. You can see these by examining the undersides of stones and searching the banks of the streams. The main insect groups are larvae of caddisfly, stoneflies, mayflies, two-winged flies and water beetles.

Access: From Rathdrum take the secondary road leading west to Greenane and follow the signs for Glenmalure. Car-parking is available at the Glenmalure Hotel and at the head of the valley near the youth hostel. Walking trails lead from the hostel on forestry tracks to Baravore Glen and up to Lugnaquillia. The majority of the glen is in private ownership, although the upper moorland areas around Lugnaquillia and Table Mountain are part of the Wicklow Mountains National Park. For more information contact the National Park information centre at Glendalough.

29. Glen of Imaal

Grassland, moorland, river and bog

Map reference: S9793 Nearest town: Donard

When the sun sets to the west of the Glen of Imaal, it casts a pink tinge on the high slopes of Lugnaquillia. The summit has its own personal cloud in summer but as the day warms up, this may evaporate and the mountain is revealed in all its glory.

Landscape: Encircled by a ring of glaciated mountains, this beautiful west-facing valley contains the headwaters of the Slaney, which flows south to reach the sea at Wexford town. The rivers and streams are fast-flowing with gravelly beds and abundant aquatic plants. The isolated nature of the valley gives it a special, undisturbed atmosphere as there is only one through road to the south-east. The rebel Michael Dywer was born here in 1772 and between 1798 and 1803 he conducted a guerrilla campaign from the mountains around the Glen of Imaal and Glenmalure.

Habitats: The valley floor is mainly damp grassland with some silage fields. There are extensive areas of conifer plantation especially on the northern and southern slopes and in the valley bottom. To the west, the heather-covered foothills rise steeply to the spurs of Ballineddan mountain, Cannow mountain and Camerahill. These are mainly covered with mountain grassland and heath with purple moor grass and bracken on the lower slopes. In places there are wet flushes with a variety of mosses and rushes. All eastward paths lead up to Lugnaquillia, the highest peak in Wicklow, whose summit is surprisingly level and grazed to a springy carpet of bilberry, purple moor grass and mosses.

Wildlife: The rivers are rich in insect life with many species of dragonflies and damselflies in summer. Badgers and foxes are common in the forests, on farmland and on the hillsides, and badger setts are found high on the dry slopes. Grey wagtails and dippers feed on the aquatic insects and herons stalk small fish and frogs in the shallow pools. Birdlife is typical of moorland with meadow pipits, skylarks and wheatears among the grassland and stone walls. Ravens are common on the hills and a pair occupies the summit of Lugnaquillia. There is always a chance of seeing a peregrine, as a pair generally nests in the cliffs around the summit of Lugnaquillia.

Access: The N81 passes just west of the entrance to the valley. Follow the signs for Glen of Imaal from the village of Donard (15km or 9 miles south of Blessington). The north-eastern part of the glen is a military range and access is limited to certain parts during exercises. There are two approved walking routes through the ranges to the north-east and south-east. Do not enter these routes when red flags are raised, as this means that firing is in progress or about to begin. Check for details of restricted areas at the Army Information and Advice Centre in the old national school at Seskin (grid reference S974935; telephone 045-54653). Otherwise, hill-walking is unrestricted although is wise to seek permission from landowners when crossing private land. Dwyer's cottage in the glen is open to the public.

30. Hollywood Glen

Heath, grassland and woodland

Map reference: N9301 Nearest town: Donard

This is an impressive feature, especially if seen from above. However, it takes a stretch of the imagination to understand how the valley was carved out by meltwater under pressure beneath a massive ice sheet. Today, it is a peaceful place although the vast scale of the glen fills one with a sense of awe.

Landscape: This is a steep-sided dry gorge cutting through the landscape on the western edge of the Wicklow mountains. It was carved as a meltwater channel from the ice-dammed lake which formed at the end of the Ice Age in the area now occupied by the modern Blessington reservoir. A band of mica schist runs along the western side of the glen marking the margin of the Wicklow granite. The ground rises steeply to the east to the summit of Church mountain (544 metres or 1784 feet).

Habitats: There are rocky crags of mica schist high above the western slopes. Weathered boulders form massive scree below the cliffs. The scree is covered with gorse and heather with bracken on the deeper soils near the road. Isolated oak, hawthorn and rowan trees grow in various places on the slopes with some Scots pine near the top. On the eastern side of the glen there are coniferous plantations. At the southern end of the glen a small stream flows under the road. Here there is a small hazel woodland with oak standards where the road forks on the slopes. It contains a varied ground flora, dominated by bluebells, except where it is overgrazed by sheep.

Wildlife: Songbirds, including linnets, greenfinches and stonechats are plentiful in the gorse scrub, while wrens and wheatears nest among the boulder scree. Peregrines hunt here during spring and summer mainly preying on pigeons which are ambushed as they pass through the narrow glen.

Access: Leave the main N81 road just south of Hollywood and take a minor road to Donard. This road passes along the floor of the glen. Forest tracks lead through the plantations on the east side of the glen.

31. Blessington Lakes (Pollaphuca)

Lake, river and woodland

Map reference: N9813 Nearest town: Blessington

Landscape: Located in the upper valley of the River Liffey, this large reservoir supplies Dublin with water and electricity (from the hydroelectric power station at Pollaphuca). It lies on the junction between the granite of the Wicklow mountains and the older Ordovician rocks to the west. There was a large meltwater lake here after the last Ice Age. Evidence for post-glacial beaches and deltas can be seen in the hills around the east of the present lake. The present dam at Pollaphuca was built in 1940, causing extensive flooding of woodland, bog, farmland and many houses. The remains of these are sometimes exposed when reservoir levels are very low. The reservoir is 11km (almost 7 miles) long and 6km (over 3.5 miles) wide with many bays and inlets. East of the reservoir the highest summit, at 700 metres (2296 feet) high, is Moanbane, while to the west the land is relatively flat.

Habitats: The sandy shoreline is colonised by spike-rush, shore weed, lesser spearwort and reed canary grass. Annual fluctuations in water level are too great for common reed but there are some marshy areas of shoreline which support a variety of wetland plants such as water mint, sneezewort and yellow flag. Willow and hawthorn scrub is common on the shoreline, which is generally backed by a fringe of coniferous plantation.

Wildlife: Mammals that regularly use the lake shore include deer, badger, fox, mink and otter. Although these are mostly nocturnal, their tracks, and sometimes food remains (such as fish scales in the case of otters), are often visible on the exposed mud and sand around the lake.

The absence of natural islands limits the number of breeding birds, but there are some great crested grebe, mute swan, mallard, moorhen, coot and snipe, especially in the less disturbed areas. Sand martins nest in colonies on the steep sand cliffs on the west side near Russborough House. Solitary herons feed in the shallower bays and on streams entering the lake. The forestry plantations hold sparrowhawk and a variety of common song birds such as coal tit, blue tit, wren, robin and chaffinch. Wintering water birds include greylag goose, whooper swan, mallard, wigeon, teal, shoveler, pochard, tufted duck, lapwing and curlew. Mallard are the commonest ducks with an average of 800 in winter but about 400 wigeon and 350 teal are common. These are surface-feeding ducks which like to graze on the vegetation or eat seeds. In contrast, the pochard, tufted duck and coot dive for food on the lake bed. Greylag goose and whooper swans prefer to graze on surrounding fields but use the lake as a safe roosting area. The best places to see the wildfowl are from Crosscoolharbour (north end of lake) and from the various bridges.

Access: The N81 road from Dublin passes through Blessington and skirts the western shore of the lakes. The entire lake and a strip around the shoreline are owned by the ESB. Safe car-parking, picnic areas and access to the shoreline has been provided at nine points around the lake. Swimming in the reservoir is prohibited and fishing and boating are only allowed under permit from the ESB. While there are many interesting locations around the lakes, the best variety of habitat is found at the northern end (car-park at Crosscoolharbour) which includes an extensive marsh area at the mouth of the River Liffey.

32. Coronation Plantation *Blanket bog, woodland and heath*

Map reference: O1012 Nearest town: Kilbride

This is the nearest thing you will find in Wicklow to the landscapes of the Scottish highlands. The old trees stand apart from one another in a sea of bracken and bog. It is a reminder of the nineteenth-century fascination with 'created landscapes'.

Landscape: This is mainly rolling mountain bog dissected by river valleys including the upper reaches of the River Liffey. The surrounding summits of Kippure, Gravale and Sorrel Hill are all rounded by glacial action and blanketed in peat. Extensive peat cuttings give the landscape a striped appearance, while cultivation ridges in some fields near the river provide ample evidence of farming practices in the nineteenth century.

In the 1830s the area to the south of the River Liffey was planted with oak and Scots pine, the remnants of which survive today in isolated stands. It was planted to supply timber for the Downshire estate and 'for the improvement of the county and the working classes'. A granite obelisk near the meeting of the Lugnalee Brook and the Liffey marks the planting, which was named in honour of the coronation of King William IV in 1831. But neither the plantation nor the inscription on the monument were completed and they remain today as a memory of a bygone era.

The long, low cottage in the centre of the plantation was once a game-keeper's house revealing one of the other purposes of the plantation. Lower down the valley, around the ruins of the former Kippure House, there are mature stands of oak, beech, pine and other specimen trees.

Habitats: This is mainly blanket bog with scattered stands of Scots pine and oak and occasional rowan in the river valleys. The canopy is generally open with purple moor grass dominating the herb layer. At the south-eastern end where oak alternates with the pine, the ground layer consists of ling heather, bilberry and bracken. Wetter areas near the river have a more luxurious vegetation with woodrush, soft rush and various tussock-forming grasses. Polypody and broad buckler fern are also present in places. Due to its high altitude and relatively high humidity, the plantation has a great diversity of mosses and liverworts.

Wildlife: As in many mountain areas, animal life is thinly scattered, but the presence of the old trees adds a feature to the habitat that is absent in many other areas of high ground.

Merlins breed in the trees and hunt small birds among the heather but they are usually seen as just a fleeting glimpse. Summer visitors include wheatear, blackcap and whinchat, the latter being a scarce breeding bird in Ireland. Crossbills have bred in some years in the plantation and up to fifty have been reported in both June and September. Ravens nest regularly in the Scots pines and forage widely over the area looking for carrion such as dead sheep. Dippers have several territories on the main river, where they are most often seen bobbing up and down on large boulders in mid-flow.

Deer graze in the area but are very sensitive and will move away if there is any disturbance.

Access: From Sally Gap take the road to Blessington, and the plantation is visible to the left. Park on the grassy area beside the road just below first concrete bridge across the river. There is a safe crossing place near here to the south bank of the river or enter on track at Joseph's cottage. The plantation is now part of the Wicklow Mountains National Park.

Select Bibliography

Beining, B.A. & Otte, M.L.(1996) Retention of metals originating from an abandoned lead-zinc mine by a wetland at Glendalough, Co. Wicklow, Ireland. *Biology and Environment. Proceedings Royal Irish Academy* **96B,** 117-126.

Bowman, J.J. & Bracken, J.J. (1993) Effect of run-off from afforested and non-afforested catchments on the survival of brown trout *Salmo trutta* L. in two acid-sensitive rivers in Wicklow, Ireland. *Biology and Environment. Proceedings Royal Irish Academy* **93B,** 143-150.

Boyle, K. and Bourke, O. (1990) *The Wicklow Way: A natural history guide.* Cospóir. Dublin.

Brunker, J.P., 1951. *Flora of the County Wicklow.* Dundalgan Press. Dundalk

Curtis, T.G.F. & Young, R. (1976) *Areas of Scientific Interest in Co. Wicklow.* An Foras Forbartha. Dublin.

Curtis, G.F. & McGough, H.N. (1988) *The Irish Red Data Book 1: Vascular Plants.* Stationery Office. Dublin.

Farrington, A. (1934) The glaciation of the Wicklow Mountains. *Proceedings of the Royal Irish Academy,* **42B**, 173-209.

Grogan, E. and Hillery, T. (1993) *A Guide to the Archaeology of County Wicklow.* Wicklow County Tourism. Wicklow.

Grogan, E. and Kilfeather, A. (1997) *Archaeological Inventory of County Wicklow.* Stationery Office. Dublin

Hannigan, K. and Nolan, W. (eds.) (1994) *Wicklow: History and Society.* Geography Publications. Dublin.

Healy, E., Moriarty, C. and O'Flaherty, G. (1988) *The Book of the Liffey from Source to the Sea.*

Hutchinson, C. (ed.) (1975) *The Birds of Dublin and Wicklow.* Irish Wildbird Conservancy. Dublin.

Joyce, W. St. J. (1913) *The Neighbourhood of Dublin.* Gill & Son. Dublin

Kelly-Quinn, M., Tierney, D., & Bracken, J.J. (1996) Impact of acidification on the ecology of upland streams with particular reference to possible effects of plantation forestry. In: Reynolds, J.D. (ed.) *The Conservation of Aquatic Systems.* pp. 171-180. Royal Irish Academy.

Malone, J.B. (1988) *The Complete Wicklow Way. A step by step guide.* The O'Brien Press.

McConnell, B. (ed.) (1994) *Geology of Kildare-Wicklow.* Geological Survey of Ireland.

McCormack, J.O. (1994) *The Higher Lakes of Wicklow.* Phylax Press. Wicklow.

McGee, E. & Bradshaw, R. (1990) Erosion of high level blanket peat. In: Doyle, G. (Ed.) *Ecology and Conservation of Irish Peatlands.* Pp. 109-120. Royal Irish Academy.

Mitchell, G.F and Ryan, Michael (1997) *Reading the Irish Landscape,* Town House, Dublin.

Moore, J.J. (1960) A re-survey of the vegetation of the district lying south of Dublin (1905-1956). *Proceedings of the Royal Irish Academy,* **61B,**

Moriarty, C. (1989) *On Foot in Dublin and Wicklow - Exploring the Wilderness.* Wolfhound Press, Dublin.

Price, L. (1967) *The Place-Names of Co. Wicklow.* Dublin Institute for Advanced Studies. Dublin.

Smal, C. (1995) *The Badger and Habitat Survey of Ireland.* Stationery Office. Dublin.

Stout, G. (1989) The archaeology of County Wicklow. *Archaeology Ireland* **3** (4), 126-131.

Tubridy, M. & Daly, P. (1992) *The Wicklow Uplands: A management strategy.* Natural Resources Development Centre. Trinity College Dublin.

Warren, W.P. (1993) *Wicklow in the Ice Age. An introduction and guide to the glacial geology of the Wicklow district.* Geological Survey of Ireland. Dublin.

Whilde, A. (1993) *Threatened Mammals, Birds, Amphibians and Fish in Ireland. Irish Red Data Book 2: Vertebrates.* HMSO. Belfast.

INDEX

The index refers to the main body of the book only; readers will find further references to places and species in the gazetteer. Italic pages numbers refer to maps or illustrations.

A

Abra alba, 152
acidification, 21, 86, 185
 lakes, 90-1
acorns, 49
afforestation, 51, 57, 64, 115
Aghavannagh, 64, 111
agriculture, 20
 early Christian period, 163
 history of, 157-9
 neolithic, 61
 plough introduced, 161
agrochemicals, 134
Ailsa Craig, Scotland, 17, 128
air pollution, 107
alder, 20, 69, 76, 110, 115, 146
alpine lady's mantle, 42, 181
angelica, 110, 145
Anglo-Normans, 62, 164
animals. *see* mammals
Annamoe, 60, *118*, 162
Antrim, County, 51
ants, 77
archaeological sites, map of, *187*
arctic charr, 19, 92, 99, 163, 186
arctic fox, 19
Arklow, 64, 102, 106, 107, 115, 181
 beaches, 122, 125
 quarries, 179
 seabeds, 151-2
 Vikings, 61, 163
Arklow Bank, 124, 149
Arklow Bay, 150-1
Arklow Harbour, 125
Arklow Head, 123
Arklow Ponds, 148
arsenic, 91
Arts, Culture and the Gaeltacht,
 Department of, 60
Art's Lough, 16, 90
ash, 63, 80, 110, 127, *135, 169*
 pollen analysis, 19, 161
 woods, 75
Ashford, 93, 106, 117, 163, *176,* 179

housing, 121
Athdown, 18, *31*
Atlantic Ocean, 14, 21
Aughrim, 64, 106, 117
auk, 123
Avoca river, 85, 125
 pollution, 152
Avoca valley, 84, 106-7, 160
 mining, 13, 177
Avoca-Avonmore Catchment Conversion
 Plan, 107
Avondale estate, 64, 114, 177
Avonmore river, 21, 85, 86, 89, *100,* 106,
 162, 179
Avonmore valley, 64, 166

B

badger, 49, 53, 76, 105, 127, 159
 habitats, 117, 119, 121
 setts, *34, 68,* 119, 121
Baird's sandpiper, 148
ballan wrasse, 151
Ballybetagh bog, 158
Ballyboy, 64
Ballycorus, Co. Dublin, 178
Ballycullen, *176*
Ballygannon, 127
Ballyknockan, 178
Ballymore Eustace, 106
Ballynabarney, 110
Ballynabrocky, 168
Ballynamona Marsh, 115
Ballyreagh, 64, 82
Baltinglass, 17, 110, 160
Baltinglass Hill, 157
barn owl, 79, 114, *132*
 breeding site, *81*
 distribution, 113
barnacles, 151
Barnacullian, 55
Barravore, 41
Barravore Glen, 16
Barrington, R M, 149
Bartlett, W H, 63, 166

basidiomycetes, 74
bass mullet, 151
bats, 76, 114-15, *136*
 protection, 182
bearded reedling, 148
bears, 15, 19
beech, 63, 64, 71, 80, 111
 shipbuilding, 166
 woods, 75-6
beechnuts, 49
bees, 77
beetles, 49, *76,* 77
bell heather, 47, 53
bent grass, 41, 53
bilberry, 41, 42, 43, 44, 47, 50, 74, 96
birch, 19, 63, 95, 110, 146
 woods, 75
birds. *see also* waterfowl
 breeding sites, *81,* 124
 changing species, 185
 distribution map, *113*
 habitats
  moorlands, 50-1
  the Murrough, 148-9
  peat bogs, 46
  reservoirs, 96, 105
  rivers, 88-9
  woodlands, 77-9
 migrant, 124, 148
 rare, 148-9
 threatened, 181-2
 wintering on coast, 147
bird's-foot trefoil, 126, *144,* 145
black bog rush, 145
Black Castle, 122
black cattle, 163
black guillemot, 123
black rat, 163
black-backed gull, 123
blackberries, 49
blackbird, 44, 53, 111, 115, 127, 148
blackcap, 79, 185
Blackditch, 145, 146
black-headed gull, 147

Blackrock, Co. Dublin, 13
Blackstairs mountains, 13
blackthorn, 110, 127, *131*
blanket bog, 172, 185
    conservation, 181
    development of, 61, 158
    erosion, 54-5, 57
Blessington, 107, 108, 117, 179
    geology, 17
    gravel, 18
    housing, 121
Blessington lake, reservoir. *see* Pollaphuca
    reservoir
blue tit, 77, 78, 105, 111
blue whale, 152
bluebells, *72*, 73, 110, 126
bog asphodel, 45, 47
bog cotton, *37*, 47
bog moss, *36, 39, 45*
bog myrtle, 45, 96
bog rosemary, 47
bogbean, *44*, 96
bog-burst, 57
bogs, *34*, 44-6, 58, 172, 179, 185
    growth of, 20, 61, 158
    pollen analysis, 158-9
boletus, 74
Boleynass, 163
Bord Pleanala, An, 60
bottle sedge, 96
bottlenose dolphin, 152
bottlenose whale, 152
boulder clay, 17
Bowman, Dr Jim, 88, 90-1
bracken, 53, *75*, 110, 126, 139
    rights, 168
Bracken, Dr John, 88
bracket fungus, 74
Bray, 11, 21, 102, 115, 166
Bray Head, 122, 124, 138
    geology, 12
Breaches, the, 145, 148-9
brent geese, *27*, 146
briars, 110
Bride's Head, 124, 157
bristle worms, 152
Brittas Bay, 125, 126, *139, 143*, 155, 157
    protection of, 156
broadleaved pondweed, 95

Broadlough, 76, 156, *174*
    estuary, 93, 128, 145, 146
    rare birds, 148
    waterfowl, 146-7
Broadlough Marsh, 52
Brockagh, *36*
Bronze Age, 61, 159-60, 161
broom, 110
brown earths, 108
brown podzolics, 108
brown rat, 163
brown trout, 87-8, 91-2
Brunker, James P, 42, *43*, 155
Brusselstown, 160, *171*
bryozoans, 151
Buckroney, 125
    dunes, 126, 155
bulbous rush, 95
bullaun stone, 162
bumblebees, 49, 112
Burgage, 94
burnet rose, 126, 139, 145
burying beetles, 146
butterflies, 49, *72*, 77, *144*, 185-6
butterwort, 45
buzzard, 112, 114

C
caddisflies, 115
Cambrian period, 12
capercaillie, 164
Carboniferous period, 14
Carlow, County, 11, 13
carnation sedge, 96
carpet shell, 152
Carrigower bog, 46
Carter, Professor Bill, 182
Castleruddery Lower stone circle, *183*
celandine, 73
centipede, 50
Central Fisheries Board, 91
Ceratopogonidae, 46
cereal crops, 20
cetaceans, 152
chaffinch, 53, 77, 105, 111, 127
charcoal, 165
Cheviot sheep, 167
chiffchaff, 75, 77, 115, 185
Christianity, 161, 162-4

chrysanthemum, 145
Cill Mhantain, 162
Civil Surveys, 1654-6, 166
Cladocerans, 91
Clara, Vale of, 166, 180
Cleevaun Lough, 16, 90
click beetles, 50
cliffs
    birdlife, 42-3, 147
    plants, 42
climate, 20-1
    change, 182, 185
Cloghernagh, 41, 64
Cloghoge river, *25, 30*
Cloghoge valley, *29,* 53, 90
Clonegal, 11
Clonmore, Co. Carlow, 163
clouded yellow butterfly, 185
clovers, 145, 181
clubmoss, 41, 42
coal tit, 51, 78, 105
coastal erosion, 156
coastal waters, 149-52. *see also* seashore
    fisheries, 150-1
    ocean fish, 152
    seabed creatures, 151-2
cockchafer beetle, *76,* 114-15
cock's -foot, 95
codling, 151
Codling Bank, 149
Coillte, 83-4
collared dove, 111
collops, 167-8
common blue butterfly, *144*
common darter damselfly, *103*
common dog violet, 72
common dolphin, 152
common frog, 92
common horsetail, 126
common newt, 92, *103*
common nut shell, 152
common reed, 145
common sandpiper, 92
common scoter, 150
common scurvy grass, 145
common spike-rush, 95
common valerian, 95
commonage, 167-8
Condit, Tom, 160

coniferous plantations, 64, 82-4, 168, 177
  acidification, 86
  effects on fish, 87
Connemara, Co. Galway, 13
conservation
  changing habitats and species, 185-6
  climate change, 182, 185
  EU directive, 180-1
  map of conservation areas, *175*
  natural heritage areas, 180
  nature reserves, 180
  threatened species, 181-2
Cooladoyle, 164
Coolatin estate, 79, 112, 166
coot, 105
copper mining, 13, 107, 152, 178
coppicing, 63, 79, 165
coraline algae, 151
Cork, County, 14
cormorant, 92, 123
corncrake, 116
Coronation Plantation, 64, *65*, 82, 83, 168
Corophium, 147
corries, 16, *29,* 42
  lakes, 85, 90
Cottagh sheep, 167
cotton grass, 45, 47
cow parsley, 110
cowberry, 42
cowslip, *104*
crabs, 151
cranefly, 115
Cretaceous period, 14
Croghan Kinsella, 178
Croghan Moira, 14
Crone, 64
Crone wood, 82
crossbill, 83
Crosscoolharbour, 105, 106
cross-leaved heath, 47
crow, 50
crowberry, 41
Crowley, Billy, 94
crustaceans, 91
crystals, 14-15
cuckoo, 50, *132*
curlew, 46, 105, 147
Curragh, Co. Kildare, 121
Curtlestown, 18

D
damselflies, 45, *103,* 115, *136*
Dargle river, 21, 85
  salmon, 87
  waterfall, 89-90
Dargle valley, 16, 166
Daubenton's bat, 76, 115
deer, *39,* 43, 47, 48, 53, 76, 83, 105
  grazing, 42
  ranges, *59*
  tree damage, 75
deer grass, 47
deer parks, 166-7
Deerpark, 166-7
Delgany, 80, 108
Deputy's Pass, 180
Derry River, 85, 165
Derrybawn woods, 63
devil's bit scabious, 95, 145
Devil's Glen, 93
dipper, 88-9, *99*
Distomus variolosus, 151
Djouce mountain, 13, 14, 21, 93
  animal life, 49
  geology, 15
  walking, 58
dock, 161
Dodder river, 85
dog violet, 110, 126
dolphin, 152
Donegal, County, 13, 89
douglas fir, 82, 84
Down, County, 13
downy birch, 75
dragonflies, 45, *91,* 103, 115
Dublin, 93-4, 106, 107
Dublin, Archbishop of, 166
Dublin, County, 11, 13, 93, 157, 158
Dublin Bay, 149, 150
Dublin Bay prawn, 150
Dublin Corporation, 105
duck, 96, 146, 147, 155
Duff Hill, 21
Dunlavin, 108, 117
Dunlavin Marshes, 116
dunnock, 111
Dunran channel, 18
Dutch elm, 63
dwarf gorse, 53

dwarf willow, 42

E
eagle, 50
earthworms, 49, 117
'eco-warriors,' 82
eels, 88, 163
eland, 167
elder, 110
Electricity Supply Board (ESB), 94-5, 106
Elizabeth I, Queen, 63
elm, 20, 61, 63, 110
  pollen analysis, 158, 161
  shipbuilding, 166
emperor moth, 49, 52
enclosures, 109
English elm, 63
Enniskerry, 29, 48, 55, 166
  geology, 17
  housing, 121
Environment, Minister for the, 106
erosion
  human activity, 57-8
  by water, 55, 57
  by wind, 57
erratics, 17
estates, 112, 166
EU Freshwater Fish Directive, 87
eucalyptus, 64
European gorse, 53
European Union, 107, 121
  habitats directive, 180-1, 182

F
Fairwood Park, Shillelagh, 166
fairy flax, 42
falcon, 186
false oat-grass, 95
Faninerin mountain, 75
farmlands, 108-21
  badger habitats, 117, 119, 121
  farming, 109
  hedgerows, 109-12
  history and development, 157-9
  houses and gardens, 112-15
  lowland wetlands, 115-16
  meadows, 116-17
  pollen analysis, 158-9
  soil types, 108

spraying fields, *134*
Farrington, Tony, *16*
Fassaroe, 17, 18
feather stars, 151
feldspar, 14-15
ferns, 42, 74, 102
Ferns, Co. Wexford, 163
fescues, 95
field scabious, 95
fieldmouse, 53, 76, 114
filmy fern, 90
fin whale, 152
finch, 131
fir, 64
fish
    changing species, 186
    ocean, 152
    in rivers, 87-8
    seabed, 151-2
fisheries, 150-1
Fitzwilliam, Lord, 166
Fitzwilliam estate, 63
flies, 45, 77
flint, 128
fly agaric, 67
fool's watercress, 115
Forest and Wildlife Service, 155
forestry, *173. see also* woodlands
    history of, 168, 177
    pollen record, 19-20
    school of, 64
fox, 51, 66, 131, *134,* 149, 159
    hedgerows, 112
    hills, 49, 50
    lakesides, 105
    meadows, 116-17
    valleys, 53
    woodlands, 76
fox moth, 49
foxglove, *71,* 110
fraughan. *see* bilberry
Friends of Coolatin Wood, 80
frog, *39,* 46, 92, 93
froghopper, 45
fulachta fiadh, 161
fulmar, 122
fungi, *67,* 74

G
Gaelic clans, 62, 63
garden warbler
    breeding site, *81*
    distribution, *113*
garganey, 148
geese, 96
geology, 27, *29, 30,* 31
    map, *26*
giant Irish deer, 19, 158
Giraldus Cambrensis, 163
glacial lakes, 17-18
glacial spillways, 18
glaucous shears moth, 185
Glen of Imaal, *98,* 160, 162
Glen of the Downs, 18, 75, *169,* 180
    meltwater channel, *29*
    woodland conservation, 80, 82
Glenasmole Lodge, 93
Glenbride, 64
Glencree, 15, 16, 58, 64, 167, *170*
    afforestation, 177
    glacial lake, 17
    gravel, 18
    oak planting, 83
    Royal Forest, 62
Glencree Centre for Peace and
      Reconciliation, *170*
Glencullen river, 93
Glendalough, 15, *27, 28,* 64, 107, 161,
      172, 201, 202
    afforestation, *71,* 73, 82, 168, 177
    charcoal burning, 165
    fish, 19
    glacial delta, 17-18
    last wolf killed, 164
    mineralisation, *28*
    miners' village, *170*
    mining, 13, 57, 63, 177-8
    monastery, 161, 162, 163
    nature reserve, 180
    oakwoods, 75
    scree slopes, *36, 43
    'the Spink,' 58
    turf cutting, 179
    Upper Lake, 88, 90-1, *72, 102*
      fish, 91, 92
    u-shaped valley, 16, 90
    vegetation, 42

visitor centre, 60
    wildlife, 49, 76, 79
Glendalough House, 60
Glendasan, 13, 15, 18, *33, 173*
    animal life, 49
    mining, 57, 63, 177
    u-shaped valley, 16, 90
Glenealo river, *28,* 88
Glenealo valley, *39,* 49, 177
    nature reserve, 180
Glenealy, 117
Glenmacnass
    u-shaped valley, 16, 90
    waterfall, 15, 89-90
Glenmalure, 15, 55, 64, 162, 167
    afforestation, 75, 177
    mining, 13, 63
    scree slopes, 43
    u-shaped valley, 16, 90
goats, *27,* 49, 75, 163
Gold Mines River, 178
gold mining, 178
goldcrest, 51, *69,* 77
Golden Falls, 94, 106
golden plover, 21, 46, 182
golden saxifrage, 42
goldeneye, 147
gold-tailed moth, 146
golf courses, 155, 181
goosander, 89, 182
goosefoot, 161
gorse, *33,* 53, 95, 110, 128, 135, 145
goshawk, 159
Grand Canal, Inchicore, 148
granite, 14-15, *27,* 128
    formation of, 12-13
    quarries, 178
grasses, 41, 44, 45, 47, 95, 145
grasshopper warbler, 148
grassland, coastal, 146
gravel, 18
great crested grebe, 105
Great Famine, 109, 167
great fen sedge, 145
Great Sugarloaf, 13, 14, 18, *27,* 54, 93, 117,
    130, 169
great tit, 77, 78, 111
greater tussock sedge, 115
Greenan, 75

greenfinch, 111
green-flowered helleborine, 126
Greenland, *30*
greenshank, 147
grey plover, 147
grey seal, 122, 124
grey squirrel, 70, 77
grey wagtail, 89, *99*
grey willow, 96
greylag goose, 96, *104,* 105, 146
Greystones, 108, 111, 122, 127, 152, 164, 166
ground beetle, 49
grouse, *39,* 40, 50, 54
guillemot, 123, 150
gullying, 58

H
habitats, changing, 185
haggs, 55, 57
harbour porpoise, 152
hard fern, 43
hare, 19, 53
hart's tongue fern, 42, *46,* 90
Haverford, 62
hawthorn, 75, 96, 110, 127, *131,* 135
hazel, 20, 61, *74,* 80, *169*
    pollen analysis, 159, 161
    woods, 75
heath, 158
heath bedstraw, 53
heath butterfly, 49
heath rush, 47
heather, *33, 37,* 41, 45, 47, 50, 53, 54, 170
heathlands, 46-7
hedge sparrow, 111
hedgehog, 53, 182
hedgerows, *135*
    vegetation, 109-11
    wildlife, 111-12
    wildlife corridors, 112
hen harrier, *35,* 51, 83, 181-2
herb robert, 110
heritage areas, map of, *175*
hermit crab, 151
heron, 92, 105, 155
herring, 150
herring gull, 123
hibernation, 186

hillforts, 160-1
hill-walking, 58
history, 157-68, 177-86
    coming of Christianity, 161, 162-4
    Great Famine, 167
    medieval wars, 164
    modern Wicklow, 167-8, 177-86
    prehistoric period, 157-61
    sheep farming, 167-8
    Tudor exploitation, 164-5
    Vikings, 163-4
hobby, 185
hogweed, 110
holly, 63, *73, 75,* 110
Hollywood, 18, 84, *129, 135*
holm oak, 63
honeycomb worm, 151
honeysuckle, 74
hooded crow, 43, 50, 111
hornbeam, 63
horse chestnut, 63
horse industry, 121
horses, wild, 19
horsetail, 115
hottentot fig, 145
house martin, 124
house mouse, 163
housing development, 121, *176*
humpback whale, 152
Hunter's Hotel, 93
Hurricane Charlie, 21, 128
Hydrobia, 147
hydro-electricity, 94-5
hyena, 19

I
Iapetus, 12
Ice Ages, 15-19, *23*
Iceland, 104
ink-cap, 74
insects, 50, 93, 114-15, 146
    hedgerows, 112
    peat bogs, 45-6
    woodlands, 77
Irish Age, 61
Irish Naturalists Journal, 152
Irish oak, 73
Irish Red Data Books, 181, 182
Irish Sea, 16, 17

iron, 13, 91
Iron Age, 160-1
iron works, 63, 165
ivy, 74, 78

J
jackdaw, 43, 111
jay, 79
Jessen, Knud, 158-9
juniper, 19
Jurassic period, 14

K
Kelly-Quinn, Dr Mary, 86, 87
Kelly's Lough, 16, 90
Kerry, County, 14, 181
kestrel, 51, 66, 90, 126, 149
Kevin, St, 162
kidney vetch, *141,* 145
Kilbride, 108
Kilcoole, 96, 142, 145, 146, 148, 182
    geology, 17
    land reclamation, 185
    rainfall, 21
Kilcoole Marshes, 52, 128, 145, 146, 148
Kildare, County, 12, 106, 116, 117, 121, 157, 159
Killincarrig, 111
Kilmacanogue, 80, 115
Kilpedder
    gravel, 18
Kilruddery, *130*
    deer park, 166
kingfisher, 147
King's river, 86
Kippure, *34,* 42, 55, 85
Kish Bank, 150
knapweed, 95, 145
Knocknacloghoge, 29
Knocknanna, 116
Knockrath, 166
Knockree, 15
Knockrobin, 147
Knocksink wood, 79, 180

L
Lacken, 94, 179
lady's bedstraw, 110, 142
lady's smock, 110-11, 115, 116

230

lakes, 85, 90–3
   fish, 91–2
   wildlife, 92–3
lampreys, 163
Land Acts, 168
Land Commission, 177
land reclamation, 116
lapwing, 21, 92, 105
Laragh, 54–5, 166
larch, 63, 64, 76, 82, 84
laurel, 75
lazy beds, 167
lead mining, 91, 177–8
Leamore, 128
Leisler's bat, 76, 114
Leitrim river, 145
lemmings, 19
lesser black-backed gull, 105
lesser spearwort, 96
lichens, *69, 74*, 146
Liffey Head, 57
Liffey Head bog, *39,* 158, 179, 181
   birdlife, 50
   vegetation, 44, 45
Liffey river, 85, 86, 106, *176*
   reservoir, 93–4
Liffey valley, 64, 160
light ship, Arklow, 149
lime, 63
lime beech, 112
limestone, 17, 128
ling, 47, 53
ling heather, *37*
linnet, 76, 111, 148
little egret, 185
little grebe, 92
little gull, 150
Little Sugarloaf, 14, *130*
little tern, *140,* 148–9, 182
liverwort, 42, 90, 102
lizard, 50
loach, 163
lobster, 151
lodgepole pine, 82
Loftus, Sir Adam, 166
long-eared bat, 76, 114
long-eared owl, *67,* 79
Longford, County, 77
long-tailed duck, 148

long-tailed tit, 78
lords and ladies, 110
Lough Bray, Upper and Lower, 16, *22,* 90, 91
Lough Dan, 15, 16, 53, 90, *97,* 106, 107
   acidity, 91
   fish, 19, 92
   otters, 93
   scree slopes, 43
   woodlands, 79
Lough Firrib, 90
Lough Nahanagan, 16, 19, 90, 91
   hydro-electricity, 94
Lough Ouler, 16, 42, 90, *202*
   fish, 91–2
Lough Tay, 16, *30, 32,* 53, 90, 106, 107
   otters, 93
   scree slopes, 43
lowland wetlands, 115–16
Lugduff, 64
Lugduff river, 88, 91
Luggala, 15, *30,* 53
   birds, 79
   woodland, *72,* 78
Luggala Centre, 60
Lugnaquillia, 11, 16, *34,* 41, *56,* 117
   animal life, 49
   geology, 15
   vegetation, 42
Lybagh mountain, *34,* 49
lyme grass, 145

M
McElheron, Anthony, 52
MacMurroughs, 164
Magherabeg, 127
Magheramore, 125
magpie, 111
mallard, 92, 105, 147
Malton estate, 63
mammals
   hedgerows, 101–2
   history, 159, 163, 166–8
   Ice Age, 19
   lakesides, 92–3
   meadows, 116–17, 119, 121
   moorlands, 48–50
   ocean, 152
   reservoirs, 96, 102, 105

   threatened, 182
   valleys, 53
   woodlands, 76–7
Manor Kilbride, 110
Mantan, St, 162
manx shearwater, 150
marram grass, 126, 139, *143,* 145, 155
marsh cinquefoil, 96
marsh cudweed, 95
marsh fern, 155
marsh pea, 146
marshes, 115–16, 145–6
Martin, Charles, 157
mat grass, 47, 53, 54
mayflies, 45, 91, 102
meadow pipit, 40, 50, 52, 127, 132
meadow saxifrage, 126, 181
meadows, 116–17
meadowsweet, 95, 110, 115, 145
Meath, Earl of, 166
Meath estate, 63
megalithic tombs, 157–8, *184*
merlin, *40,* 52, 181–2, 185
   breeding territories, *59*
mesolithic period, 20, 157
metal ores, 13
mica, 14–15
midges, 46, 91, 102, 115
Military Road, 48, 58, 172, 179
milkwort, 95
mining, 13, 57, 61, 177–8
   pollution, 107, 152
   use of trees, 63, 168
mink, 92, 93, 102, 105
minnow, 91, 92, 163
   stoneloach, 87
mistle thrush, 111
Mitchell, Professor Frank, *31,* 161
mites, 49–50
Mizen Head, 126, 155
molluscs, 91, 152
monasteries, 161, 162
Moore, Thomas, 85
Moore's horsetail, 126
moorhen, 92, 105
moorlands, 46–7
moraines, 17, *31,* 90
mosses, 42, 90, 102, 145
mossy saxifrage, 42

moths, 77, 115
motorbikes, 58
Mount Kennedy estate, 63
Mount Usher Gardens, 93
mountain bikes, 58
mountain hare, 43, 48-9
mountain lakes, 90-3
mouse, 49, 75, 114, 131
Mullaghcleevaun, 16, *34*, 41, 54
    vegetation, 42
mullet, 148
Murrough
    pumping station, 151
Murrough, the, 96, 127-8, *141*, 145-9, *174*
    aerial view, *153*
    grassland, *144*
    marshland, 145-6
    protection of, 156
    rising sea-levels, 182, 185
    sand hills and saltmarshes, 145
    shingle beach, 128, 145
    songbirds, 148
    wet woodland, 146
mushrooms, 74
mussels, 151
mute swan, *101*, 105, 147-8

N
N11, 80
National Museum of Ireland, 152
National Park. *see* Wicklow Mountains
    National Park
National Parks and Wildlife Service, 84,
    180
natterer bat, 76
Natural Heritage Areas, 84, map of, *175*,
    180
nature reserves, 180
    map of, *175*
neolithic period, 20, 61, 157-8
New Ross, Co. Wexford, 13
Newcastle, 104, 127, 128, 150, 182
    beaches, 142, 145, 146, 148
    castle, 164
    geology, 12
    land reclamation, 185
Newrath Bridge, 93
Newtownmountkennedy, 18, 46, 114
newts, 92, *103*

nightingale, 185
nightjar, 182
Nimmo, Alexander, 90
North and South Prison, 16, 41
Norway spruce, 82, 84

O
oak, 20, 64, *66, 68,* 73-5, 80, 110, 168, *169*
    and beech, 75-6
    forest clearance, 63
    National Heritage Areas, 84
    pollen analysis, 19, 20, 62
    shipbuilding, 166
    threats to, 74-5
    Tomnafinnoge, 79-80
oakwoods, 78
O'Byrne family, 164, 166
O'Donovan, John, 164
Office of Public Works, 80
oil pollution, 150
open field system, 109
orchid, 155
ordnance survey maps, 64
Ordovician period, 12
osprey, 148
O'Toole family, 164, 166
Otte, Dr Marinus, 91
otter, 53, 92-3, 102, 105, 182
overburning, 46, 47, 50, 54
overgrazing, 42, 46, 54-5, 57
Ow valley, 83
owls, 66, *67,* 79, *132*

P
painted lady butterfly, 77, 185
Parnell, Charles Stewart, 114, 177
Patrick, St, 162
peacock butterfly, 77
peat bogs, *34,* 44-6
    peat-cutting, 58
peat pipes, 55, 57
pedunculate oak, 73
perch, 88, 163
Percy's Table, Lugnaquillia, *56*
peregrine falcon, 35, *40,* 42, 52, 90, 181-2,
    186
pheasant, 111
phytoplankton, 91
pied flycatcher, 79

breeding site, *81*
    distribution, *113*
pig, 20, 163
pigeon, 40, 52
pike, 88, 163
pine, 20, 63, 64, 78
    pollen analysis, 158
pine marten, 77, 163
pinkeens, 87
pipistrelle bat, 76, 114
placenames, 61
plaice, 150, 151, 152
plane, 63
plantation period, 63
plantations, 51
plants, threatened, 181
ploughs, 161
plover, 125
pochard, 105
podzols, 53, 108
pogge, 151
poison, 50, 114
Pollaphuca reservoir, 54, 85, 94, 95, 96,
    104, 106, 178
    management of, 106
    waterfall, 89-90
pollen analysis, 19-20, 158-9, 161
pollution, 107, 116, 178
polycholorinated biphenyls (PCB), 150
pond skaters, 45
poppy, 145
population density, 167
porpoise, 152
Porter's Rocks, Arklow, 125, 152
Powerscourt, Lord, 48, 166-7
Powerscourt estate, 48, 112, 179
    birds, 79
    forestry, 168
    waterfall, 15, 42, 85, 89-90, *100,* 167
Praeger, Robert Lloyd, 111
prawn, 150
prehistory, 159-61
    map of archaeological sites, *187*
prickly saltwort, 126
primrose, *67,* 110
puffballs, 74
purple loosestrife, 115, 145
purple moor grass, 47, 50
purple orchid, 110

pygmy shrew, 114
pyramidal orchid, 126, 145

Q
quarries, 18, 57, 156, *174,* 178-9
quartz, 14-15
quartzite, 13

R
rabbit, 43, 53, 76, 93
    sand dunes, 126-7, 142
ragged robin, 115, 116, *135*
rainfall, 21
raised beaches, 157
rat, 53, 67, 114, 163
Rathdrum, 64, 106, 114, 117, 157, 179
Rathgall hillfort, 160-1
Rathnew, 108, 110, 121, 179
raven, *35,* 42-3
razorbill, 123, 150
reafforestation, 76, 84
    mining, 63, 168
    17th c, 165-6
red admiral butterfly, 185
red algae, 151
red deer, 39, 48, 159, 167
red grouse, *39,* 40, 50, 54
red squirrel, *70,* 76-7, 83
redshank, 95, 147
redstart, 79
    breeding sites, *81*
    distribution, *113*
reed bunting, 92, 126, 148, 155
reed canary grass, 95, 96
reed grass, 115
reed warbler, 148
    breeding sites, *81*
    distribution, *113*
reeds, 146, 148
    removal of, 155
rccfs, 151
reindeer, 19, 158
reservoirs, 85, 93-6
    management of, 105-6
    vegetation, 95-6
    wildlife, 96, 105
rhododendron, 75
ring barrows, 161
ring ousel, 44, 182

ringed plover, *138,* 155
river valley management, 106-7
rivers, 85-9
    acidification, 86
    map, *113*
roach, 88, 163
road kill, 114, 119, 134
road-widening, 115
robin, 77, 105, 111, 115, 148
rocky headlands, 122-4
Rocky Valley, 18
rook, 111-12
Roundwood, 12, 93, 108, 109, 117
Roundwood reservoir, 93
rowan, 96, 110
Royal Dublin Society, 109, 167
rudd, 88
ruff, 148
rundale system, 109
Rural Environment Protection Scheme, 116, 180
rushes, 47, 95, 126
Russborough estate, 105, 112
Ruttledge, Major Robin, 150

S
saddle quern, 157
sage, 161
St Kevin's Church, Glendalough, *172*
St Kevin's Road, 162
St Patrick's cabbage, 42, 43
Sally Gap, 54, 57, 58, 162, *172,* 179
salmon, 87, 163
saltmarshes, 145, 185
Sambur deer, 167
sand, 18, *174*
sand couch grass, 126
sand dunes, 21, 124-7, *142,* 185
    dune slacks, 126-7, 155
    inland from, 127
    plants, 125-6
    protection of, 155, 181
    sandy beaches, 125
sand eel, 149
sand gaper, 152
sand hills, 145
sand martin, 18, 31, 105, 124
sand mason worm, 151
sandpits, *174*

sandwich tern, 124
sanicle, 42
scallop, 150
Scalp, the, 18, 55, 158
Scarr mountain, 13, 14, 15
schist, 15, 41
scoter, 150
Scotland, 14, 17, 92
Scots pine, 61, 63-4, *66,* 71, 75-6, 80, 82, 110-11, 168
Scott, David, 51
scree slopes, 43-4, 55
scrub vegetation, 76
scurvy grass, *141,* 150
sea aster, 145
sea beet, 128, 145
sea bindweed, 126, *142,* 145
sea buckthorn, 145
sea campion, 128, *141*
Sea Empress, 150
sea holly, 126, *142,* 145
sea lettuce, 145
sea pink, *137*
sea purslane, 128
sea rocket, 128
sea rush, 145
sea samphire, 128
sea sandwort, 126
sea squirt, 151
sea trout, 88, *98,* 163
Seabank, 125, 126
seal, 124
seashore, 122-8, 145-56
    coastal features, *154*
    coastal waters, 149-52
    the Murrough, 127-8, 145-9
    protection of, 155-6
    rising sea-levels, 182, 185
    rocky headlands, 122-4
    sand dunes, 124-7
seaside pansy, 126
seaweeds, 145, 151
sedge warbler, 115, 126, 148
sedges, *36,* 41, 45, 47, 95, 126, 146
seed mussel beds, 151, 152
Seefin, 157, *184*
Seefingan, 157
sessile oak, 73, 95
shag, 123, *138*

sharp-flowered rush, 96
sheep, 43, 47, 50, 54, 163, *171*
    farming, 167-8
    grazing, 42
    National Park, 58
    tree damage, 75
sheep's fescue, 41, 53
shellfish, 150
Shillelagh, 63, 108, 109, 117
    deer park, 166
    woods, *68*, 79, 165
shingle, 127-8
shingle beach, 128, *141*, 145
shipbuilding, 63, 165, 166
shooting, 43, 146
shore crab, *143*
shoreweed, 95, 96
shoveler, 105
shrew, 49, 53, 126
shrimp, 151
sika deer, 39, 48, 53, 167
silage cutting, *129*
Silurian period, 12-13, 14
silver birch, 75
Silver Strand, 124
silver-washed fritillary, *72*, 77
Simuliidae, 46
siskin, *69*, 83
sitka spruce, 82, 84, *173*
six-spot burnet moth, *204*
Six Mile Point, 127, 150, 151
skua, 150
skylark, 50, 116, 127, 144, 155
Slaney river, 85, 87, 165
Slaney valley, 160
slate quarries, 179
Slavonian grebe, 148
slugs, 49, 67
Smal, Dr Chris, 117, 119
smooth hawk's beard, 95
snails, 49, 67
sneezewort, 95, 96
snipe, *37*, 46, 105, 115
snow cover, 21
soil erosion, 54-5
soil types, 53, 108
    distribution, *120*
song thrush, 111, 127
sorrel, 42

Spagnum moss, 45
Spanish chestnut, 63
sparrowhawk, 79, 105
Special Areas of Conservation, *175*, 180-1
speckled wood butterfly, 77
Sphagnum moss, *39, 44*
Sphagnum papillosum, 45
Sphagnum rubellum, 45
spiders, 50
spike-rush, 96
Spinans Hill, 160
spine hedges, 112
sponges, 151
spotted flycatcher, 79
spotted orchid, 110
spotted redshank, 148
spring quill, 122
spring-tails, 49-50
spruce, 51, 63, 64
squirrel, 53, *70*, 75
standing stones, 159-60
starfish, 151
starling, 21, 111, 131
starry saxifrage, 42
starwort, 115
state plantations, 64, 82-4, 83-4
stickleback, 87
stitchwort, 110
stoat, 53, 76, 163
stock dove, 90
stone circles, 159-60, *183*
stone loach, *103*
stonechat, 50, 148
stoneflies, 45, 91, 102
Stout, Geraldine, 157-9
Stratford, 108
subterranean clover, 145, 181
sun stars, 151
sundew, 45
sunshine, 21
swallow, *132*
swan, 96, 147-8, 178
swift, 124
sycamore, 63, 71, 110, 127
Synge, J.M., 11

T
Table Mountain, 41, 55
tanneries, 165

teal, 105, 147
tern, 155
thistle, 161
threatened species, 181-2
thrift, *137*
thrush, 21, 131
tin, 13
Tinahely, 117
tit, 53
toadstools, 74
Tomnafinnoge Wood, *68*
    conservation of, 79-80
Tonduff, 55
Tonelagee, 15, *29*, 41, 91
    animal life, 49
    vegetation, 42
tormentil, 45, 145
tortoiseshell butterfly, 77
townlands, 167-8
Travilhawk Strand, 162
treecreeper, 78, 111
Trinity College Botanic Gardens, 181
Trooperstown, *100*
Trudder, 164
tufted duck, 105
tundra, 19, *30*
turbary rights, 168, 172, 179
turf cutting, *172*, 179
turkey oak, 63
Turlough Hill, 19, *36*, 61, 94-5
turtle, 152
two-winged flies, 50, 146

U
Uplands Council, 60

V
Vale of Clara, 180
valleys, 16
    u-shaped, 16, 90
    v-shaped, 18, 55
    wildlife, 52-3
Vartry reservoir, 86, 91, 93, 95-6, *102, 176*
    grasslands, *104*
    management of, 105-6
Vartry river, 46, 85, 128, 147
    otters, 93
    salmon, 87
Vartry valley, 166

vetches, 116
Vikings, 163-4
viviparous lizard, 50

W
wader, 92, 146, 147
Wales, 63
walnut, 63
Wapiti deer, 167
wasp, 49, 77
water birds. *see* waterfowl
water boatmen, 46
water erosion, 55, 57
water mint, 96
water rail, 148
waterfalls, 15, 85, 89-90, *100*
waterfowl, 52, 123-4
    the Murrough, 146-8
    seabirds, 149-50
watermint, 115
Webb, 42
Wentworth, Sir Thomas, 166
wetlands, 185
    lowland, 115-16
Wexford, 85, 151, 165
Wexford, County, 11, 13
whale, 152
wheatear, 44, 50, 111, 124
whinchat
    breeding site, *81*
    distribution, *113*
whirligig beetle, 45
whiskered bat, 76, 114
White Hill, 58, 60
white trout, 88
white-tailed eagle, 50
whitethorn, *131*
whitethroat, 50, 148
whooper swan, 92, 96, 105, 146
Wicklow, 61, 102
Wicklow, County
    climate, 20-1
    dimensions of, 11-12
    first people, 20
    geological development, 12-14
    during Ice Ages, 15-18, *23*
    influence of geology, 14-15
    vegetation, 18-20
Wicklow Arbour, 128

Wicklow Bay, 150-1
Wicklow County Council, 60, 80, 107
Wicklow Gap, 15, 94, 162
Wicklow Harbour, 122, 127, 178
Wicklow Head, 122, 124, *137*, 138, 162
Wicklow mountains, 11, 13, 14-15, *59*, 162
    animal life, 48-52
    description, 41-60
    management, 54
    moorlands, 46-7
    overgrazing, 54-5
    peat bogs, 44-6
    scree slopes, 43-4
    snow, 21
    wildlife, 42-3
Wicklow Mountains National Park, *38,* 55,
        60, 76, 84, 172, 173, 179, 180
    established, 58
Wicklow People, 152
Wicklow town, 108, 111, 121, 127, 145,
        147, *174,* 181
    swans, 148
    Vikings, 163
Wicklow Uplands Council, 60
Wicklow Way, 58
wigeon, 105, 147
wild angelica, 95, 110
wild asparagus, 126, 181, *202*
wild boar, 159, 163
wild cat, 159
wild garlic, 73
wild thyme, 142
wildlife. *see* birds; mammals; plants
Wildlife Act, 1976, 80
William IV, King, 64, 66, 82
willow, 19, 76, 96, 110, 115, 146
    creeping, 126
willow warbler, 111, 115
Wilson's filmy fern, 42
wind, 20
    erosion by, 57
windhover, 51
wolf, 19, 62, 63, 64, 163, 164
wood anemone, 73, 110
wood mouse, *67,* 126
wood pigeon, 90, 111
wood sorrel, 74, 110
wood warbler, 79
    breeding site, *81*

distribution, *113*
wood white butterfly, 77
woodcock, 79
Woodenbridge, 152
woodlands, 67-84
    coniferous plantations, 82-4
    conservation of, 79-80, 82
    early clearances, 158-9
    effects of forestry, 83-4
    flowers, 73-4
    history of, 61-7
    maps, 66
    oakwoods, 73-5
    other broadleaved woods, 75-6
    placenames, 62
    threats to, 74-5
    timber exploitation, 164, 165
    wet, 146
    wildlife, 76-9
woodpecker, 159
woodrush, 42, 74
wood sorrel, 77
woolly mammoth, 15, 19
World War II, 172, 179
wren, 36, 44, 53, 77, 105, 111, 115, 127,
    148

Y
yarrow, 95
yellow flag, 96, 111
yellow horned poppy, 128
yellow rattle, 96, 116
yellowhammer, 111
Yorkshire fog, 95

Z
zinc, 13, 91

COMPLETE LIST OF MAPS

Map 1   Location and main features of County Wicklow 10

Map 2   Glaciers and ice movement during the later stages of the last Ice Age...............23

Map 3   Simplified geological map of County Wicklow and surrounding area 26

Map 4   The extent of Wicklow Mountains National Park 38

Map 5   The main hill deer ranges and merlin territories...................................59

Map 6   The changes in forest cover in County Wicklow 1886 *v* 1995 66

Map 7   Some scarce breeding birds in County Wicklow 81

Map 8   Main rivers lakes and reservoirs in County Wicklow 113

Map 9   Soil types and land use capabilities in County Wicklow 120

Map 10   Land cover classification of County Wicklow 133

Map 11   Main coastal features of County Wicklow 154

Map 12   Protected areas in County Wicklow in 1998 175

Map 13   Archeological sites in County Wicklow 187

Map 14   Location of sites to visit 188